TIME TO WRITE

SUNY Series, Literacy, Culture, and Learning: Theory and Practice
Alan C. Purves, editor

Time to Write

The Influence of Time and Culture on Learning to Write

John Sylvester Lofty

STATE UNIVERSITY OF NEW YORK PRESS

Published by
State University of New York Press, Albany

© 1992 State University of New York

For information, address State University of New York Press,
State University Plaza, Albany, N.Y. 12246

Production by Marilyn P. Semerad
Marketing by Dana E. Yanulavich

Library of Congress Cataloging-in-Publication Data
Lofty, John Sylvester, 1946–
     Time to write : the influence of time and culture on learning to
write / John Sylvester Lofty.
          p.   cm. — (SUNY series, literacy, culture, and learning)
     Includes bibliographical references and index.
     ISBN 0-7914-0901-5. — ISBN 0-7914-0902-3 (pbk.)
     1. English language — Composition and exercises — Study and
teaching — United States. 2. Educational sociology — United States.
3. Time — Sociological aspects. 4. Literacy — United States.
5. Sociolinguistics — United States. I. Title. II. Series.
LB1576.L59 1992
370.19 — dc20   91-21447
                                                                              CIP

10 9 8 7 6 5 4 3 2 1

For the students and teachers
in a Maine fishing community
where I had the privilege of teaching English
and
To my parents Marjorie and James
and my sisters Janet and Susan

Contents

There above the circle of pointed firs we could look down over all the island and could see the ocean that circled this and a hundred other bits of island ground, the mainland shore and all the far horizons. It gave a sudden sense of space, for nothing stopped the eye or hedged one in, —that sense of liberty in space and time which great prospects always give.

Sarah Orne Jewett, *The Country of the Pointed Firs*

And so it goes. And so it goes. And so it goes. And so it goes goes goes goes goes tick tock, tick tock, tick tock, and one day we no longer let time serve us, we serve time and we are slaves of the schedule, worshippers of the sun's passing, —bound into a life predicated on restrictions because the system will not function if we don't keep the schedule tight.

Harlan Ellison, " 'Repent, Harlequin!' said the Ticktockman."

WRITING AGAINST
THE CLOCK

In the world of language education, and in fact in the worlds of language and of education, there emerge few books that have an immediate and telling message. These books startle by the very simplicity and obviousness of what they say; they give us the shock of recognition. One can number among them authors like Mina Shaughnessy, whose *Errors and Expectations*, which shows how surface errors in writing are related to the writers' perceptions about text and reader; or like Shirley Brice Heath, whose *Ways with Words* which shows how the practices of literacy in school can differ from that of the community, and thus how school can put some children at a loss.

Now, John Lofty has produced a volume that again is deceptively simple. In examining the ways in which student and school appear at odds in their attitudes towards writing and its production, he finds that one of the major differences is in the perception and use of time. School time is clock time—divided, industrialized, punchable through time clocks. In such an orderly world, writing becomes a matter of the clock of fitting composition into neatly organized periods. As it is with writing, so is it with much of school learning: A science experiment cannot last more than a 38-minute period. Discussion of an issue like war cannot extend beyond the bell.

Against the world of the clock-and-bell school stands the world of the lobster fisher, the clam digger, the farmer, the cook, the writer, and the scientist. These are people for whom everything falls into its season, for whom the time to do things is not a regimented divisible time, but a time that evolves from the nature of the task—and from nature—the movement of the earth on its axis and around the sun.

Lofty illuminates the fact that school writing is an unnatural act. School instruction in writing prepares students not to be writers in the grand sense of the term but functional writers, writing against the clock, meeting deadlines, preparing viable drafts, committing words to paper in order to get a job done, but without the commitment that constitutes the writer's craft and art. Students like those in the community Lofty analyzes with depth and honesty perceive this anomaly and either opt out of school writing and school, or they take to it and turn towards the world of the school. The latter become successful students and will be successful scribes, those who have the craft of writing well enough in hand to use it in a variety of ways demanded by the information age.

But these people are not writers, not those who can worry over the nuance of a word, who see that writing is a "craft or sullen art." School writing instruction leads people to become clerks and scribes, not to become writers. Many schools recognize this distinction and offer special courses called "creative writing." This kind of writing cannot be done according to the clock; these writers work with the season and the day as do the lobster fishers. Theirs is a rhythm developed according to more natural patterns than that set by the school bell.

As Lofty points out, the attempt to establish the rhythms of the artist within the framework of the school clock as has been suggested by many of those who espouse process writing is to set up a contradiction. The cycle of planning, drafting, revising, and editing that marks the writer at her métier cannot be done by the clock. *Time to Write* admirably describes the anomaly.

It also presents what I see as a most humane way of dealing with that anomaly. One could see the book as another "critical" attack on schools as they are presently constituted; but, like Shaughnessy and Heath, Lofty is above that easy answer, and like them he writes out of love for all those he describes. The schools are a product of, a preparation for, and a reflection of a technological world that a large number admire and are unwilling to forego. That a number of students chafe and resist and drop out.means not that either the schools or the students must change. Awareness of the differences and the anomaly is a first step towards the offering of alternatives. Just as we should not force everyone into the orderly world of the clerk, neither should we impose the creative model on all. We should be able to offer alternatives and to help our students become increasingly aware of the options, the benefits, and the risks of each alternative. Such, I think is the view offered in Lofty's four questions at the end of this volume. These questions cast no blame but open the possibility for dialogue between school and community, between teacher and student, that should, I think, be the aim of any educational endeavor.

ALAN C. PURVES

Acknowledgments

When in the autumn of 1990 one of my former middle school students, now with a young family of her own, asked if I was still writing "that book," I realized how long it had been in the coming. Since the work began seven years ago, many people have supported the study as it developed, from fieldwork to dissertation to book. Consequently, the interest and value this work might have owes much to many groups and individuals.

My deepest appreciation and gratitude to the students, teachers, principals, and members of the New England fishing community where the study was first begun. For their many hours of conversation and for patiently showing me their work, a heartfelt thank you to the people on the island. The continuing approval and support for the project by the School Board and Superintendents made possible each round of school-based research. To respect a community that values its privacy, I regret that the island cannot be named, but I hope that each person will hear his or her own voice speaking in this work.

I wish to give special recognition to my dissertation committee at the University of Michigan. Jay L. Robinson continually reminded me to ground my observations in the local context; Val Polokow taught me the importance of looking at the world through the eyes of children; Ralph Williams provided a superb model for how to listen to people's stories, to represent them with respect for the teller, and to scrutinise their meanings; Bernard Van't Hul gave me the gift of his editorial pen. When I asked Alton L. Becker whether to consider also the phenomenon of space, he said that it would be enough to hold on to the dimension of time. His belief in the importance of studying the temporal dimensions of people's lives and language has informed my own work at each stage. Particular thanks go to Robert H. Paslick for his discussion on the philosophy of time. Wise counsel on beginning ethnographic research from Shirley Brice Heath helped me to keep my mistakes in "entering the field" to a minimum.

Several colleagues were generous enough to put down their own research to wrestle with mine. In particular, I am indebted to the support of Lilita Gusts, who believed in the work, from my island teaching to my professional writing. John Briggs tried to steer me away from writing academese, which he thought I did badly, toward a narrative voice more consonant with the spirit of the community and the project. Jan Armon was so influenced by his reading of Shirley Brice Heath's *Ways with Words* that he suggested the title of "Ways with Lobsters" for my own first chapter, a fitting emblem for the many ways in which he supported my work.

Because of the generosity of the people on the island who offered me places to stay during the fieldwork, costs were kept to a minimum. Special thanks, however, go to Mary Jarrett in the Rackham Office of Financial Aid for support and to the English and Education Program at the University of Michigan who defrayed the cost of interview transcription. The English Department at the University of Colorado, Denver helped me to bring the work to completion with a grant and leave time for final fieldwork. Rick VanDeWeghe, Hannah Kelminson, Mark Clarke, and my graduate students each offered thoughtful criticism for the final revisions. A grant from the Center for the Humanities at the University of New Hampshire, director Burt Feintuch, enabled the index to be compiled.

I learned to see the difference between snapshots and photographs, and perhaps to take a few more of the latter, with the help of Nancy, a photographer friend from the island and from Martin Tessmer. I very much appreciate the art work generously contributed by two professional artists: scratch-board engravings for the front and closing illustrations by Siri Beckman and a wood engraving by John Bischof for the end of Chapter one. The island students who provided the drawings—sometimes offered instead of class writing—cannot be named because of the need to maintain the anonymity of the community.

At each stage of book preparation, the editorial guidance, support and tireless patience of Priscilla Ross helped me to see the final shape of the manuscript. Alan Purves' suggestion that I look at how professional writers think about time and writing deepened my understanding of the topic. If both editors had not encouraged me to visit the island one more time and had not been willing to wait a little longer for the manuscript, I would have missed the opportunity to record many of the changes now evident in school and community. Marilyn P. Semerad's artful technical skills and editorial supervision brought the work to completion in a timely manner. My thanks go also to Malcolm Willison and Carol L. Inskip for the final rounds of copy editing and proof reading.

The professional advice of Anne Ruggles Gere and Thomas Newkirk helped me to find a wider audience for my work, and I particularly appreciate Newkirk's readings as the manuscript progressed. Conversations with Richard Blot, Max Van Manen, Susan Manning, Donald Murray and David Spurr helped me to complete the book. The bibliography will situate my thinking about time and language within the wider community of scholars who have shaped my work and to whose scholarship I am indebted.

Without the encouragement of my long-term friend and colleague Ellen Westbrook, so many of my observations and interpretations would have stopped short. Her questions, close reading, and suggestions have been an integral part of the process from start to finish. And a special thanks to my family who each summer have provided time and place of a unique quality in which to read and to write up this study.

Introduction

In 1978, on an island off the Maine coast, I began teaching two classes of junior high school students who enjoyed class discussion but who resisted writing. By the time the first winds of autumn blew down the bay, many students were studiously refusing to write more than a single draft. Writing only scant amounts in moody silence, they worked in a routine and often begrudging manner and asked why they could not simply tell me what they knew. Few students seemed pleased to see their writing displayed, to hear it read aloud, or to receive high grades. When I read their writing, I found it spare and shorn of the rich descriptiveness of their talk. A small but very vocal group successfully disrupted class by asking in both their words and actions, "Why do *we* need to learn how to write?"

Their question not only echoed their skepticism about the value of writing itself but challenged the way in which I was teaching writing by a process approach.[1] Despite my attempts to orient the classes to students' interests and to current issues in the community, before the first snow students were hostile toward the kinds and amount of writing entailed by this approach. Although many students questioned also the value of reading, their entrenched resistance was to writing. Workbook exercises in grammar and usage, however, were tolerated, I think, because students were inured to rote work and saw it as the real basis for English.

When I had previously taught students who did not want to write, their resistance was often because they had been given too few opportunities for personal writing and too many analyses of literature. The resistance of these island students was qualitatively different, however, and I had not heard their question asked with the same insistence before. While my students actively challenged writing, in many other ways they sought a personal relationship and shared their world with me.

1

Had I been entering the school in 1990 rather than in 1978, the teacher-researcher movement might have offered critical ways to explore what was happening in our English classes. But my immediate focus then was on how to work with groups of students whose attitudes fascinated even as they frustrated me. Since I wanted students to write every day, their resistance successfully undermined our work together. By the end of the first year, my efforts had united the students into a spirited community of non-writers. My second and third years of teaching both junior and then senior high English were slightly more successful. We knew each other better, and students agreed to write a little to maintain our relationship, but not, I think, because they saw any greater value or took appreciably more pleasure in the activity.

With a view to understanding more about how social contexts shape students' responses to writing, in 1981 I left the school district to begin graduate studies in English and Education. During the next three years, I thought about why my teaching only partially had met the needs of some students and had failed to reach those who quit school. In 1984 I returned to the island to make my students' insistent question, "Why do *we* need to learn how to write?" the subject for an ethnographic research project. I began by accepting the invitation of my ex-students to go fishing and to learn more how their lives beyond the schoolhouse had formed and informed their time within it. I had realised that the hostility to writing was part of a broad-based resistance to schooling and reflected what I saw as a disparity between home and school. When students had described their lives at home, ways of proceeding had emerged that contrasted significantly with the patterned ways and values of life in school. One of the most visible features of the difference between the cultures of home and school[2] was in how time was conceived and realised in daily activities. This observation led me to ask: Was my students' resistance to writing grounded in how community representations of time related to those of the school?

Community

To provide an exhaustive account of resistance to literacy in this one community would require several avenues of enquiry. One might explore how the kinds of reading and writing that the community values are different from school-based literacy. In this fishing community, writing tends to be used more often to transact formal business and to share information publicly than to record what is memorable in a fast-changing life style. Within this community there are highly literate individuals, but many regard the ability to talk and to listen as skills sufficient to meet their communicative needs, an observation that would hold true also for communities in which literacy is highly valued.

Another account of resistance to writing would consider that in 1978 students first identified themselves with a life directed toward the sea in contrast to a life in school. In part, students' anti-social behaviour during writing class was a dramatic critique of the perceived relevance of writing to their future lives. In 1978 most of the island's young people planned to remain on the island to fish or to become homemakers and to raise families. For the most part, reading and writing were not seen as means essential to reaching these goals. To secure much more than a survival-level literacy appeared a superfluous achievement. The major value of a high-school education appeared to lie in being able to say that one had earned the diploma, a literate document to celebrate a homecoming after a rough passage.

The Culture of Time

Rather than explore each possible source of resistance, I chose to hold onto my question about time. I believed that it would connect with and lead to other sources and make visible a constraint on learning that I seldom had seen discussed fully in the literature. The answers that emerge, however, cannot be generalised to account for the behaviour of students in other classrooms.[3] What I learned about the relations between time and literacy in island life is context-specific knowledge that will increase our understanding of how lived time relates to schooling only if other teachers ask comparable questions in their own schools. Although I will argue that the culture of time will always be a constraint on learning, we cannot predict how its influence will play out in different arenas.

With the purpose of reflecting broadly on the influence of time on learning, consider the master schedule that organises education in most American high schools. The day is often divided into seven periods, each lasting for fifty minutes. After classroom rituals, office communications, and transition time, a resourceful teacher and highly motivated students will do well to have more than thirty minutes for learning. By the time our students are settling into the rhythm of work, the bell rings, and they stream off with three minutes to reach the next class and to begin a different subject. Talk with students ends mid-sentence and the once-common ritual of leave-taking is reduced to a hasty "Gotta go. I'll be late." Like Alice's white rabbit, we teachers also look at our watches to verify that we are behind and have not "covered" the syllabus for that day. Back in the staffroom, teachers ask for more time in which to teach while our students complain that being in school is like stepping onto a production line.[4]

If we pause to examine the qualities of time that shape our work in school, then we notice that this clock-driven experience of time controls virtually all aspects of our daily life. Pervasive in modern industrial societies, clock time measures the heartbeat of the production of goods and services.[5] Although the temporal contours that we have drawn around our lives enable us to coordinate and synchronise activities among people and organisations with diverse time needs, these boundaries quickly assume the absolute status of the laws of nature.[6] Despite the apparent absence of human signature to our clock culture, people shape time to embody and to represent the values currently most important to their social, economic, and political life.

The metronomic[7] approach to the temporal organisation of life and work in modern society has been inherited by most of our schools and imported into our classrooms. With the rationale of making education efficient, educators have established a series of time standards that measure in Carnegie units the number of hours students are to receive instruction in each subject before they can graduate. When we question the rationale behind school time, the answers given are grounded frequently on time-honoured values embedded within the cultural habits of daily life. Educators have argued, for example, that time and learning are most efficient when divided into discrete units.

The effects of the temporal organisation of education on students' learning has remained largely an unexamined domain (see Leichter, 1980, pp. 360–363). As a profession, educators do not know enough about how the quality of time in school influences how our students feel, think, and act. This area of knowledge is difficult to scrutinise[8] but is beginning to receive critical attention from a range of different research traditions. As teachers of English, we recognise that learning to write is influenced by students' sociolinguistic backgrounds and specifically by their oral language, but we often overlook the influence of cultural frameworks so fundamental as the learners' modes of perceiving time and space.[9]

In this study, I have focused on time as though this category of human experience existed in isolation from space. Many readers will rightly see this separation as artificial as it would be for us to separate form from content. Issues of cultural and physical space will be evident to the reader, for example, in my discussions of classroom life, in observations on the imaginative space that student writers create, and in descriptions of linear and cyclical scheduling of local activities. My primary focus in the time-space modality is on time, because this dimension always appeared to be more significant than space to students. A more complete account of the influence of cultural frameworks on learning in this community, however, would need to look at each phenomenon and how each relates to the other.[10] My purpose in this study is two-fold: first, to describe how the sociotemporal mismatch between home and school has serious consequences for education in this particular community; second, to invite teachers, administrators, and those concerned with the quality of schooling in both urban and rural settings to look at the ways in which the culture of time may influence their own students' responses to literacy.

Literacy

Since this book is about the relationships between time and literacy, readers will look for clear definitions of each key term. In recent years, however, we have seen increasing public debate over what literacy can, if not should, mean for those in school and particularly as preparation for work. With the move from the age of industry and technology to that of information, the need for a differently and more highly educated labour force has increased bringing new concepts of literacy (Purves, 1990).

The boundaries we have assigned to literacy have ranged from the minimal ability to sign one's name to the power to bring oneself into being by transforming word into world. (Freire and Macedo, 1987). In our attempts to define literacy, we have had difficulty reaching clarity and consensus on how literate people think, feel and act, on what they know about language, and on how they might use it in different rhetorical situations. As Robert Arnove and Harvey Graff observe:

> Literacy takes on meaning according to the historical and social setting. Notions of which skills constitute literacy change over time and differ by

setting, causing estimates of illiteracy to vary enormously from time to time and from place to place. (1987, pp. 202–206)

As our understanding of literacy has broadened, we have moved away from defining literacy wholly in terms of the ability to demonstrate for the purpose of school-based assessment a set of discrete skills, abilities, and performances. While such competencies are indeed essential, we now believe that definitions of literacy must reflect also the needs and purposes of language users in particular sets of circumstances. We have recognised the need to study the social and pedagogical contexts in which literacies are situated (Robinson, 1990).

Within this study, I will discuss literacy as a set of communicative practices shaped by and in the engagements between home and school.[11] By watching how the island students approach writing, the uses to which they put their spoken and written words and the social constraints on those uses, we can begin to understand the role that literacy plays in their lives. In Lorri Neilsen's words (1989, p. 2): "Because I believe literacy is not a skill that we acquire but is a reflection and creation of who we are, my findings show these people in the process of living."

My focus then will be to describe students' approaches and attitudes toward the task of writing, to examine the value that writing had in their daily lives and to consider the role that literacy played in how these students created their identities. I will use the broad term of literacy where the students' responses to writing are embedded in and conditioned by their responses to reading and talking and on those occasions when it is especially important to think about reading, writing and talking as connected activities.[12]

Time

Agreeing on what we mean by literacy is problematic, and to suggest how we understand time is equally so. To begin by admitting the problem is commonplace among those who write about time.

Time is everywhere, yet eludes us. Time is so bound up in our universe and ourselves that it resists our efforts to isolate and define it. Time haunts our experience like some invisible spirit of things, some irretrievable truth. (Grudin, "Preface," 1982)

In *Time the Familiar Stranger,* J. T. Fraser (1987, p. 35) uses the key distinction between *time felt* and *time understood* to account for St. Augustine's difficulty in defining time in *The Confessions.*

> Bk. 11, sec. 14: "What then, is time? If no one asks me, I know. If I wish to explain it to someone who asks, I know not." (p. 35)

Augustine locates time in the mind.

> Bk. 11, sec. 27: "It is in you, my mind, that I measure time . . . . As things pass by, they leave an impression on you. . . . It is this impression which I measure. Therefore this itself is time or else I do not measure time at all." (p. 34)

When I arrived on the island in 1978, I confess that I was not thinking about time as the personal impress of change. From my teacherly perspective, I identified time with the public measures of clock, calendar, and schedule. Being raised in the Britain of Greenwich Mean Time, I had inherited through school and community a set of somewhat rigid time values that in turn informed how I organised classroom life. For example, events happened *on* time, not *in* time; punctuality was a virtue, lateness a venial sin. Although such values had equal currency in the mainstreams of American life, these norms had far less purchase on the lives of my island students than I had expected and wanted. A more social sense of time was making impressions on my students' minds and bodies which were invisible to me. In not recognising the many non-verbal signs and markers of time, I failed to understand the extent to which the students' sense of time is a key dimension in the social contexts of learning. My own oversight reflects the scant attention that educators have given to this area until quite recently.

As a topic of study in education, time has been approached from a range of perspectives. Miriam Ben-Peretz and Rainer Bromme (1990, p. 64) offer the following categories, acknowledging that they overlap and provide a provisional rather than a definitive framework: instructional time, curricular time, sociological time, and experienced-personal time. Instructional time is defined as "classroom time, allocated and prescribed by teachers, and engaged in and used by students" (Ben Peretz and Bromme, 1990, p. 64). Researchers study teaching by measuring instructional time in evaluating the "teaching-learning process," determining what occurs during "academic learning time," studying the effects of the order of classes on the intensity of learning, and assessing the time requirements of individual students, of different subjects and more broadly of schooling itself.

Curricular time is defined as "time allocations, and specifications for time use, prescribed by curriculum developers" (Ben-Peretz and Bromme, 1990, p. 67). Because this perspective views time as a scarce curricular resource, it raises political issues of how time is to be distributed for particular subjects as well as for social experience and issues encountered in schools. Going beyond questions of time allocation, curricular time examines from developmental perspectives the effects of timing and pacing on learning. When and at what rate do we introduce material in instructional sequences?

The sociology of time, a new area of investigation, studies the "*sociotemporal order,* which regulates the lives of *social* entities such as families, professional groups, religious communities, complex organisations, or even entire nations" (Zerubavel, 1981, p. xii). Studies in sociological time look at the qualitative difference between such different kinds of time as the sacred and profane, the private and public. In *Hidden Rhythms: Schedules and Calendars in Social Life* (1981), Zerubavel describes as forms of temporal regularity the four parameters that we commonly use to present the profile of a social event or activity, namely, the dimensions of sequential structure, duration, temporal location, and rate of recurrence (p. 1). These terms provide a useful set of references for describing the time orders both of communities and schools. English class might be scheduled every day from 8:05 until 9:00 a.m., to last 55 minutes and be followed by Math. These parameters establish norms that students and teachers often come to regard as natural, even though they are socially constructed. By making social situations orderly, predictable, and coordinated, however, temporal regularity helps to provide the participants with a sense of "cognitive well being" (p. 12).

Experienced-personal time is one of the least studied perspectives of time in education. Ben-Peretz and Bromme (1990, p. 73) define this perspective in terms of "the perception of the temporal order by individuals [who] perceive time in different ways and may be viewed as assigning personal meaning to time."[13] As public as the units of time might be, these measures take on personal meaning only as we interpret them in the context of our own lives. Ben-Peretz and Bromme cite

Rousseau's dictum that the most important educational principle to "lose time" illustrates one approach to how personal time might be conceptualised:

> The growth and development of a person should not be dictated by the tyranny of the clock. Each person is conceived as an individual, different from others. Therefore, each has his or her own pace of development, and the passage of time is experienced by each in a unique way. (1990, p. 73)

The reader might argue that what we lose is not time but our awareness of how it is represented. While this qualification is an important one, the point is well made that we need to attend closely to how students in school view time, and what it comes to mean in their individual lives:

> 1.18. For the real problem of time is not in nature but rather in our position toward nature, not in what we see but in the way we look. (Grudin, 1988, p. 9)

Although my own approach to the study of time makes reference to and has implications for how we think both about instructional and curricular time, my focus is primarily on how students experience time in the writing class and more broadly in school. My descriptions of the life worlds of students in school and communal life are informed, in part, by a sociological view of time.

When Thoreau spoke of time as "the stream I go a-fishing in" (p. 68), he pointed to time literally as the medium in which we create our sense of self. Members of the island community construct the contours of the stream to serve a life of sea-related work. Identity is predicated on an essential freedom to schedule activities in accord with the natural cycles of tide, season, and daylight, and their attendant time values. Because we cannot separate a context from our interaction with it, time and the stream of activities are one and the same.[14] Time is perceptible only in the impress of one activity on another.

> 11.12. Time is not an influence affecting things and relationships, but rather an essential element of things and relationships. The cosmos is not so much a thing in motion as a thing of motion, a complex interplay of energies and paces. (Grudin, 1988, p. 21)

Time is fishing, time is writing, and time is children in school.

So far I have spoken of literacy and time separately. How might we relate time and literacy? Both constitute and organise daily experience and allow us to orient ourselves in the world. They enable us to make meaning from and to give shape to our experiences, two fundamental means by which we establish personal identity.[15] Saying who we are has both linguistic and temporal dimensions. As human systems, time and literacy are socially constructed, but they are structured and evaluated differently across social groups.

In moving between home and school, island students observed differences in the forms and uses of time and language, and experienced discontinuities between how each system was evaluated in its setting. To establish an identity in school controlled and evaluated by measures of time different from home was a major issue for these young people. I will argue that these disjunctions affected students' ability and their motivation to write. While I focus primarily on the time order of students' approach to writing, the time order of the writing itself deserves comment.

In narrative writing, I had noticed interesting departures from textbook English in how my students managed tense and aspect and in how they located themselves in narrative time. For example, students shifted frequently between past and present, favoured progressive verb forms, and structured their stories without a clear delineation of beginning, middle, and end. Although we cannot assume that linguistic time, for example, tense and aspect, directly reflects the lived time of the narrator, I thought that the ways in which students managed discursive time within their stories, the time of telling, would represent at some level their lived experience of time.[16] By examining what their teachers regarded as temporal miscues, I believed that I could gain insight into the larger cultural configurations of time that clearly had shaped my own students' responses to instruction in writing.

Although both time and language are culturally constructed, I soon discovered problems in attempting to relate the time order of written or spoken narrative to how the language user appeared to perceive time. At best, I was able to make inferences about cultural attitudes toward time but was unable to show any predictable correspondences across the kindergarten through twelve narratives examined. To understand the temporal logic of student narrative, I have included several in which the writer's handling of time deserves the scrutiny that Mina Shaughnessy (1977) applies to errors. It is too easy to assume merely that temporal miscues need correction rather than attempt to establish the narrative's temporal logic for its author.

Summary of Chapters

The lives of the people in this fishing village are depicted through the voices of students and adults describing life and work, first in the community and then in school. My focus in these chapters is on how time and identity are related to each other within the settings of home and school, and on the role that writing plays in mediating and revealing the contours of this relationship.

Chapter One takes the reader through a day in the life of Mike, a young lobsterman who, finding nothing of value for himself in school, quit in grade nine to go fishing. We see how the fisherman's work and identity is grounded in the challenge to develop a schedule that accords with the natural and changing cycles of tide, season, and daylight. The patterns of activity, time values, and attitudes toward work taught in school are seen to contrast sharply with those of work on the water.

Chapter Two describes the life and seasonal work of people ashore doing such traditional things as clam digging, home making, and crab picking. I argue that the social and economic values represented in the temporal organisation of these kinds of work influenced how Mike approached and valued his school learning. Through students' perspectives both on failing to meet their school's expectations and on finding an education appropriate to their needs, we come to understand why many of these students put minimal efforts into school or quit school altogether. The patterns of communal life that emerge in Chapters One and Two establish a context against which the lives of students in school are presented in Chapters Three, Four, and Five.

Chapter Three moves from the world of lobsterboats and clam flats into the elementary classroom where we see school through the eyes of Fay. The different ways in which young children (K–2) become aware of time at home and in school are presented, for example, through television shows, teacher announcements of a change of activity, schoolbells, and the arrival of the buses. Fay and her friends are then shown responding to being taught to write by a process approach followed by a critique of how time is used for in-class writing.

Chapter Four portrays life in grade six from the perspective of Mark and his friends. As they describe their process of composing, we see a change in attitude from students' enjoyment of writing to asking,

"Why write?" Students are being taught to write by an approach that recognises neither the insistence of their question, nor the time values of people in this community. Despite the teachers' efforts to make learning personal and to involve students in planning activities, the power of schools to depersonalise learning emerges in this chapter. Contrasts are drawn between home and school learning to illuminate the cultural influences on how students regard school-based literacy.

Chapter Five presents the attitudes of Christie and her friends in grades eleven and twelve toward how their time needs are recognised by school and the English class. Drafting, peer review, meeting due dates, and students' responses to teacher evaluation are discussed here. The influence of gender on students' attitudes toward the writing process and toward literacy emerge in this chapter. We see how culture-based knowledge of how artifacts are made serves as one paradigm for approaching writing. Attitudes toward pursuing a traditional life style in contrast to alternative careers broaden the concluding discussion to assess the roles that literacy and formal education might play in the future of these students.

Chapter Six identifies the different kinds of time evident in this community, and describes their coalescence into "island time," a multi-faceted form of time that contrasts sharply with the monolithic time of schools. I raise the political issue of what kinds of literacy will be needed in the future if local people are to manage their island and to govern the schools. Although many teachers do not work in communities where time values are predicated on the activity patterns of rural life, I argue that all students are affected by the time values of the school. Examples of how professional writers use their time are provided as a reference against which teachers of English might enhance their effectiveness by developing alternative timescapes for literacy.

Chapter Seven suggests the character and directions of social, educational and economic change through field note observations. For example, when I arrived in 1978 to teach on the island, approximately twenty-five percent of the graduating seniors planned to go to college; by 1986 the number had risen to over fifty percent. That change was becoming a major theme in many aspects of life was increasingly evident in 1990.

The Appendix is for those readers interested in the approach taken in this study. I describe why this approach was appropriate to the problem I chose to study, as well as how I gathered information and shared my readings of school and community life with those I described.

The logical order of the chapters within the study might suggest a nexus of causal relationships between the adults' daily activities and the students' approach to writing in school. But in fact, the chapter sequence reflects my own shift in focus from teaching students to write to exploring the contexts that influenced how they approached this task. The nature of the relationships between the temporal rhythms of communal life and the students' attitudes toward literacy will emerge in the chapters ahead. My reason for immersing the reader in what might appear to be an overly detailed account of the fishermen's lives and life ashore is to show, by way of a particular example, that teachers in schools will always need local knowledge of their students' life world. To teach students effectively, we must study the contours of their world as we engage them with ours. This is an account of how such knowledge was gathered in collaboration with a group of people who encouraged me to tell their story in full detail.

A Note on Transcription and Voice

I have represented as closely as ear and eye allow the speech and writing of islanders in its unedited form, a practice now broadly accepted when presenting variations of American English. In making transcriptions, I have sought to preserve the integrity of regional voice but without attempting to represent speech phonetically. By the use of "eye-dialect," I have suggested dialect variations within the community but have otherwise followed standard American orthography.

To preserve features of my own voice, I have followed a variant form of British spellings except where reporting direct speech. Following this convention will remind the reader that as narrator I am from another country. Consequently, the interplay of language and culture in my conversations with islanders, and in my own teaching there, have been more complex perhaps than if I had been raised and educated in America. While I can observe and study island life, I can never be of it.

Brothers Fishing.

Docking Lobster.

Chapter One

WAYS WITH LOBSTERS

"When it's time, you know it."

At the end of one more English class that Mike and his junior high friends had successfully disrupted, Mike confided, "I ain't got nothin against you personally, but I just don't want to be here." I believed him. By the time the leaves had begun to turn into the yellow and brown of a New England fall, Mike and his friends were refusing to read, write, or participate positively in their seventh-period language arts class. As their new teacher, I had tried and largely failed to develop a curriculum that focused on writing about local issues. Earnestly and at length I now talked with Mike about how he would need reading and writing for his future work. Politely he listened to what his eyes told me he had heard from his teachers too many times before. When I asked Mike what he thought about the problems we were having in class, his answer was to pull out of his jean jacket a salt-stained piece of paper that entitled him at age thirteen to fish for lobster off the Maine coast.

I was unwilling to accept that talking about lobstering could have much to do with why Mike did not need this class, but now it was my turn to listen politely to what counted in his world. Mike's real day did not begin until he got home from school, went down to the cove behind his home and untied the boat built forty years ago by his grandfather, who from well-seasoned cedar and full-grown oak frames had fashioned a fourteen-foot "peapod." It was a boat that followed the lines of the canoes used by the Indians who fished these waters little more than two hundred years ago. Mike's peapod had been refastened and replanked several times, and its once proudly curving lines had flattened with age, giving a middle-aged spread to the beam. Mike described his boat with immense pride and was ready "to scale" across the schoolyard anybody who dared to suggest his boat had "gone by." He fished about twenty traps from his small boat and took advantage of its shallow draft and manoeuverability to set his traps closer to shore than was possible with a larger boat. His father had shown him how to steam bows of oak to frame his traps, and his mother taught him how to net their entryways. Down on the beach he found storm-damaged traps that to Mike were worth repairing. At thirteen he planned to begin his career, here, out on the water; he achieved his goal by quitting school the next year. I never was able to teach Mike to write in the ways that I had envisioned in our after-school conversations.

Six years later in 1984 — at 4 a.m. on a chill autumn morning — it is Mike's turn to teach me what he knows about fishing. Unlike the fishermen, I do not wake up before sunrise winter and summer. A local storekeeper tells me that he sells clocks only to summer visitors. As I drive to the fish dock, dim lights shine from windows along the main road as the fishermen get ready to go fishing. On the road ahead, taillights flicker and fade around the bends into town. The buses parked by the school are ready to pick up Mike's younger brother and sister three hours from now. Two figures in thigh boots, jeans, and hooded jackets walk from their pick-up trucks toward the fish Co-op, a large wooden building at the center of dockside activity.

The figures disappear behind the fish-packing factory that waits in darkness for the first shift of sardine packers to arrive at seven o'clock. Boats come alongside the Co-op to pick up net pockets stuffed with ripe-smelling herring and redfish, the bait for the lobster pots. The small company store supplies the fishermen with their fuel, raingear, gloves, bait needles, and most anything else they need. Through a narrow walkway lined with sacks and barrels, the sternmen enter the building to wait for their captains to bring in the boats off the moorings. Although a few lobstermen both drive the boat and haul the pots themselves, most operations are run by the skipper with one or more sternmen. And not only men go out to haul. Several boats in the local fleet are husband-and-wife teams, and if a husband is sick, the wife will sometimes fish alone. I know of only one woman, however, who holds a licence to fish full time for lobster.

The lobstermen standing around the barrel stove briefly pause in their bantering to look at the stranger wearing a trenchcoat and new sea boots. Mike explains me away as his old English teacher who now wants to go fishing. Lobstermen wear their clothing to tatters before replacing them. Mike's outer jacket is a paint-streaked and oil-stained bomber top that he seldom fastens even in the foulest weather. His pockets bulge with assorted oddments: a shucking knife, cigarettes, a can of soda, and rubber gloves to prevent salt-water sores. Beneath his jacket, an orange thermal top and vest hang out in ends frayed from constantly rubbing against the side of the boat. Tight jeans worn hip-low string out at the knees; new jeans he saves for a dance. When asked if he ever wears a hat, Mike laughs and replies, "You mean like those captain's caps that the summer people wear?"

Around the stove conversation slowly continues. Mike's Uncle Amos begins, "I was awake at two. Couldn't get to sleep last night."

"So wasn't I," adds one of the other men, "and I wasn't doin nothin either."

Mike's uncle teases him with, "I heard the older the buck the harder the horn."

"Naw, it's all in the head," his friend replies.

Mike is eager to leave the dock and to start fishing. He keeps looking across the moorings for a light on his skipper's boat. No two boats will fish for the same number of hours, and boats go out at different times in the morning. While most are leaving the moorings by 4:30 or 5 a.m., some even earlier, others will remain until as late as 7 a.m. An older fisherman comments, "Those seven o'clock guys are unbelievable. They wanna see you, 'Where in the hell've you been?' Man, I've hauled up a hundred traps before seven!' "

The late leavers who eat breakfast at the local restaurants or talk away down on the waterfront tend to be regarded as "slack." In contrast, the "drivers" are the first to leave the moorings, and they are respected for their long hours on the water, one measure of a fisherman's worth. This fisherman now explains, "One guy is going out, and they're not going to let the other guy get ahead of him. If he's out there, they're going to be out there, too. It's that predatory, individual-instinct business."

The sternmen sit around talking in a small room filled with old chairs and an overstuffed settee. The roof is massively constructed of roughly-squared beams suspended from a stout system of iron tie bars braced against the ridge pole. Outside, the roof is lined with screeching seagulls waiting for fish waste to be dumped out of the packing factory.

At five o'clock it's almost daybreak, and most of the boats are heading toward their first trap of the day. The few men remaining around the stove drink coffee or wander to the sales office and idly scan the faded want ads and notices.

> WANTED: TRAP HEADS TO KNIT MARY DAVIS, CORNER OF STONE ST.

> ATTENTION: IT IS UNLAWFUL TO REMOVE LOBSTER FROM TRAPS OR TO CUT OR CARRY AWAY LOBSTER TRAPS, POTS, BUOYS, ROPES OR CONTENTS FOUND ON THE BEACH OR SHORE.

> A CLAIMANT'S WEEK OF UNEMPLOYMENT AND HIS REG- ISTRATION FOR WORK SHALL BE DEEMED TO COMMENCE ON THE SUNDAY OF THE CALENDAR WEEK IN WHICH HE . . . .

Mike's skipper, Dave, arrives, and we go aboard the *Stella*, a thirty-eight-foot wooden boat built here on the island in the 1960s. Since Mike dropped out of school three years ago, he has been Dave's sternman. At quarter after five, the *Stella* swings away from the dock and heads south for the fishing grounds. Moving slowly at first, we wind out among the moored boats and enter the narrows where the outgoing tide draws us away from the shelter of the land toward the open sea. Mike comments on who has left the moorings ahead of us and who has not shown up for work yet. The coming and going of boats and of people is public knowledge. Boats are frequently named after girlfriends, wives, and daughters, whom everyone knows.

The water is dotted with the white, green, and red lights of other boats heading out to fish. The town lights fall astern, soon to be lost in the spray blown from our wake. In a series of short bursts, the engine is eased up to eighteen knots, a fast, wet ride in a fishing boat. We pound hard, once outside the protection of the inshore islands. Our bow rises sharply to meet the short steep rollers of the open sea. From setting his lobster pots down this bay for seventeen years, Dave recognises each of the dark silhouettes of the hundreds of islands scat- tered off this part of the Maine coast. He knows to the yard the contours of the bottom, and tells me, "You have to if you are going to know where the lobsters are." A summer visitor once asked a local skipper how he ever remembered where all the rocks were situated. He replied that he had a hard enough time keeping up with where there weren't any to try to remember where there were.

In the warmth of the wheelhouse, Mike smokes a cigarette, a bright glow of red in the darkness above the green light circling across the radar screen. At the wheel, Dave watches the other boats on the screen and then continues to stare into the blackness ahead. The moon is setting in a star-filled sky. On the VHF radio, the fishermen talk about the weather, if the fishing is good and what is happening ashore. Across a sea of talk, the fishermen keep in close contact and will help each other quickly if an engine fails or a sternman is injured.

The ride down to the fishing ground takes a scant half hour, and we reach the first string of pots a little before sunrise. To the east, heavy night clouds catch the sun's rays across their lower edges. Black turns into a pale wash of pink and blue. We cut the engine and wait for daybreak. Hauling before sunrise or after sunset is illegal, because in poor light it is difficult to see the coloured identifying bands painted around each man's pot buoys.

Dave and Mike time their departure from the dock to bring them to the first string of pots at around daybreak. Depending on the time of year, this will be minutes earlier or later than the previous day. Fishing is most active between early spring and late fall. Except for a few offshore fishermen, the harsh winters and attendant migration of lobster offshore preclude much serious fishing in the winter.

We turn slowly on a flat, still sea and drift a few yards off a shoreline of steep granite bluffs topped with stands of spruce and fir, a dangerous place with a tide running or an on-shore wind. Mike slides the engine cover off and takes his warmed orange coveralls from above the motor. Each man pulls on his work gear, a one-piece plastic suit with snugly fitting sleeves that stops the icy water and bait juice from trickling into their warm underclothing. Mike says that his blood is "thin" this morning and that getting going is taking longer than usual.

Waiting for activities to begin is a good time for a story of how things were done and of what life was like in the past. When I ask Mike and Dave how fishing has changed since colonial times, they recount what they have heard and read of the island's seafaring history.[1] They tell of deep-water men who, almost two centuries ago, fished for cod and mackerel in two- and three-masted schooners as far away as the Grand Banks off Newfoundland, the coast of Labrador, and Bay Chaleur off Cape Breton Island. In the early 1800s, fish were caught by "jigging" with hand-held lines either from dories launched by the schooners or from the decks of the mother ship.

For boys between eight and twelve to be cabin boy and cook was not unusual. The little formal schooling that they did receive came only in the winter. Accounts of young boys quitting school to start fishing reach back to the earliest days of the island's history.

Clams were used for bait and the clam digger was paid in goods at the local store. As is the case now, credit was needed to survive through the long winter months. By the 1880s seine nets were introduced which allowed more fish to be caught. Split and packed into barrels between layers of salt, mackerel were shipped in the nineteenth century to markets in Gloucester and Boston, or off to the Caribbean as a trade cargo. But the prosperity that the mackerel fisheries had brought to the island in the early years of the century declined rapidly after the Civil War. One explanation is that once slavery was abolished the market for cheap fish in the South ended. As the salt and custom houses of the mackerel industry began to disappear, commercial lobster fishing began to boom on the island during the 1880s.

In the colonial period, lobster were so plentiful that one could gather them from the beach at low tide, and farmers tossed them onto the fields as fertiliser. Lobster as large as forty pounds were not uncommon, and there were even cases reported of fishermen being trapped in gargantuan claws. Increased demand both at home and abroad for Maine lobster led to the canning of seafood and an exploitation of the resource. People became aware of the need to protect and conserve the lobster fishery and in 1895 a state law was passed to prohibit the sale of lobster less than ten and one-half inches from nose to tail.[2]

Before the days of engines, the smaller boats were moved by oar and the larger ones by sail. Mike proudly explains to me that until the early years of this century, much of the inshore lobstering was done in the same kind of small open boat in which he started fishing. From the beginning of the eighteenth century until the later years of the nineteenth, fishing under sail was from pinkies, a double-ended boat of up to forty tons. From the 1880s until the 1940s, Friendship sloops then became the mainstay of the inshore lobster fleet. Both craft now sail these waters as pleasure yachts. A century ago, few lobstermen[3] fished

Painting pot buoys with identifying colours.

more than a hundred traps in contrast to the five to eight hundred set today.

When I ask Mike and Dave to tell me about the steamboat ferry services from Boston Down East, they remind me that all this talk about island history will not get the traps hauled. For Mike and Dave, the low grind of the hydraulic pot hauler marks the beginning of the day's fishing. The hauler, a grooved wheel about ten inches in diameter hauls up the line, or "warp," connecting each pot buoy to the pair of pots on the bottom. Around the steadily turning drum, Mike wraps the pot warp, and within minutes the pots are hauled to the surface. These machines are now common on virtually all the boats, even on the smallest outboard rig. Before mechanical haulers, pots were hauled with muscle power, arduous work across the constantly rolling decks. Another young fisherman, who is sternman to his sixty-year-old father, told me that between them they still haul by hand a hundred traps each day. Some traps set on long lines in water up to a hundred and twenty feet deep can weigh with their rock ballast as much as sixty pounds. He laughs, "You just have to hope they are full after pulling them up."

Although Mike has little use for a watch while he is working, he can estimate clock time with remarkable accuracy by observing the height of the sun above the horizon. My watch reads six o'clock; he guesses about a quarter after and points to the sun now breaking the backdrop of hills to the east. The green and red bands on the pot buoys glint brightly, and Dave deftly hooks the first one. The business of hauling has begun. Barring the inevitable snarl-ups of gear, this task will continue without interruption until the last trap of the day has been hauled, picked, baited, and slid back into the ocean to "set" until tomorrow.

Attached to the buoy are between five and fifty fathoms of pot warp that leads down to each pair of pots set about seven fathoms apart on hard bottom or rocky ledges [one fathom equals six feet]. Each pair of pots is secured to a line with four other pairs to make up a "string." The pots are set at the maximum depth offshore where strings are set on warps of forty fathoms or more.

In this fishing community, about a hundred and fifty boats each haul up to eight hundred pots a day. Lobster fishing is done in basically the same way on each boat. Variation in skill accounts for top boats making in excess of $100,000 a year, while other fishermen sell their boats and gear and find work ashore. Knowing where and when to set pots requires a remarkable blend of local knowledge, years of experience, and intuition.

Mike stands ready to bait the pot now breaking the surface. Two bait needles loaded with fresh pockets of red fish are ready to replace the empty pockets in the main pot and trailer pot that he will soon empty. Already he has baited up a tub full of pockets on the ride out here, because:

> "If you haven't got it done beforehand, then it's takin up hours of your day. I've got it figured out between strings how much time I've got to bait needles and put pockets of herring on. For the next trap that comes along, I've got to have so many fish. The time ain't measured in minutes by the watch but in your head."

The margin of profit has been a slim one this season on the *Stella*, and Mike baits their own bait pockets to save money. He tells me about his Aunt Mary, who baits pockets for other boats. Between five-thirty and seven-thirty every morning, she works at the bait shack alongside the fish factory and baits anywhere from 230 to 500 pockets at five cents a pocket. This is one of several ways in which island women support and in turn make a livelihood from the fishing. Women and young girls were a key part of the industry past and present. Before lobster canning was prohibited, they were employed in the canneries to pick out and pack the meat. Many women will dig clams for a living when clams are available.

This season has been slow for everybody, and the constant concern has been about when the lobsters will start to move out of the rocks and into deeper water where they can be trapped. Many fishermen believe that the lobsters migrate offshore into deeper and warmer water during the late fall, den into mud holes and remain inactive. At this time they are hard to trap, and most fishermen then pull their boats ashore or rig them for scalloping. The fishermen believe that a cold snap will start the migration and by mid-October the catch should be better. In the early spring when the icy waters begin to warm, according to lore, the lobsters migrate back inshore to feed and breed among the rocks. Many fishermen set and move their traps around according to this belief. On the other hand, marine biologists question the extent to which lobsters are migratory. Their arguments are based on the results of following the movements of tagged lobster.

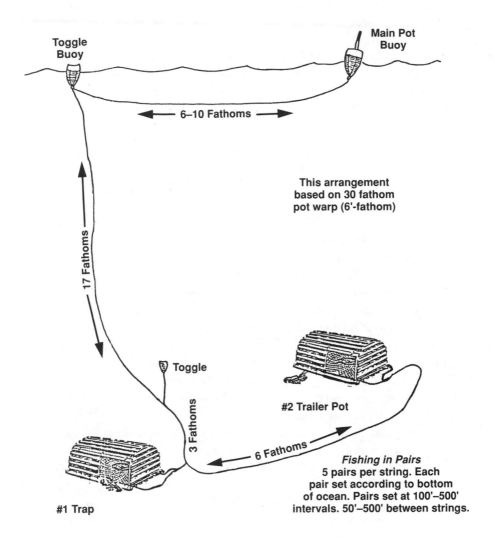

Toggle Buoy

Main Pot Buoy

← 6–10 Fathoms →

This arrangement based on 30 fathom pot warp (6'-fathom)

17 Fathoms

Toggle

#2 Trailer Pot

3 Fathoms

← 6 Fathoms →

#1 Trap

Fishing in Pairs
5 pairs per string. Each pair set according to bottom of ocean. Pairs set at 100'–500' intervals. 50'–500' between strings.

Fishing gear: The arrangement of buoys, line, and lobster pots.

The fear that perhaps the area has been fished out lies below the surface of the fishermen's talk. They hope that the lobsters will come back in a season or two, as they have done in the past. Setting trap limits and limiting the number of operators are possible solutions that the conservationists in the State Department of Fisheries offer. While most fishermen want to preserve their future livelihood, few can afford to defer the economic needs of making an adequate living now. The time perspective of many of the younger fishermen is grounded in the present to the point that they are reluctant to hear the stories of those who observe a steadily diminishing catch.

On this late October morning hopes for a good haul run high after the cold snap of the weekend. More than a hint of autumn is in the thin clear air. Birch and oak leaves have darkened already to dark green and vermilion. The colour changes of autumn are associated by some fishermen with the movement of lobsters. Fishermen say that when the leaves are red on Green Island Mountain, the lobsters will strike at Little Fog Island. Oak leaves floating down the bay are taken as a sign that lobsters will soon be trapped.

Today we are hauling mainly short warps of about twenty fathoms along the thickly wooded shoreline of Green Island. By afternoon we will haul a few strings in deeper water to see whether lobsters are moving out yet. The winch draws the warp into a tight line that breaks the water a few feet away. Dave and Mike watch the streaming feathers of spray fall toward the dark shape of a rising lobster pot. After leaving the pots set-out over the weekend, the first string gives a good indication of the day's fishing. Mike explains, "It lets you know how your day is goin to do." As the pot comes aboard, the hopes of a really big haul fade. Crabs, sea urchins, and a couple of small lobsters scrabble in the bottom. The last occupant of the pot is a sculpin, a curious-looking fish with bulging eyes and fleshy lips. Mike snaps it back overboard. Occasionally a cod or other edible fish is trapped and taken home for supper.

Dave swings the first pot aboard, slaps it down onto the washboard, and slides it swiftly aft down the polished brass runners to Mike. Twenty-five seconds have passed. Mike unties the string that secures the leather-hinged door to a securing button. In a series of quick movements, his gloved hands reach in and pick out the contents of the pot. Large crabs are dropped onto the deck; their meat-filled claws will be removed later. A handful of prickly urchins and one snapper—a lobster shorter than the legal limit—are tossed disgustedly over the side. One fair-sized lobster is carefully placed into a division of a wooden holding box where it will soon be measured. Only lobsters between $3^3/16$ and 5 inches from the eye socket to the far edge of the carapace can be sold in Maine. The oversize limit is one attempt to produce more lobster from larger female lobsters carrying seed. The lobster in the tray is measured with a brass gauge and then dropped into a drum of circulating salt water. Lobsters soon suffocate if put into still water. As Mike removes the empty bait pocket, reaches for the bait needle, and skewers a full pocket of sardine and red fish, the second pot, the trailer, hits the washboard. The two pots are separated by about seven fathoms of warp so that the two pots are not fishing too closely together on the bottom.

Dave now starts to pick his own trap fifteen seconds after Mike, who is closing his pot and tying it up. Mike flicks it down the washboard and positions it ready to be dropped back over the side. Dave's pot has a couple of good sized counters—lobsters of legal size—and enough crabs to keep his wife busy picking out the meat in the evening. He baits, ties off the pot, and puts the boat into gear. We have been stationary for barely a minute. Dave nods to Mike, who slides the first pot back into the ocean. As we move ahead, the pot warp snakes and whips across the afterdeck back into the ocean. Mike tells me how he once saved a friend from being dragged over the stern when his leg was caught in a gillnet line. Grabbing his boot, Mike held onto him until he was disentangled.

The second trap must be thrown at exactly the right moment when the seven-fathom line joining the pots is just tight enough:

> "You've got to have that pot thrown properly. If you throw it out too soon, the line kinks. It's going to have a slack rope. The pots fish too close together. If you throw it out too late, it's going to get a whip to it, and it's going to draw away from the trap, and your trap is going to go upside down. So it's got to be flung at just the right moment."

Before the count of one hundred, the second trap settles into our curling sternwave to be followed by the trailer buoy and then the red and green pot marker buoy. Scarcely a minute and a half have passed since Dave gaffed the first buoy. This same cycle of hauling, picking, baiting, and setting will be repeated several hundred times before the last trap is hauled, and the *Stella* heads back up the bay to the moorings and home.

Time and timing play an important role in the whole business of fishing. Mike explains to me:

"Your whole day is bein used in time, in different segments, you might say. You've got big times. You've got small times. You've got times when it's goin to matter and you've got times when it ain't. But if you use your time wrongly, when it matters, then you are goin to do somethin wrong. You could damage your gear, go over the side or kill yourself, if you wasn't thinkin or watchin, and if you didn't do somethin quick enough."

I look at my watch to measure the progress of the day's haul but realise that this constant measure of time is inappropriate for understanding an experience whose temporal frameworks change throughout the activity, and as I learn later, change with tide, day, and season. In Mike's words:

"Time at certain points is extremely important, and you measure it down to the smallest unit. And yet at other times it's nothin at all. It don't bother you. It's constantly varyin dependin on whether you are goin between traps or whether you are droppin the trap back at the right moment. Time is everythin as far as breakin it down and makin it seem as nothin."

Mike's comment on the paradoxical nature of time on the water begins to explain the frustration that he experienced with the metronomic pace of activities in school.

We move from pot to pot closely following the rocky ledges off the shore until we reach the westernmost point of Green Island where their fishing territory abruptly ends. The distance between traps is seldom more than about a hundred yards—just long enough for the *Stella* to plane a broad white swath across the calm waters. Mike uses the running time between the strings of pots to accomplish essential tasks before hauling begins again. How much time he has depends on how far apart the strings are set in the particular area being fished. Sometimes he will have only a couple of minutes; at other times he may have ten minutes or more in which to get his work done. He plans this time ahead accordingly:

"I say I am goin to drink a little soda, bait some pockets, and get all the lobsters binned. I figure I am a minute away from the trap. I try to get all my lobsters done first, otherwise they are goin to be pilin on top of each other from the traps. And I figure I've got to get my bait pockets done. You are tryin to bait up ahead as much as possible. If you haven't got it done, then it's takin hours of your day. When you get to the buoy, you have about half a minute before the trap is goin to be at the surface."

Running between pots provides short intervals for the other tasks necessary for getting healthy legal-sized lobsters to the dealers on shore. Each lobster must be measured to ensure that it falls within the size range determined by state law. Mike can see immediately whether a lobster is within the permitted size or is border-line between being a "counter" and a "snapper" or a counter and one oversize, an "old bull." He takes a smallish lobster and carefully lays the curved brass measure across the soft back of the shell. This lobster has recently shed its shell and can be damaged easily by careless handling. His careful handling of lobsters has earned him the reputation of being a dependable sternman who docks good lobsters that aren't "banged up." It's almost big enough but not quite, and Mike drops it over the side.

Mike believes that what the sea does not give him now it will give later. He does not see his time as an irreversible flow of opportunities that he must take now or lose forever. He plays a waiting game and knows that the lobster he cast back today will be trapped again when it has had a chance to grow some more. Mike and his friends seldom understood my urgency in school about getting writing in on time and completing a prescribed number of essays. Students would tell me, "Stop buggin us. It's comin."

The next lobster twists and squirms around in Mike's gloved hand. It measures up to size and a thick rubber band immobilises its powerful crusher claw. The band is expanded over the snapping claw with a pair of scissor-like tongs. Banding is necessary to prevent the lobsters from attacking and damaging each other in the holding tank. A few lobstermen still secure the claws by forcing them shut with short plastic plugs. The days when plugs were whittled out of basswood on a winter's evening have gone by.

I watch Mike baiting the pockets as we head to the next string. He grabs a pocket, unties the slip knot, opens it and dumps the half eaten contents over the side. Overhead the constantly circling seagulls dive into our wake and fight over the scraps. Into the pocket goes his fist full of bait—maggots and all. The drawstring pulls it tight. He twists the pocket around his first finger, grabs it with his other two fingers, slips the knot through and whips it closed. Looking over his shoulder, Mike sees Dave gaffing the next buoy. Mike grabs another pocket and hurriedly flips it open. The buoy rattles across the davy block, and in ten seconds the trap is on the deck waiting to be picked. In a blur of fingers, the pocket is baited and ready for Mike to stuff in the trap as it slides toward him. Mike's hands go through these finger-aching motions several hundred times a day.

If there are lobsters out here to be caught, Mike and Dave will fish these waters for the rest of their working lives, for as long as they are physically able. A fisherman is old only when he is too tired and worn out to fish any more. For some, retirement is at sixty, or even younger. Others like "old man Eaton," who fishes a small outboard rig like the boat in which Mike started out, will still be fishing into their eighties. Mike hopes to save enough money to buy a boat large enough for scallop dragging by the time he is twenty. With less than a year to go, he is close to this goal and is already "squintin and dickerin" among the boats for sale.

Working as sternman to Dave has given Mike experience in waters that take years to know. A large part of the art of fishing depends upon local knowledge of where to set traps from one day to the next. Dave's father has fished these waters since he was fifteen and knows virtually every ledge, hole, and stretch of hard bottom where a lobster can be found. In infinite detail he remembers the contours of a sea bed that rise and fall like mountain ranges. Using eyes and ears, fishermen recall the precise location of several hundred traps dotted across a hundred square miles of sea. To the unfamiliar eye, the islands appear similar. In fog the few differences between one pine, spruce, and birch-capped island and the next are blurred into a featureless smear of grey and green.

Yet through the fishermen's eyes, small differences are sharply contrasted, and they can locate their pots quickly by using range marks. One bearing might be a transit formed by lining up a solitary oak on a hill with an outcropping of rocks on the shore. A second transit positions a summer camp in the foreground against a small clearing in the background. These transits intersect in the area where the strings are set. Once in the general area, the colours of other fishermen's pots help to orient him toward his own pots. In bad weather when the visibility is down to yards, a skilled fisherman can determine his position by

Picking the pots.

Baiting the pockets.

Measuring lobster.

turning off the engine and listening to the waves breaking against the shore. The sound of the surf changes along the coast, as does the way the current runs across the ledges; no two places look or sound alike. The land and seascapes of their working world change constantly, and each change must be remembered, if one is not to depend wholly on electronic aids.[4]

Dave's father does not rely on a nautical chart to show him what he has learned through experience about his home waters. In countless conversations, he has passed to his son the knowledge in his mind and hands. Little if anything of what he knows is written down. In contrast, Dave and Mike are from a new generation of fishermen who find their way with the help of radar. In thick fog, they can plot a position, find their pots or the way home. New math and high technology rely less upon a well-developed memory and all the senses finely tuned to the life of the ocean. Yet Dave sees the value of both ways of finding his way among the islands and around the rocky ledges of the Maine coast. His father's skills and whole relationship with the sea impress him deeply.

At the same time, Dave recognises that fishing is changing and computers will soon be as familiar an aid to navigation as the lead line was to his father. High-school students will need to take courses in electronic navigation, if they are to handle the sophisticated electronic equipment essential to fishing competitively and going outside home waters in all weather. Fishermen need to be able to read technical service manuals, notices to mariners and to translate complex information into practical actions. If they cannot do this, they will be disadvantaged by having to seek help from those more literate than themselves.

Time-space values are related closely on the water, and this is especially evident in the time-honoured rights of a family to fish a particular area. Dave and Mike need to know where their traps have been set not only so they can locate them quickly, but also because fishing grounds are territorial. Although nobody owns the sea, and a lobster licence nominally entitles a fisherman to set traps wherever he chooses, tradition establishes the rights for father and son to fish a particular stretch of coast. The boundaries between areas are established by undrawn but closely observed lines that fishermen cross only at the risk of losing their gear. In the last century, a fisherman staked out his territory by making fast several dories in the coves he intended to fish. This procedure was traditionally done on town meeting day, the

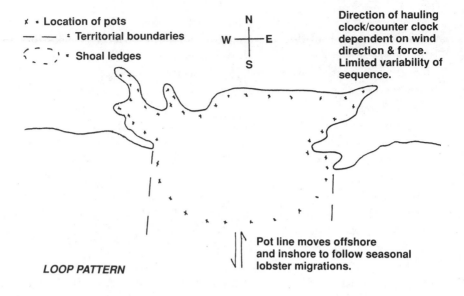

x • Location of pots
— — : Territorial boundaries
⌣ ⌢ ⌣ • Shoal ledges

N
W ─┼─ E
S

Direction of hauling
clock/counter clock
dependent on wind
direction & force.
Limited variability of
sequence.

LOOP PATTERN

Pot line moves offshore
and inshore to follow seasonal
lobster migrations.

Direction of hauling
'zig zag' dependent
on wind direction/force
and state of tide. Both are
highly variable sequences.

Mark
Island

TIDAL PATTERN

Alternate sequences for hauling lobster pots.

first Monday in March, when the season started.

Now, one or more families will fish an area and seldom attempt to extend their territory unless by invitation. Consequently, newcomers will probably be allowed to start fishing only in marginally productive waters. After the local fishermen approve a newcomer, a process that can take years, they may then invite him to move a few traps into the better fishing grounds of the established fishermen. The conservative rate at which a change occurs in the distribution of fishing rights illustrates the initial response to many of the island's newcomers and to the different approaches that they bring to all aspects of life. This phenomenon was particularly apparent in parents' initial skepticism to new ways of learning in school.

Each stretch of the coast has a different topography that requires an individual to vary his approach from that of his neighbour's and from one day's fishing to the next. The diagrams show two representative patterns of how the pots might be set. In both areas, the patterns are determined by how each fisherman chooses to fish throughout his territory. He decides where to place traps, when to move, and what the daily sequence of hauling will be, decisions that ensure no two days will be alike either in terms of route taken or time on the water.

The length of day is determined by the number of traps owned and the territory over which they are distributed. The number of traps he fishes within that area is influenced only in part by available capital, much more by choice. Many of the fishermen out of Long Harbor go down to the Eastern Isles, a journey that takes about one-and-a-half hours before hauling can begin. Others haul close to home and have minimum travel time. Some fishermen constantly move their traps around in search of lobster, while others are content to wait. Distance between strings varies from a couple of minutes to perhaps a quarter of an hour, depending on the length of an individual's route. And besides these variables, there are those caused by seasonal cycles.

Mike's Uncle Amos traps down the shore line of Green Island from North Point clear down to the Eastern Ledges, a distance of about two miles. In late September, his inshore pots follow the gently curving shoreline running up into an occasional cove or inlet. At the end of the bay, a rocky headland forms a natural boundary line. Sometimes several fishermen share an area, but here the territory is sharply divided. Beyond the point, pots of a different colour lay claim to another man's territory. Amos' pots follow the point to where it disappears under breakers of spray. From here his route curves off into deeper water for about a mile and then parallels the inshore line back up the bay. Each day's run is for Amos a long loop with jagged ends.

Whether Amos begins hauling at the eastern or the western end of the loop depends on the direction of the wind in the morning. He starts each day at four o'clock by opening his bedroom window to feel and hear the direction of his day's work. If there is a strong wind from the south, he usually doesn't haul that day because the advantage of fishing in the lee of the land is lost. An onshore wind lifts the shoal water into a short steep chop that makes hauling difficult and danger-ous. On these days he will work on something else or take a day off. For Amos, the freedom to work in this way is part of the continuing appeal of fishing.

He explains that his fishing grounds have the advantage of being uninfluenced by the height of the tides:

> "Tides don't affect me as much as they would Dave. When the tides are slack, he can get all his gear, but when the tide is running all of it will be under. Pulls the buoys down and he can't get them. That's when the tide is like this week, running eleven feet."

On the other hand, Amos can get each of his pairs any time during daylight hours and at any state of the tide. Consequently, he doesn't need to worry about timing his arrival at certain stretches of the route to coincide with slack water. Dave sets his buoys in narrow channels where they are pulled under when the tide is running fast. An eleven-foot tide produces a tidal current of up to five knots. He must time his arrival to coincide with either the top or the bottom of the tide when there is no current running. Each boat makes different decisions about how best to use time and tide.

Even though the tides are one variable that Amos does not have to contend with, his routine does vary. "When I'm here on this route, I might jump out a little bit, run off with a pair of traps just to see if the lobster have moved off from the shore." Although the precise contours of Amos' loop pattern of hauling change daily as he moves pots among the rock ledges up and down the bay, moving pots extends the day often until dusk. Conceivably, two fishermen can own the same num-ber of traps, fish in comparable waters, and yet one will finish several hours before his neighbour, who hunts for his lobsters by moving his pots into the water where he believes they are going.

Because many fishermen believe that lobsters migrate in response to water temperature, availability of food, seasonal breeding, and the growth moulting cycles, fishermen either choose to set their traps and wait for the lobster to arrive, or to hunt for the lobster. Mike regards the latter choice as the mark of the good fisherman and admires this in his uncle:

> "A lot of people just sit there and wait for the lobster. Uncle Amos goes looking for them. He chases them where they're moving. He moves right with them moving traps one step ahead of the lobsters. One day he'll catch them over there, and the next he'll catch them over here. He can catch lobster when nobody else can."

Uncle Amos adopts the approach more of a hunter than of a gatherer, a practice that reflects his awareness of the comparative scarcity of a quarry that can no longer be harvested simply by setting traps and waiting for lobster to be trapped in the fullness of time.

Mike and Dave fish in waters where the variables of tide and current must be considered. Their route is one that encourages them to make detours and change the sequence of hauling. The tides are full this week, and Dave is anxious to reach his strings around Mark Island before the tide turns at noon. He glances at the sun and tells Mike that they'll catch the rest of the offshore strings in the afternoon. Dave does not haul his traps in the same order each day. "Sometimes I go one way and sometimes another, dependin on the tide and wind. Sometimes I zig-zag one way down the route and sometimes another."

"Sometimes," "it depends," and "yes and no" are answers that fishermen give frequently to my questions. Sometimes their pots come up full while at other times they come up empty. The length of the workday depends on the size of the haul, the weather, and the energy of the fishermen. Sometimes the pots can be reached while at other times they are inaccessible. This kind of indeterminacy in being able or willing to give a definitive answer or to make an exact prediction is attributable both to the nature of the work itself and to working in a setting controlled by daily, lunar, and seasonal cycles. For example, fishermen predict that when the moon comes up full, the fish will back off and be difficult to catch. This world of constantly changing circumstances and constraints contrasts sharply with Mike's perception of an unvarying and inflexible routine that controlled his life in school.

Mike's pace of hauling noticeably alters through the day as the fishing goes well or goes slowly. At times both the men pick out the haul in a frenzy of excitement occasioned by almost full pots; at other times they slow down and lethargically toss the numerous snappers, crabs, and sea urchins over the side. Mike tells me:

> "If lobsters comin good, then you'll speed up. Slow down with poor haulin. If you get lobsters, you feel like workin harder. If you aren't doin nothin, you don't feel like workin. Sometimes you get a few in the mornin but a lot in the afternoon."

Fishermen are free to work as fast or as slowly as they choose. The rate at which they work will not influence the size of the day's haul but will affect the length of their day. In school, teachers will say that their students have a personal tempo for working and nothing that teachers can do or say will induce students to alter it. No authority tells Mike and Dave at what pace they should work or reminds them of a quota to be reached. But whether pots come up empty or near full, they keep on hauling. "You put your head down, and somewhere along that route you'll get enough to make a day's pay."

Mike and Dave will fish through the lean times expecting the lobsters to "come back" as they have done in the past. Similarly, clams, scallops, and many other fish are believed to come and go in cycles. Dave remembers a time a few years ago when his scallop drags were rusting behind his barn. But two seasons ago they were almost too heavy-laden to lift off the bottom. Now scalloping is not so good again. A few fishermen see the cycles of lean and plentiful seasons within a larger time frame and believe that however good this year's catch might be compared to last, the general trend is for fewer lobsters to be caught each year. Some fishermen argue that to conserve the fishing more cooperation is needed to manage a resource with a limited capacity for regeneration under the onslaught of more boats each year carrying larger numbers of traps.

Mike points to a bucket of empty bait pockets and says that when it's rounded off at the rim, the day's hauling is half done. At this point they normally take their lunch break. It's ten o'clock by my watch. Mike guesses a quarter after. The time for lunch changes slightly each day in accordance with the sunrise and the tempo of how well the lobster are coming. For almost ten minutes hauling gear stops as we head for the next string two miles away. Mike jokes that he is into health foods and munches on carrots and drinks another soda. They have hauled continually for the past four hours with only a pause to warm their sea-soaked gloves against the engine's exhaust pipe.

In school Mike ate lunch at precisely 11:25 a.m. During the last few minutes before the bell rang, Mike's impatience invariably led him and his friends into trouble, and he never accepted explanations for why he couldn't go now. If he attempted to assert his need to have some control over how his time would be used, then he risked the punishment of points lost, a detention hall, or possible suspension. To stop work early, to come to class late, or to work on a different topic at the wrong time was regarded as infractions of the clock-governed time boundaries that organise all school work.

The division between morning and afternoon is marked differently by some fishermen than by many people who work ashore. The lunch break does not necessarily separate morning from afternoon. Mike explains. "You don't call it mornin after ten. It's afternoon. That's what it feels like." On another occasion, I hear the division within the day explained differently:

> "It's mornin 'cause you are gettin up. Mornin is gettin to work. Once you are out fishin it's day time. You've entered the day. You get in, in the afternoon. Doesn't matter if it's ten o'clock. Afternoon is when the day is all heated up and everythin is out and goin. Traffic goin. Everyone goin."

Working independently of a clock schedule, no foreman tells them when to start, when to stop, or how to allocate their time. Dave is proud of the fact that he is his own boss and can quit when he wants. Freedom to structure their time according to the varying demands of the work and to their own needs brings a level of independence that is a large part of the continuing attraction of fishing. Yet the cost of this perceived freedom is a willingness and ability to go out and fish whenever possible to make a livelihood. Although the boats are in frequent contact, they do not coordinate activities or make collective decisions while out fishing. During the net fish season Mike will work day and night with scarcely a break for rest. But on storm days in the winter or when he's tired of fishing, he can take off time. Even if he loses his job as a sternman with Dave, he can find another boat that needs a crew, or dig for clams.

On the *Stella,* we are now approaching Mark Island; a mile off-shore, away from the lee of Green Island, the sea is noticeably chop-pier. Fishermen claim that there is often better weather before noon. This belief is borne out by the fact that as the sun rises, the shallow coastal waters warm up and create an onshore breeze. At ten-thirty the wind is freshening up, and we begin to roll. Dave eases back the throttle to ease the pounding. Mike puts on his gloves again and checks how many lobsters there are in the bin. It's not yet half full. By the end of the day, they hope to see claws above the top of the rim. Last season the second bin was filled each day, but now it stands full of assorted gear with a low line of yellow rust marking the level of the previous season's haul. Mike and Dave hope that the slow haul of the morning will be improved with the afternoon's haul, as is often the case.

Time on the water is measured by how much work has been done and by how many traps remain to be hauled. In clear weather on the sea, the horizon is visible, and the sun's height above it immediately shows how much daylight has passed and how much remains. Time is associated much more powerfully with the height of the sun's arc than with the hands on the watch. On cloudy days when the sun is hidden, Mike looks for light spots behind the clouds. Mike looks up many times in the day to see how far it has passed. He explains why he does this:

> "I know when it's goin over me. I get up in the mornin when there ain't no sun. When I'm leavin in the mornin, I see the sun breakin. I see the sun breakin when I'm comin in. I kind of look over the westage, and she's just breakin Green Island. That time it's realized. [by Mike] I'm passin between strings, and I'm grabbin my lunch. I kind of look up in the same spot, and she's there. No clocks needed. When you're passin between strings, and you look up and the sun's there, you know you're on schedule. Around here you can't have a watch on. If you are diggin clams, your arm is under water. The island is wet when you are workin. When it's time, you know it. Just somethin you relate with and get used to."

Today the sky has a hard, full brightness to it, and it's difficult to imagine the coastline with its hundreds of islands blanketed in fog. A solitary beacon marking a ledge of shoal water booms every few sec-onds to the west, a constant reminder that visibility can be lost in minutes. Mike catches and picks the first of the afternoon pots with an enthusiasm that he expressed in school when he was talking about a hunting or fishing trip. His interest waned, however, once I asked him to write down these experiences.

The pace of fishing quickens as the offshore pots begin to catch more lobster. Mike and Dave joke about whose pot, the main or the trailer is catching the most; Dave picks the trailer and Mike the main pot. Both work harder now that more are being caught and the bin is more than two-thirds full. By one o'clock the lobsters are almost level with the top of the barrel. A second bucket is almost filled with empty bait pockets. When it is "rounded over," we will have hauled most of Dave's pots. The sun is already starting to slide down toward the horizon again. Since the lunch break at ten o'clock, nothing has broken the steady rhythm of work except for an occasional snarled line.

The constant sound and motion of the boat, and the steady hauling, picking, and setting of traps creates a mesmeric rhythm that Mike now describes:

> "I do this and that and don't really think about it. Hands doing one job and mind doing another. I've been really interested in diving, and thinking about it don't interfere with my work. Kind of automatic. Weird isn't it? I never got into a routine while in school."

Their routine of hauling, picking, and setting the traps gathers momentum and any talk, apart from its difficulty being heard above the engine, appears to intrude on the privacy of their thoughts. The rhythm of their work creates a quality of time that allows Mike and Dave to experience fishing as the focal activity that makes sense of their lives.

Within view of the *Stella*, twenty other boats are hauling their traps. Some are visible only as a streak of smoke against the skyline while others are close enough to recognise individuals and to wave. Mike sees Jeff, a fellow student from junior high days who is now in a programme that allows students to be released from high school for two days a week for job training. Some students try out nursing while others are introduced to servicing marine engines in local repair shops. This programme has done much to encourage students, who might otherwise have quit, to remain in school long enough to consider a career other than fishing, but Jeff has wanted to fish since he was a child. He works as a sternman with Uncle Amos, who laughs when Jeff pulls off his gloves to scribble in his salt-stained notebook details of catch size, pot location, fuel burned, and details about what Amos is teaching him about fishing.

On the *Stella*, hauling the last trap of the day is as important a time marker as the first. Dave gaffs it aboard and laughs that if we'd only thought to haul this one first, we'd have been done a long time ago. Today's hauling has been moderately successful, more than enough to pay the overheads. I ask Mike what it feels like to reach the end of a long day:

> "Last trap of the day. Take it easy when you put that buoy on the hauler, relax. You've got the pockets all baited—good time, good feelin, and everythin. You see the barrel almost full. You know you have a good day's pay there. And then you have to think of cleanin up. Time to wash her up."

With the last trap hauled and returned to the ocean until tomorrow, most of the day's work is done. Earlier in the day, Dave talked with other boats about how the fishing was going. Now he calls ashore to tell his wife that we are finishing up and that he should be home soon—her signal to start getting supper ready. As he heads the *Stella* for the moorings, the sun is setting on the ridges of Green Island mountain. Mike lights a cigarette and goes below for buckets and soap.

Physical movements have been confined to the small spaces on a lobster boat. Dave has stood at the wheel all day and gone below once to check the engine. Another time he stood on the stern, downwind. Mike has moved around a lot more since he picks, baits, traps, bands, and bins the lobsters. From time to time, he hosed down the decks to keep them clear of the treacherously slippy scraps of gurry, or fish waste. Now he takes pride in ensuring that from deck house to stern deck their boat is clean for tomorrow. With boiling hot water from the engine exhaust and detergent, he scrubs the working area, windows, and bridge deck, and hoses down the decks. Next the holding barrel is drained of sea water in readiness for bringing the lobsters ashore at the dealers. Gear is straightened and oilskins removed.

The few remaining crabs scuttling beneath the side decks are collected ready to be brought home. Picking out and dressing crab meat are traditionally women's work. In a confessional tone, Greg, a senior, once told me that he would do any work in order to pay for a car—even pick crabs and make Christmas wreaths. Crabs can provide

Picking crab meat.

a substantial supplement to the income gained from the lobster fishing of the menfolk. When the Boston and New York markets are strong, many of the island women pick out up to twenty pounds a day and can make a hundred dollars or more. But crabbing is usually a limited market, and the local dealers will not buy crab meat in appreciable quantities unless the price of seafood is high.

Not all boats trouble to bring crabs back to shore for mothers and daughters to pick out in the afternoons and evenings. Dave sees the income from his wife picking out crab meat as well worth the little time it takes for Mike to break off the claws of the small crabs and to toss the live bodies back into the ocean, where they are reputed to grow new claws. The large crabs have sufficient body meat to make picking out the whole crab worthwhile.

Pat, a senior, has picked crabs during the long summer vacations and in the evenings since she was in elementary school. Like Mike, she first learned about work from watching her parents as a young child:

"I'm so used to doing them. That's what my mom and dad used to do. Dad used to be a lobsterman until his boat got wrecked. He used to bring in the crabs and me, mom and grandma would do them. We'd all sit at my home and pick crabs all day. It seemed like all day, but I was young then, took no time. We whipped it right up. I enjoy picking crabs. I'm fast with my hands. It's natural. I can do a crate of crabs in an hour and a half. That's me and another person."

Each crate holds a hundred pounds of live crabs that when dressed out produce about nine pounds of meat, for which Pat gets around five dollars a pound. Pat and her friend can pack anywhere from five to seven crates a day for the dealer. Her hours are flexible as long as her dealer has enough crates when he goes to market:

"We could do them whenever we wanted. If we wanted to leave early and do the rest the next day, we could. When I was picking crabs, I could do what I wanted to do. The guy never said anything."

For Pat, the freedom to work her own hours is as much part of the appeal of this work as it is for Mike and Dave.

As we pass by the old stone quarry, the tall steel gantries stand as reminders of a granite industry that brought skilled Italian stonecutters to the island in the 1870s. Massive blocks of stone and marble were cut and shipped out to construct public buildings in places like New York City and as far away as Colorado. At the height of the quarry industry in the 1940s, up to three hundred men were employed here working two shifts, from 7 a.m. to 3:45 p.m. and from 4 p.m. to midnight. The high cost of shipping stone and the availability in less remote New England quarries have closed the quarry for several decades.

We pull in alongside the fish dock and tie up. Mike and Dave unload the catch. The fish dealer weighs it and writes out a slip for the number of pounds landed. At least part of the payment will go for gas and boat maintenance. The remainder is divided between captain and sternman. Mike's share is less than Dave's, since he does not have to make boat payments of several hundred dollars a month nor replace lost gear.

For the first time that day Dave asks me what time it is. He wants to pick up his daughter from basketball practice and then go shopping with her off island. The carpenters on the island have a saying that the work will be done in the time allotted to it. The freedom to allocate one's time among work, home, and other activities is a mark of independence that is evident throughout the community. Dave, a father of two daughters and a son, has chosen recently to spend less time fishing and more time with his family. "My day ends about noon. I make it that way. I want to spend time with my family. My wife brought the kids up. I'd go 3 a.m. until 8 p.m. I've lost those years. The kids are growing up. I want to be with them now."

We put the *Stella* back onto her mooring and row ashore in the dinghy. Many moorings will remain empty until the boats return around sunset. When I ask a retired dealer why some boats come in so much later than the others, he smiles.

> "I know of a fisherman who would come in like late at night, and he would pull into a harbor, wait, set there. Just so he could say he was the last guy in. And we're all there waiting for him, seven o'clock at night, you know, trying to get home. And the clown is sitting out there trying to be a hero, just to be the last guy in. They're very proud people. There's no question about it."

At the end of this day on the water, Mike wryly asked me if I thought that it wasn't a bit different from our being in school. I could only answer, "Yes." As a teacher accustomed to organising all classwork within the context of the master schedule, I had been struck by the extent to which the work of Mike and Dave had progressed without reference to a clock that measured the location and duration of activities. References to clock time were never made except in answer to questions that I asked as the observer. We have seen how Mike, Dave, and the other fishermen organise their time according to the demands of the work, the tide, and the weather. At each stage of the work, the fishermen are responsible for deciding how best to use their time.

The length of each day's work varies appreciably not only among different boats in the fleet but from one day to the next on the same boat. The factors that influence this variation include the distance from shore to the fishing ground, the number of traps owned, their distance apart, the depth at which they are set, and the pace at which each fisherman hauls them. In addition, the length of the day is influenced by the daily route, a sequence dependent upon topography, weather, tide, and the fishermen's willingness to hunt for the lobster by moving pots around in anticipation of their migratory movements. If weather permits, traps are hauled on a daily basis during the season. The only exceptions are Sundays, when many fishermen respect a religiously grounded day of rest, and "storm days" when few fishermen will put their gear and life at extreme risk.

Fleet rigged for the scallop-dragging season.

The consequence of these variables is that each day's hauling is different, and this variety is part of the appeal in this arduous, uncertain living. Fishermen perceive a freedom to work in the manner that they choose and in so doing maintain a life style independent of external control or close supervision. This independence, however, is closely balanced with, and in a sense undercut by, the economic need to make an adequate income during the present recession in catch size. Most fishermen work for much longer hours than the potential freedom suggests we might expect. In short, there is a tension between a perceived freedom and an economic determinism, the resolution of which will be examined later in a discussion of what I will call "existential time."

In contrast to the experience of time described above, Mike and his friends had complained to me as their teacher about the monotony and boredom that the unvarying inflexible schedule conferred on much of their school work. Every day was like the preceding and following ones. A major consequence of students' focus on the schedule was that the demands of the task and the potential interest and value of our work became eclipsed by students watching the clock and waiting for the bell to take them to the next forty-two minute block of schooling. This precise measuring of class time appeared arbitrary and unrelatable to the students' time needs for the task at hand. Similarly most students viewed due dates as devices designed for the convenience of teachers and the discomfort of students.

The controlling aspects of time in school took on a punitive quality when students were kept in during break or after-school detention. Time became the enemy in the way that writing can, when used to punish students by making them write out repeated lines. Mike and his friends seldom were able to develop a meaningful routine and rhythm in schoolwork, and their one-speed pace of working contrasted markedly with the tempo of the few students who did find interest and value in their schooling. After seven periods of schoolwork, Mike was finally free to go home and start the day's work that was important to him.[5]

John Bischof

Chapter Two

WORK ON THE ISLAND

Although Mike and Dave's day on the water is usually over by two o'clock, the first shift workers at the fish factory still have another hour of packing. The constant cloud of gulls that circle around the fish factory breaks for a few moments as Mike drives past on his way home. Today packing is in full swing, and women are working in shifts around the clock. But the work is not always so heavy, depending on fish, market demand, and the weather. Judy, the floor supervisor, tells me, "If mother nature decides to be bad, then we are bad, too."

A silver stream of herring slides down the center of the room past the packers' tables. Some women, like May, have stood here for forty years, while others have packed only during their summer vacations from school. Judy has noticed that fewer young women come here now than when she started eleven years ago:

> "The younger ones don't like the smell at first, and they aren't so steady. It's the last thing they want to do. They've heard it's really hard work. There's a lot of other things out there for them, too, now. Many women start in after they get their families in school because they need to make extra income. Some start in their teens and then return as adults."

Once they get used to it, many of the women enjoy the work and can make good money. But packing fish does not sound the siren call to women that lobstering does for many young men. Judy believes that "You've got to enjoy cutting fish to do the job. Always something different. If you don't have a liking for it, forget it."

Sixty women work two at a table next to the endless belt of fish waiting to be packed, shipped and eaten as far away as Japan. The factory is the largest employer of island women. Taking up two fish at a time, Janet, one of the fastest packers, deftly cuts off the heads and

Cutting and packing fish.

Piece-rate packing needs fast fingers.

Women at work.

tails and flips into the can four pieces head to tail. In the past all of the women wore uniforms, but now they work in loose-fitting dresses, sleeves rolled and hair netted or scarved, the colours of their clothing bright against the silver fish. Janet slows down just enough to show me each time-saving move that allows her to pack up to three thousand cans a day. Two cases per hour makes minimum wage; four to five cases, up to seventy dollars a day. New workers are given four to six weeks to bring their hands up to speed. Very few of the packers are men. When I try, Janet laughs and tells me I would never make any money. "Stay with the teaching."

She has done this work for twenty years, and still finds a challenge in cutting the fish into different sizes to pack into the various cans: "snacks, steaks, three-packs, and ovals." Working close by your friends and being able to talk with them is good. The talk is of family, the state of the fish, where they were caught, the ease or difficulty of packing certain kinds. Janet sometimes thinks of doing other work, of running a bakery perhaps. Laurie, who left school in grade nine, would like to be a nurse, if she can find the time to complete her high-school diploma and raise her family. Susan looks down at her reddened chapped hands. "Just look at 'em. I used to dream of being an air hostess, lots of stop-overs in different places. Now I have my son Mark, and my mom and dad just adore him." Other hands bear scissor scars and bandaids from fingers coming between fish and blade.

When the factory isn't running, the women go to other work, depending on the season. In July and August they can rake blueberries in the barrens; it is a short season that also attracts families of migrant Indians who come down from Canada. For a person with a strong back, good money can be scooped up in a few weeks. After the berries have been raked off the bushes, they are refrigerated and pressure-packed, labour that offers still more temporary work to women for about a month. Seasonal work offers employment to many of the island women who are not either full time in their home or working regular year-round jobs. One of the local restaurants closes for the winter, and the other three are open only for limited hours. Tables to wait are scarce during the slow season from November until May, until the summer tourists come to eat in the seafood restaurants.

Relatively few local women or men work in the professions, businesses, services, or trades, although their numbers are increasing rapidly as new work other than fishing becomes available. In the past, most of the professional jobs went to people from "away" who had received a college education and possessed comparatively high levels of technical training. A nursing home was opened recently for residents of the county. This center has offered not only another choice of work for women but also specialist training in medical care. For high-school seniors, such training increases the likelihood of island women and men also being able to find skilled work in other places.

Wreath making for the Christmas season provides work in many homes and in a small factory from early November until Christmas. The work involves the whole family down to toddlers, who help to carry spruce boughs out of the woods. But in late October Christmas is still more than two months away, and money has to be found now by digging clams when the tide is right, picking out crabmeat, baiting pockets, or finding other occasional work. Island people are resourceful and able to get by on very little during lean times. They know that spring will follow winter even if it is slower in coming some years than in others.

The coming of winter marks the end of lobstering for most inshore fishermen; a few drag for lobsters in the deeper waters offshore. In the words of a local saying, "when the rockweed freezes, it's time to take up your traps." In a month's time the newly cut woodpiles will be flanked by stacks of lobster pots. Although lobster fishing in these waters is not controlled by the seasons, many fishermen bring their boats and gear ashore for storage through the winter. Those few who do not haul their boats ashore in October and November often keep on lobstering into December in the hope of making a little extra money for the winter.

Winter and summer are the major seasons that divide the year into two unequal parts. The climate of coastal Maine is moderated in the winter by some of its weather originating over the ocean, which cools off initially more slowly than the land. Solid ice covers the land, extends across the mud flats and often joins the islands together in the depth of winter. Fishing boats are frequently frozen in on their moorings and cannot reach open water for days and sometimes for weeks at a time. Ice tightens in around the boats and has to be broken up to prevent the hulls being crushed. In the winter, people think in terms of survival until the spring mud season. Then boats ashore are "put over" into the water. The ice melts out of the bays, and the land starts to green over.

Alton and Mike have been close friends since elementary school, and both of them dropped out in grade nine, Mike to go lobstering and Alton to dig clams. He describes here what winter means to him:

"In the winter time, you just work to get by, comfortably; you think about the present. In the summertime, you start thinking about the future. In the winter it would disgust you to try and save money. You go clamming and bring home $30 that day. You know you've got to take $20 out to take care of expenses. You take that last $10 and try and save it, and you can't. You are going to need it the next day. You are barely going to have enough money to live off, but you'll be all right."

Mike arrives home and prepares to cut wood until supper time. By early September, stacks of firewood stand in many door yards. People plan to cut their next year's supply of wood in late winter before the sap rises in early spring. Mike describes the change of seasons:

"This is the end of the summer time, right now. I don't care what the calendar says. Fall's here 'cause leaves are changin, even though the calendar don't say it. You can see it. You start to feel it. You can't go barefoot and stuff like that anymore. Then you know winter's comin, so you gotta get ready for that."

Mike's family heats their home with about six cords of wood each year. Although oil, gas, and electricity heat many island homes, oil and gas are costly here and require the expensive installation of furnaces and duct work. Wood heat is traditional in New England and still keeps people warm through the six months of winter. One elderly woman decided to have her wood stove removed and a gas furnace installed for convenience. When asked how she liked her new system, she replied, "Yes, it keeps me warm, but it's a lonely flame." The locals repeat the saying that heating with wood warms them three times over. "Once when you cut it, again when you carry and stack it, and finally when you burn it."

During the fall and until the first snow flies, Mike will cut cordwood for a couple of hours after fishing. With a chainsaw and hydraulic log splitter, the work goes fast, and a few afternoons' work provides enough wood for his family. Mike's father owns a ten-acre woodlot. His father remembers when it was full of oak and ash, but now it's mostly spruce, fir, and some silver birch. The money from selling additional cords will "carry him" through the winter. He sells locally and occasionally takes a truckload up to the "big city" and parks outside the supermarket; there he can get a better price for his wood, and go to a movie too. Some of the wood that Mike cuts now will not be burnt until next winter, by which time it will be fairly dry.

Although many decisions are made on a day-by-day basis according to the weather, the need for money, and time for oneself, long-range planning is essential for much seasonal work. On this warm afternoon in late October, it is hard to think about winter coming and the need to prepare in advance. But gardens have to be planned well ahead for the next spring, and the ground turned and composted before it turns solid beneath the ice of winter. Each day's work takes account of the changing seasons.

Time is used and valued differently in the woods than out on the water. The hour becomes important as a measure of time for Mike as he cuts wood.

> "I've got to cut at least a cord of wood in so much time to make my money. That's when you probably would use a watch. On schedule, clock time. The rest of time is off a schedule. Your money is already made with lobstering. Go out and take the lobsters out. You ain't makin no money to time. But if you have to have five cords cut and two hours have gone by and you've only got three, then you know you are behind schedule, so you work harder."

Like almost all of the houses on the island, Mike's home is built from wood. Mike's father started building it some years ago and plans to finish shingling it soon. He framed the house from an assortment of two-by-fours from the lumberyard and poles cut from his own land. The house is built over a basement remaining from the old house site where his great-grandfather built his home. After raising the new house, Mike's father covered in the frames on the outside with plywood and then filled in the spaces between the frames on the inside with rolls of insulation. The plywood he covered with sheets of tar paper held down with nails and thin wooden laths. These crisscross the outside walls and provide a place to nail down the final covering of cedar shingles. The wall facing north was shingled long enough ago for the pale brown colour of freshly split shingles to weather into a light grey. Mike has grown used to the look of tar-paper walls, and they look finished enough and right.

In front of his home is the kind of yard that tells at a glance that Mike's family are fishermen. The remains of a lobster boat stand by the

deeply rutted drive. The deck house was pulled off last summer to
become a home for a few hens and rabbits. Although the hull planks
have sprung off the bow, and its once sweeping sheer line is now
starting to sag and "hog down" at the ends, the beauty and fineness of
her lines are a continuing tribute to Arno who built her almost forty
years ago. Behind the house, a couple of old cars jacked up on stumps
wait for parts from the junk yard. In a corner sit a set of scallop drags,
big steel buckets red with rust from seasons of disuse. Mike plans to
use them when he has his own boat. Everything in this yard seems
alive and waiting for some different use. In the distance, Nancy, Mike's
mother, collects the last of the vegetables before the first frosts predicted for tonight.

Mike already has a long woodpile that snakes its way down the
side of the house, never farther than a few steps from the door on a
winter's evening. Working with a chain saw is a fast way to cut wood,
but the high-pitched scream of the saw teeth gives the work a chore-
like quality. Mike flips the blade against the four-foot logs that I drop
across the sawhorse. In seconds the logs are cut into stove-length pieces.
Exhaust fumes and sawdust blend in a heady smell. The speed of
cutting is set by the saw's whining engine, which usually runs full tilt. I
remember a friend in Tennessee who bought a chain saw to save time
and later sold it. He preferred the slow rhythmic strokes of a Swedish
bow saw that did not deaden the sounds of the forest. But Southern
winters are kinder than those of New England.

Mike cuts steadily away at the log pile and speeds up a little as
the sun reddens low among the pines behind his home. Judging from
the pile, I guess we'll have cut over a cord before dark. Earlier today,
Mike mentioned that the days were closing in now, less daylight for
outside work, less time to get things done than in the seemingly endless
hours of summer days. Daylight time is important to him.

Mike continues to work steadily at the end of the day without
more food after his earlier lunch of sandwiches, occasional sodas, and
candy bars on the boat. While we have been cutting wood, Nancy has
been preparing supper since the *Stella* docked. From the front window,
she can see the moorings, and the high green hull of Dave's boat is easy
to spot among the rest of the fleet that now all swing toward the fish
factory. A summer visitor once asked him, "When you park the boats,
why do you line them up in a different direction every day?" Dave
guessed that city folks didn't know too much about the wind and the

tide.

Mike continues to live at home with his sisters, Christie and Fay, and his younger brother, Mark. Christie is serious about going on to business college when she graduates from high school next spring and already has a couple of offers. She has never lived anywhere else, is ready to see other places and wants a broader choice of jobs than her mother had when she graduated. Christie's boyfriend already has his own boat at 19, but she is not ready to be a fisherman's wife until her schooling is completed. The yellow school bus drops her off at home around 2:30 p.m. every day. By 3 p.m., she will be bagging groceries at a local market until 9 p.m. to save money for next year and pay for her car.

Mark, in grade six, gets off the same bus as Christie, heads straight for the kitchen, then changes into his old clothes and clam boots. Today he was mad because low water was at 2 p.m., and he's already missed the best part of the tide while sitting in school. From the woodpile, Mike watches Mark head off for the mud flats in a hurry carrying his clam roller and hoe. He doesn't reappear until dark. Mike recalls for a few moments clamming with his father when he was a seven-year-old child:

> "He was a full-time digger. Half the time I was with him. If it was really late tides, I wouldn't go, and if it was really early tides I wouldn't go. First time I hit the clam flats, I dug three pecks. I'd never been clammin before. Screwed around with the fish comin in with the tide. My mother and father clammed for the longest time. My mother would dig eight bushels. She used the hand method. We had a skiff, and we'd fill her till she almost sank. I've never seen nothing like it. I wish I could see it to this day. If I ever had a tide like that, it would be totally awesome."

His mother and father made their living clam digging for many years. When they dug, a good clammer could get eight bushels a tide. Now, two bushels or less is good. Even though the price has risen, reflecting the dwindling supply, few people now dig clams for their major work. In any case, Mike's father has been unable to dig for the past eighteen months because of a bad back. The constant stooping and bending eventually slipped a disk. Now he works in the store at the shipyard selling marine hardware. He likes the work, but he would rather be out on his own, and he continues to set a few traps from a small skiff.

As we work on the woodpile, Mike's father is fitting a new wooden flatbed on his truck. The metal bed corroded away from constant exposure to the salt air. Mike cuts the saw and decides to split wood for the last half-hour of a day that started before dawn out on the water and is now finishing in darkness ashore at his home. Again Mike uses a non-traditional way of splitting wood. Instead of setting the fat rounds of birch and spruce on end against the flat base of an old tree stump and splitting them with a wedge and sledgehammer or a maul, he uses a hydraulic splitter. The pile grows rapidly in the "brown of the evening." Only when the sawed logs are all split do we stop.

Dark has come quickly, and in the last light, Mike carries the saw into the woodshed and heads to the house for supper. Although the days still feel like summer, it is cold enough at night for a fire. Above the stove, wet gloves steam away, giving off a warm, damp smell. A pile of logs are stacked on one side of the stove and on the other side sleeps Fay's kitten. Fay, who is in first grade, plays beneath the dinner table on an old braided rug with Ninja, her pet guinea pig. I sink down into a deeply cushioned chair covered with an afghan made by Mike's aunt, to watch Mike as he carries in more wood from outside. Finally he pulls up a colonial-style rocker and slows down to rock. He relaxes and tells me, "Dark is when you can hardly see the clam holes. Dark is when you are sittin in your home, takin it easy and callin it a day." Such items as the axe by the door, wooden netting needles hung from a nail and the handbraided rug contrast with the chromium standing lamp by the television, the noise of Nancy's blender in the kitchen, and Fay's Cabbage Patch doll.

In the kitchen Nancy is picking the meat out of the crabs that Mike brought home, and making supper—potatoes, carrots, peas, and lamb bought from Bruce who runs a small flock on one of the outer islands. Many homes have a small garden plot that provides a fairly constant supply of fresh produce from late May through early November. Planting the garden and then tending it usually falls to Mike's mother who works on it with a little help from Fay, usually in the afternoon after housework is finished and the evening meal planned. Since spring she has spent time first working the soil, then setting in seedlings, and later in the summer weeding. Almost time now to dig in some seaweed for the winter. She grows vegetables and flowers that she can sell with her baked goods at the village hall to make the extra dollars.

Caring for the children of other working islanders.

At other times, she will babysit her neighbour's children while their parents work, hours that keep her fully occupied in playing games, reading stories, and the endless cycle of changing diapers. She's done it for so long that she cannot imagine a home without children. With little time for herself, she likes to collect books from the book barns down the coast. She says that her husband reads a lot, too, and would read anything that didn't move. Mike thumbs through a *National Geographic* exclaiming at pictures of great white sharks off the barrier reef. He points with pride to a stack of magazines piled on a corner table.

Mark comes in soon after dark with a roller full of clams. After supper, he'll take them down to the dealer and probably make around twenty dollars for about three hours of digging. He scoops out enough clams to make a side dish for supper and goes to wash up. Supper is served between 4 and 7 p.m. depending on what time Mike gets in and how much work he and his father want to do before dark. When I ask Mike's mother if her children expect mealtimes at home to follow the regularity of school scheduling, she replies, "No, they've done it [eaten at irregular times] all their lives."

As in many other small communities, social life is with family and friends, with the occasional visit to a large city for shopping, movies, and eating out. Like the fishermen, the women who work at home spend much time alone but easily find company when they want it. Mike's mother tells me:

"The [local] restaurant is really the only out. We look forward to that every morning. A bunch of us do go for coffee every morning at 8. And at 8:45 I'm back home again. Get your beds made, start your cleaning. We usually take a lunch break. Sometimes we go out for lunch, meet at each other's homes."

Mike's mother goes on to describe the importance of social contact:

"Communication is really important around here. I like the privacy of my own home, and I don't visit other people's and bother them. Unless a bunch of us get together and sew, make crafts or do something. My mother makes quilts all winter. She just finished one for Mary Anne. It was beautiful. A lot of women do that. They get together. It takes awhile, and there's a lot of handwork in them, and it costs a lot. Families are large around here, so you make them for your own brothers and sisters, aunts, uncles, and grandchildren. We usually start at 10 a.m."

In both of these quotations, the times for meeting are marked with a preciseness uncharacteristic of how islanders more usually plan their social activities. I found that on occasion people would give answers in terms of clock time when they believed that this would be important for me to know; they recognised the importance of this measure to others, but infrequently used it themselves.

Supper is a leisurely affair, a time to talk and swap the day's stories. While Mike's family eat supper, Christie is coming to the end of the second session of her day's work. Mark sits with us just long enough to watch his fried clams being eaten and then excuses himself to watch a show or two on TV before reluctantly starting his homework. He has to maintain a "C" average to stay on the basketball team, his major interest in school right now. Low grades in English threaten his place on the team, and he leaves us muttering about how he can make more than his schoolteacher by digging clams. Mike's father laughs, "Not any more. Those days have gone by." Fay listens to us talk for a while and then goes outside to feed her rabbits before joining Mark at the television. In first grade, she does not have homework but likes to draw and writes stories which she proudly displays on her wall.

Mike's mother clears away the dishes and escapes the noise of Mark's TV show by going upstairs to read in her bedroom. Mike tells me how much his mother loves to read, which she does by the hour. Long after everybody else in the family has gone to bed, he says, she reads whatever she can find in the town's small library and from the shelves of romances at the store. She swaps books with friends and once in a while buys and sells them through garage sales.

I remember how Mike would bring magazines such as *Field and Stream* to school. Sometimes he was reluctant to read them aloud in our seventh-grade class. I encouraged him to try, and he usually would read well for a paragraph or two and then miss a difficult word and stop. After he told me how he felt about reading aloud in high school, I wish now that as one of Mike's teachers I hadn't asked and encouraged him to read aloud:

> "When they wanted me to read to them, I couldn't read to them. It embarrassed me a lot. I try hard to read out loud, but I just don't. I stutter. When they wanted me to do a report on somethin, it would be done. But if they wanted me to read somethin, they'd give me a bad grade because I couldn't read out loud. It embarrassed me a lot. That

doesn't seem right to me, so I said, 'What the hell. These guys aren't goin to pass me when I'm workin my hardest. You know, I can be makin my own livin right now. Why should I be here wastin my time on them?'"

I asked Mike if he had talked with his teachers about this situation:

"Yea, but they got so many other students. What can they listen to, do for you? They gotta be workin with all these other students. Why can't they explain to me why I can't, explain to me why I can't read out loud? You know there's a reason somewhere."

By the ninth grade, Mike was torn between the demands of his time in school and his desire to be out fishing:

"When I got home, I didn't do homework. That's what messed me up. I didn't do homework, because I was always off buildin traps and helpin people out fishin. My mind was on fishin, what I wanted to do. I was in the ninth grade for two years. I went one year and finished it out, but you know I wasn't there half the time, out lobsterin. Then I continued the second year of ninth grade, for a month or two, and I found that fishin interested me more. The teachers just wouldn't pass me because I wouldn't do homework. I could do the work and was doin the classwork. I just feel that schoolwork is made for school and after school is made for after school. If you had done all your work in school efficiently, if everythin was planned, you could do all your work in school. You would have your own time at home to do as you wished. That's the way I feel things should go."

During the time that Mike was in school, he thought constantly about the work that he wanted to do, and now does with an obvious pleasure even when he makes little money. In the seventh grade, he and Alton used to dig clams. There wasn't much extra money around in either of their homes. By the time they were fourteen, their parents expected them to buy their own clothes and to provide any extras they might need or want. Consequently, the time they spent in school came to be associated with time lost for making money. Mike explains:

"The students have got to have money to get along and to understand the community. They've got to get clothes for the year. Parents figure the kids are old enough to go and work on their own. After grade six, the parents see what the kids can do. The parents 'round here depend on the kids to make their own future. They aren't goin to make it for them. The parents are goin pretty much hard as it is. So they figure the kids have got to understand this while they're young. And they put them right out there. Make a kid learn while they are young."

At certain times of the month, clam digging is far more profitable than at other times because of the increased range of the tide. The tide flows further out and much more of the mud flats can be dug by the clammer. The frustration of being in school during times of these "low-drain" tides was enormous for Mike. As though he is still a student, although he has not been in school for over two years, he remembers the experience of those times with the immediacy of the present.

> "This is the good time of the year. Say clam tide is from ten to twelve in the afternoon. While you are in school, you are thinkin that I can be there diggin clams—that big—right now, two and a half bushels, makin a hundred dollars, and here I am sittin behind this desk, listenin to that teacher tellin me somethin that I already know. You don't learn much that way. You're thinkin if you want to make money, you've got to do it with the time you've got left at the end of the day. You've only got four nights a week, not even that, when you can only go clammin at the end of the day."

When he was a seventh grader, his future work became a part of the present; in turn, what is now a past experience becomes part of the present as he relives those years.

At the same time that Mike is out fishing, doing what he loves, many of his old classmates are still in school completing their senior year:

> "If I went back to school now, a full day, a term, it would drive me nuts. Just, doin, you know, sittin. My nerves. I've got to be doin somethin constructive. I've got to be doin somethin I want to be doin. If I had to be in a classroom for that many hours, it just wouldn't feel right. I'd be wastin time—count the minutes. Every minute would be noticeable. Because every minute I know I can be doin somethin else that would be profitin to my knowledge. They took me as somebody not really dumb, but I didn't know as much as other students. But actually I just wanted to get it over with."

Later I talk with Mike's old classmates, my former junior high students, and begin to understand why for some the school is a place of confinement, while for others it is a place where a valuable education can be found. For Mike and Alton this experience became a waste of time, a series of daily tasks whose value they could not discover however hard they tried. When Mike left school in grade nine to go fishing, he had developed his reading skills sufficiently to teach himself about his work:

> "This is what I read right here. Of course you got *Maine Life* and that's my outboard manual. In the bank or up the chimney, you figure out how to read. You figure out how to read, learn about your houses, so you don't waste any money. I read stuff that interests me. I read in *Maine Life* about how to grow gardens and build stuff. That book tells me the whole story on my outboard engine right there."

He picks up an outboard manual that he used to rebuild a 1957 Perkins engine and proudly reads:

> "'Inspect the indicator to make sure the float arm is not bent and the float is not damaged or oil soaked.'. . . I find no problem in reading that right there, no problem. But if you wanted me to read that to somebody, I mean, I couldn't. It just, it just wouldn't come out right. But I can take an outboard and rebuild it in one day."

Yet despite Mike's lack of confidence, he does read well, and with a greater fluency and interest than I ever recall him reading in school. When I tell him this, he looks encouraged and reads more about the mysteries of fitting brass bushings to engine shafts.

Mike has started diving and has learned how to use complicated equipment by buddying for a friend and then reading up on what he needs to know about safety and marine photography. He has already started to photograph and write about marine life on the seabed. Most lobsters are seen only in the pots or moving sluggishly around in holding tanks. He hopes to write descriptions of lobster movements in their natural habitat that would be informative for other fishermen and encourage students to read about the life off their own shorelines. Here is an excerpt from a letter Mike wrote me about what he had seen while diving:

> When I last dove I found that some lobsters had not left for their offshore destination. They had burrowed under big rocks as if to make a

Six hours from high to low tide.

permanent home. When I approached these holes the lobster would come out just enough to keep an eye on me. When I was getting too close for comfort, he would shoot into his home with lightening speed only to return again as if to regain my location. I took one of the spiny beasts from his home and set him out on open bottom. When I released him, his claws immediately raised, and he turned facing me. He did not attack but put on one hell of a show to try and scare me. He slowly maneuvered around me and slid back into his hole as fierce as ever.

Mike loves being out on the water and diving beneath it. It's a different world from that of the clam flats where Alton digs. Shortly after supper, Alton stops by at Mike's home to visit. In the ninth grade, Alton quit school and went to work full time as a clam digger. Although he does well to make two bushels a tide, he has been able to support himself for the past three years. He and Sylvia live together in a small trailer that they have fixed up into a comfortable home. They hope to save enough money to buy a small piece of land and to build a log house.

Alton digs clams with a hoe from among the boulders at the high tide mark and by hand in the soft mud left by the ebbing tide. Below the rocky shore line off the Maine coast, vast expanses of mud are alternately uncovered and covered by the ebb and flow of the tide. He digs clams in these tidal mud flats from the high-water mark down to the low-water tide line. This expanse of grey is usually covered by a skim coat of water left by the falling tide. The flats are an unstable blend of earth and water. The farther you walk below high water mark, the softer the mud becomes until every step sinks down to knee level.

I first learned about the appeal of the clam flats from reading students' descriptions. Here Bobby in grade seven writes about the drop of the water from high to low tide.

At high tide you can see the oil floating on the water. All the boats are afloat and the air smells clean. You can see sea gulls' feathers and crab shells tangled up in the greasy seaweed. As the tide starts to go down, you can start to see the barnacle covered rocks. As the tide gets down a little more, you begin to see sand with broken glass, sand dollars, and old pieces of wood or pipe. Some of the old "Sally G" comes out of the water. Then all of the posts of the old dock come out all brown and barnacled. You can never tell what you will find on a beach or in the clam flats. As you get down a few more feet, you can see clam flats with old scallop shells covered with barnacles.

At low tide you see mostly clam flats. You can smell the rotten seaweed. You can see the constant squirting of clams. You can see old abandoned clam shells. Old scallop shells and machinery frames look like someone don't like the ocean good enough to keep it clean. The broken glass people collect for a great collection. There are lots of ledges covered with mussels. There are also lots of mud crabs, eels, and mud worms crawling all over the flats. There are boats pulled up on the mud from the clam diggers. You see lots of sea gulls flying all over the place. You hear the constant cracking of clam and mussel shells dropped onto the rocks by sea gulls getting their food for the day.

Students were very willing to talk about this world but reluctant to write about it. My requests for further written information or details were frequently answered by the advice, "Go and see for yourself." Students believed that to know their world one must be prepared to enter it directly—an experience that could not be conveyed adequately by reading about it. Although Alton dropped out of school, he admits that he did like his art classes and enjoyed writing his own stories.

Children who are born into clamming families learn how to handle clam hoe and roller soon after learning to walk. They learn how to move steadily across the flats, their eyes searching ahead for the telltale breathing holes of clams buried beneath several inches of mud. In hard mud the clams are dug out with a clam hoe, a kind of rake with six long steel tines set at right angles to a short wooden handle. The fingers are slipped between the tines, which are then pushed down into the mud around the clam's breathing hole. The handle is rocked back and forth until the mud is loosened and flipped over.

Once Alton finds a place that looks promising, he works the tide in the following manner:

> "As you dig, follow the tide out, and when it comes back in, dig into the shore; dig in a half circle in front of you. Keep digging as far as you can. Then begin another circle. You dig in these circles because of the mud that is dredged up. Just look along as you dig. You're looking ahead all the time. See where the holes are. You dig all kinds of ways. I have had a place where the water is six inches in one place. I just take my foot in, back the mud out. Keep pushing it back more all the time. Dam it up. You push the mud back, and that keeps the water back."

Clam digging.

Student's sketch.

CLAM-BOOTS

Students' sketches, cont.

In the right spot, several clams at least two inches long will be uncovered. These are then tossed into the wooden carrying roller, and the movement is repeated. The practiced clammer digs across the mud in an unbroken rhythm of graceful movements. Bending with each flip of the hoe, the digger moves across the mud behind the falling tide. He or she steadily follows the tide out until the mud is too soft to bear weight. Alton explains that the digger must have a sense of touch:

"You feel them with your hands while your eyes are looking for the next holes. You can start while the tide's out and be digging in a hard area and then find yourself in the soft, and you look and the tide's out."

An alternative method of clamming is known as hand digging. Instead of using the hoe, the digger, wearing rubber gloves, reaches down directly into each hole and pulls out the clam. It's a faster method than hoe digging but direct contact against the razor-sharp edges of the clam shell is much harder on the hands. Mike claims his father was the first person on the island to dig in this way and dug more clams per tide than anyone else.

As every schoolchild knows, the movement of the tide is determined by the gravitational pull of the moon and to a lesser degree by that of the larger but more distant sun. At the time of the new and the full moon, the combined pull of sun and moon causes a greater than usual tidal range known as a spring tide. These tides (which occur throughout the year) produce higher high tides and lower low tides. These low-drain tides are a time of great activity for the clammer who can reach seldom-dug sections of the clam flats where the clams have had a chance to grow to a larger size in greater numbers. Alton describes such tides:

"If you get a low-drain tide, say two and a half feet, then you know the tide will go so far out you ain't even going to be able to see it. You just go for it. But when it comes in, it comes, like, whoosh—a wave about that high across the mud. You say I ain't been here this year. Nobody has been here this year from what I can understand. The tide is going to leave here today. I'm going to dig here, and there's going to be big clams. And when it happens, you are there. And you make yourself $200 a day for that day."

The really big tides last for about one week out of each month. Just about everybody who can carry a roller is out on the flats. The junior high principal claimed he could plot and predict absenteeism by the time of spring tides. What young clam digger wouldn't squirm in school if the clam tide fell during school hours? As I was a new teacher, he also cautioned me to expect unusual unrest and more behavioural problems around the full moon. As an experienced teacher and veteran digger, he knew what the big tides meant.

When the moon is in its first and third quarter, the moon and sun are in opposition and their combined pull on the earth is reduced. At this time of neap tides, the tide range is smaller than normal which usually means very poor clamming for about a week. The mud that is uncovered then has been dug over many times and is "beat out." On these days, Alton is likely to help Mike build his camp or help Charley in the garage until better tides return in a few days.

Fishermen's optimism is borne out by their belief, close to a superstition, that luck will turn with the tide and that fishing will pick up after the next full moon. In lean times they remember times of plenty and know that a tide of ill fortune must eventually turn. And the fishermen have learned how to wait.

Clams are scarce now, but a successful digger still can find two to three bushels a tide while his neighbour might find only a bushel and a half. Such differences are accountable in terms of knowledge of where to dig, eye-to-hand skill and economic motivation. The issue becomes how much money a person needs to live comfortably between the big tides with enough left over to save a little through the winter. Slim, an experienced digger, describes his approach to this work in the winter.

"Today I was digging in a little cove. There was a little dish in the rocks where the sand was, rocks all around it except for one side. I just ploughed up an area; bulk of that area was 10 feet by 12 feet. I got up in the morning. Had to check the weather first. Couldn't dig where I dug yesterday 'cause I would have froze to death. I had to get some place in the lee. I dug in a place where the ice had gone out just two or three days ago. I was on a little survey trip.

You always do that looking for the next day. Have to look ahead. Pay check isn't going to come normally. Have to look ahead. You know what seasons are coming. You know where you were successful last year and you might be this year. Some people keep little maps of places where they dug, but I don't."

Knowledge of place and time are important for the clammer's work. The clammer must know when the tide is right, and he or she must know how long the tide will last. Alton explains the importance of the tide in his work. "Today's tide—it went out and soon as it turned low tide it came right back in, so today's tide only lasted about an hour all together." His first concern is the time of low water. Because he digs every day, he knows when this will be. The time of the tide is about fifty minutes later each day, "You pretty well get used to it because you remember what time you went the day before."

Sitting with Alton and Mike in his home, I remember the first time I went clamming with Alton. We arrived at The Creek, a narrow finger of water flanked by spruce-covered hills to the west and salt marshes to the east. Since the water was still well above the mud flats, we sat down beneath a stand of trees to wait for the tide. The sun was already settling on the tips of the tallest first. Alton built a small fire of driftwood and pine cones. At the end of the cove, a blue heron dipped into the water, flashing silver glints of fish in its beak.

Waiting for the right time to do things is an experience familiar to most people whose work is not regulated by the clock. I asked Alton what he did when he had to wait. Since waiting is often part of this activity, it's not regarded as anything special and therefore not worth thinking about. But he knew why I asked and answered with an example:

> "We built a fifteen-foot alligator down the shore on the sand yesterday. Me and Keith, we were sayin this alligator is goin to come out of the sand when we've built it. We didn't take no time, but we took our time. We tried to make it look as real as we could. It's all made of gravelly sand and crushed granite."

Keith's father ran a sawmill, and Keith loved to work with wood. He spent as much time as he could in the industrial arts shop but was frustrated continually by the experience of trying to work within fifty-minute blocks of time. Having to keep stopping in the middle of his project because a bell rang made little sense in terms of how he or his father worked at home, where work continued until it was completed, until another job became more important, or until the sun set. By comparison, he saw work in school organised within time frames whose logic escaped him. Class could have started at 11 a.m. or 11:30 a.m. and run for fifty minutes or two hours. He did not see an equivalent principle of organisation at his father's workplace.

Unlike the fishermen who are governed by the area restrictions that influence lobstering, clammers are free to dig anywhere they choose unless an area has been closed. Once an area has been dug over to the point where it's "totally beat," the local authorities will close the area until the remaining seed clams have had a chance to grow to the legal size of two inches.

Slim explains that territoriality is still there among the older, full-time diggers:

> "People would say, 'Stop following me around. There's plenty of places to dig. Why are you following me around?' It's not very direct. People aren't very direct around here. Only so much time for people to deal with this stuff, too. If you dealt with all your conflicts, you'd never have time to deal with anything. Wouldn't have time to eat your supper."

In the same way that Mike and Dave need to know where the lobsters are before they set traps, so Alton needs local knowledge of the best spots to go digging:

> "You've got to keep up on your clams. If you're goin to clam for your livin, you got to know every spot on the island. You've got to know where they're growin, when they're gonna be ready, so, when you think they're gonna be ready, you go there. Otherwise you can be missin out on your clams."

Keeping up on the clams requires an excellent memory and a keen ear for the reports of other clammers. Alton explains the importance of memory in his work:

> "I remember in my head where I've already covered in that year and the size of the clams. You have to. That's the main thing of clammin. I know the time that they are goin to be good, the time when they will be still small. Because I'm always there. I go back there because you want the clams."

The stove around which we are talking in Mike's home is getting cold. Time to put more logs on the fire and to think about tomorrow. At eight o'clock Mike and Alton are looking tired and ready for sleep. They've been up since four o'clock in the morning. Planning the next day's activities is the last thing they do before falling asleep. As Alton recounts:

"You do it when you're goin to sleep. Just sort of lie there and think, think, well, tomorrow, I better . . . . what has got to be done, you put in front of everything else. It's a sight. I dream it! I dream it. I see myself doin it. You say, 'Well, I'm gonna dig down in the hangers tomorrow.' Then you see yourself ploddin round the hangers. Where are the best clams gonna be? You think, well, let me see, they gotta be down here somewheres. Where have you seen all the foot tracks?"

Alton plans several activities in a day, the sequence of which depends on the time of the tide:

"If I gotta go clammin in the afternoon, night before, I've gotta figure out what I'm gonna do till the afternoon next day before I go clammin. I can't overstretch myself for time o' nothin, 'cause I gotta be there at a certain time. You can do twenty different things sometimes. Some things ain't that big to do. Some things are. Sometimes schedules get interrupted. You get in from work, you're really tired. You had a bad day. Sit down and relax, watch TV for a little while, and get calmed down, go to bed and get ready for the next day. Sometimes you have to skip somethin you had planned."

This kind of flexibility characterises how many of the fishermen approach their work and other activities. This need for a high degree of control over one's own time is an integral part of the independent lifestyle here. On the other hand, people give help freely when needed; for example, parts of houses are still built with neighbours' help. Roofing and shingling parties are common here as in many other rural areas. The high frequency of mechanical breakdowns and bad weather also demand that work schedules are kept flexible. Even though these problems mean a loss of income, fishermen complain little—a stoic attitude that comes from having developed endurance in the face of constant hardship and economic uncertainty.

When Mike and Alton aren't working, they like to visit with family and friends. When urgent and important work needs to be done, however, they see this as potentially a waste of time:

"Sittin round, sittin round, goin places, vacation you might say, when you're supposed to be workin. That's Friday and Saturday night. Go hang around, visitin people, that's wastin time, in a way, when you gotta be workin to support yourself. It's like sittin down watchin soap operas all day."

Visits are seldom planned by the clock or the calendar. Many people will drop in on their friends any time of day or evening. "Stop by any time you see the house lights on or when my truck is in the yard," is the kind of open invitation that island people offer. Social time is likely to be integrated with work time when opportunities for conversation arise. Slim recalls an instance that illustrates how the need to make money is tempered by a sometimes greater need for social time:

"Some people go down to the shore, park alongside some other guy, pull down their windows, talk. You know. Then sometimes they'll say, 'Jesus, we've talked so long it's too late to go. Let's go home.' I couldn't do that, not now. If I am going to be there to begin with, I might as well do something."

From conversations with Mike, Alton, and many others in this community, I learned that time is measured in far more ways than that recorded by the schoolhouse clock, the metronome for institutional life. The time zones that Mike and Alton encounter in their work are presented here in spatial terms in a piece written by Mitchell in grade nine. He describes his return home from an offshore fishing trip with his father:

OFF SHORE

You are off shore and all you see is the rough seas rolling in. Once in awhile a fish or seagull will be going by, and you are off shore 100 miles. Then you are heading on in and there are the seas still rolling in and more fish swimming by and seagulls flying on by and you are at 50 miles now. There is the sight of land and all you see is the green of the trees and the nice flat seas and seagulls all over the place. Not no fish around to see when you're at 20 miles in. The outline of trees, land and seals all around the ledges with gulls all around. Maybe see a little bit of houses at 10 miles from the land. There are the pot buoys all around and lobster buoys, hauling traps, and land just like you want to step on it. Everything seems like you can touch it. But the touch is far. Seals and seagulls are all around. There the beautiful sight of trees, rock, and clouds makes it feel good at five miles off home land. Then there's the sight of land, the white of the houses and the boats off the home coast at three miles away.

Coming into the cove are the water-drenched rocks with their dark murky colors. At one mile there's the mooring and the shape of the boat just sitting there going up and down. Then half-mile you're up on the bow just waiting to gaff the mooring and jump in the boat. The trees are so clear you feel like you can climb right up there with the blue sky, right above the dark green trees. At 25 yards you're in the wharf and in the truck and all ready to go home and go to bed.

Reading Mitchell's description of coming into land after an off-shore fishing trip, we cross four time zones, areas in which time is measured and valued differently. On a chart, these areas correspond to the sea offshore, the coastal waters, the intertidal zone, and the land. The temporal distinctions among these areas overlap in such a way that it is difficult to recognise absolute time frames for work except for those jobs controlled by the clock.

Those who fish around the banks and sea canyons, situated perhaps a hundred miles offshore, are away for days at a time. They fish around the clock, day in and day out, for the duration of the trip. Sleeping and eating are scheduled during the infrequent breaks in the almost constant activity of running out and retrieving the fishing gear. This kind of fishing represents work that is least influenced by the time of day or available daylight. Reasonable weather, that is, winds below thirty knots and seas below fifteen feet, sufficient fuel and space enough for the catch are the major factors that influence how the work will proceed. What little I know about this kind of fishing, I have learned from talking with offshore fishermen. I include this zone because it represents work least affected by the temporal constraints of those following.

The second time zone is bounded to seaward by the limitations of the twenty-five to forty-foot in-shore boat that Mike and Dave fish from. They seldom venture more than twenty miles from shore. By keeping relatively close to land, bad weather usually can be avoided and traps can be set in water deep enough to catch migrating lobsters. The inner limit is around the level of low water. Some pots may be uncovered briefly during low-drain tides. In-shore fishermen have to pay closer attention to the tides than do the offshore fishermen.

In contrast to the offshore fishermen, in-shore lobstermen can work legally only within daylight hours. They often will leave and return home during darkness so that daylight hours are spent hauling pots and not travelling to and from the fishing grounds. Mike leaves for the moorings as early as 3:30 a.m. in the long days of summer and as late as 6:30 a.m. in the short winter days. Consequently the variation in his day on the water might be as much as three to four hours between the shortest and the longest day of the year. Each day will be either longer or shorter than the preceding one by about a minute and a half.

This lengthening and shortening of daylight becomes most crucial in the fall when certain tasks must be completed before winter. Mike's uncle who works both on land and on sea tells me:

> "I follow the sun in my work and especially at this time of year when the days are shortening, and you have to work faster to get everything done. The sun ain't good for a thing except shining in your eyes from November until April."

Although Mike can predict the potential length of his day from one season to the next, the actual length is unpredictable because of factors such as the need to move traps to new locations, the inevitable snarl-up of gear, and the time it takes to haul and pick empty or full pots from varying depths. Mike knows that in the spring and summer he can haul almost every day, but in the late fall and winter, storms will keep him at home for days at a time. For the in-shore fisherman, the height of the sun and the varying length of the days are the key measures of time.

The inner limits of the fishermen's working world overlap the outer edges of the clamdiggers'. Crossing the line of low water brings us into the intertidal mud flats, the third time zone. Here the state of the tide completely determines when and for how long Alton and Slim can work, who must consider this factor, however, in relation to the available daylight. Although in the past, clammers have dug during darkness using flashlights, it has not been economically worthwhile to do so in recent years. By going to a tide chart or, as is more often the case, remembering the time of low water from the previous tide, the clammer can predict when and for how long he can dig.

Predictions of the tide are as approximate as every other event influenced by nature. The time and height of the tide are controlled primarily by the gravitational pull of the moon and the sun. The actual time and range of the tide, however, are influenced also by local topography and the weather conditions. A low pressure system can reduce the range of the tide, and a high pressure system increase it. The strength and direction of the wind also affect the tide. Slim explains this to me after I ask him how the weather affects his work:

"Today it wasn't supposed to be a very good tide, but the wind was quite strong, out of the north-northwest, and it blew the tide way out, as far as a very good tide. But then on the contrary, if it's supposed to be a good tide but the wind's southeast, sometimes it will hold it, sometimes it won't. Something you have to know, and you don't always know."

Slim and Alton know that tide-chart predictions are at best only estimates. They plan their work accordingly and are ready to do other work if the tides do not fall right on a particular day. Their time is important to them, but it is seldom measured against the clock. Their decision to go clamming is dependent on a scale of priorities. The need to make money is balanced against the need to cut wood, work around the home, or to visit. Maintaining a high degree of independent control over when and for how long work is done is very important. Their pride in being able to do this is in part an assertion of their independence, the counterbalance to an uncertain income and times of poverty.

As young children, Alton and Mike became accustomed to seeing their fathers and sometimes their mothers go out to work at different times each day and being gone for varying amounts of time. During the winter when the ice was too thick to dig through, clamming stopped for days and sometimes weeks at a time, and their parents stayed at home. Mike and Alton learned that work was organised within a schedule that changed with the tide, the day, and the season. In contrast, their work in school was regulated by the unvarying master schedule.

The boundaries within which Alton and Slim work stretch from the line of the lowest spring tide to the high-water mark where they can hoe among the rocks framing the shoreline. This line marks another boundary; above it we enter a fourth time zone that controls the work of those who work ashore. We encounter a broader range of variation in the kinds of time frames that organise land work than the time frames organising work either in the intertidal zone or on the sea.

Seasonal work, such as cutting wood, gardening, and raking blueberries, can only be done during daylight. In contrast, seasonal work such as wreath making can be done at any time indoors. During wreath-making season between November and Christmas, a woman who works in her own home is able to choose not only how many hours of her day she will work but when they will be. Given that much of her day will be taken up already with caring for a family, a woman will likely work early and late in the day, if she is to make a significant income. On the other hand, if she chooses to make and decorate wreaths at the nearby "factory," she will be on shift work and be required to pace her work to the piece rate.

Another group of seasonal workers includes carpenters, painters, and masons. This group of shore workers, like the lobstermen and clammers, "follow the sun." The length of their workday and the opportunity to make a living change with the seasons. Clock time becomes important to them when they need to deal with someone who works on a different kind of time, or when they need to coordinate activities. For example, a group of carpenters arrange to unload a boatload of lumber and agree to meet the boat at the dock around 8 o'clock, the time of high water on that day. For much of their day, however, outside workers do not relate their activities to clock time. They eat when they are hungry and quit either when it is too dark to see, or when they have completed the tasks they planned for that day.

A relatively small number of people work in jobs that are regulated exclusively by a clock schedule. These people include the shift workers at the fish factory, builders and painters in the shipyard, men and women in small businesses, nursing home staff, bank and town office employees, and teachers and support staff in the schools. Since the essential character of clock time will be familiar to all readers, I will discuss how it shapes attitudes toward learning in the next three chapters about life in school.

The four time zones found in this community show evidence of two different ways of thinking about and experiencing time. One way represents it as a cycle around which events and activities occur and recur at predictable intervals. The cycle is tied to the natural rhythms of the turning world governed by the movement of sun and moon. This revolving view of time tends not to make as sharp a distinction between segments of past, present, and future as does the second, linear view of time, which situates events in non-reversible order. The distinctions between cyclical and linear views of time are both arguable and complex.[1] The contrast, however, provides one useful way to understand the consequences of the dichotomy between time in school and the time order of the natural world.

Since each way of thinking about time entails a contrasting set of values and implications for action, conflicts and confusions can and do result between people whose affiliations are primarily with one or the other view of time. Mike and Alton, for example, know that "short" lobsters or undersize clams put back today will in all probability be trapped in the future by which time they will have had a chance to grow to a legal size. Because they see each new tide, day, or season as another opportunity to make money, Mike and Alton tend to accept the fruits of each day's labour for what they are and do not regard opportunities as likely to be once-only phenomena that must be acted upon immediately or lost forever. In contrast, Mike and Alton learned that opportunities in school to complete a piece of work usually were offered once and then graded with an "F" if not completed by the due date. The opportunity to repeat work, to make up for "lost time," came in the form of being held back a year and not being promoted with one's class—an option that carried a high social stigma for these students. The natural rhythms[2] of the daily and seasonal activities of people in the community establish one particular kind of time order at sharp variance with the order established in the schools.

If we understand the movement of time as circular, as island people often do, then we see that what is now past will move into the future again with the turning of each day and season into the next. Within each season, the daily pattern of work is highly repetitive, even allowing for variations in both the time and duration of the workday. Work that is closely attuned to natural rhythms and is repetitive in character has the effect of breaking down divisions between sharply differentiated frames of time.

Units of time, such as hours, days, weeks, and months, become blurred together for Mike and Alton who do not need to make precise distinctions between these units in much of their work or in their leisure-time activities. Consequently, the segment on the line that we refer to as "the present" becomes extended for them. For Mike and Alton, the present is a sense of "now" that encompasses yesterday, today, and tomorrow. Most of their activity is ongoing, and what appears to be completed today will be started again tomorrow. A beginning and an ending are not two points along a line but two words used at different times of day or season for the same place on the circle.

Our grammatical system of tense and aspect makes fine distinctions between events in the near and far past, the duration of those events and whether they are completed or ongoing at the time the events are narrated.[3] The progressive aspects of Mike and Alton's thinking about work is well marked in their speech. In sections where they now talk about their past experience of being in school, we see a use of the present progressive that suggests their past experience is remembered and relived as a present ongoing experience:

> "While you are in school, you are thinking that I can be there diggin clams that big now, makin a hundred dollars. Here I am sittin behind this desk, listenin to that teacher tellin me something that I already know."

What Mike and Alton did not know as they sat in their eighth-grade classroom was that five years later they would be teaching me about their sense of time and language.

My reason for examining time from the perspectives above has been to suggest that different conceptions of time will entail different ways in which people establish their personal and cultural identity in this community. For those who work by the water, identity is based on the perceived freedom to use each day according to the demands of a range of activities. Yet as the natural stock of fish and clams has declined, people have had to work for longer hours or accept a lower standard of living. Fishermen experience a significant tension between the perceived freedom to work as and when they choose and the economic necessity to work for much of the time in order not to forfeit all luxuries, and in some cases life's necessities. The freedom is perceived, rather than actual, for all but those few fishermen who have been economically successful. The fishermen have chosen the economic uncertainties of work on the sea to the economic predictability of a "regular job" with a boss who follows the clock.

The individual creates the authenticity of his or her own life by living out personal values in the context of the tension between the need to control one's own time and the economic need to work for most of the available time. A former student explained the essence of these values to me when we met by chance one day. Robert had been clamming since early childhood and now did this for a living. I asked him how his work was going, and he told me that it was bad but that he could still find enough clams to make a living. Without any prompting, he then went on to tell me what he thought was important to the people in his community. Robert listed strength, pride, and trust. Without these virtues, he said that life for him and his family would amount to nothing.

He explained this further by way of a story about a friend of his who came to the island with a wife and children but had little money. It was winter, and he couldn't find a job. So each day he went out and broke through the ice to dig for clams in the frozen mud. His actions showed physical endurance and pride in his capability to provide for his family. In turn his wife trusted, as he did, that together they would all make it through the winter. She had the strength to make do with very little and was proud of what he could provide in circumstances that would send many families running to their parents or to the bank.

The values illustrated in Robert's story, while not limited to this community, illustrate how he interprets an ethical code within his own world in his own terms. When I watched Alton slowly filling his roller with clams as he followed down the tide, and Mike hauling lobster pots until the barrel was full, I thought of Robert's story. As they worked, they created their own personal time in which each could be the person he chose. When I had taught these students in school, seldom had we been able to achieve a quality of learning in which work and time could coalesce as they did now. To an outsider, the people in this chapter might appear to be culturally shaped by the demands of their work. The conclusion to which my time on the island brought me was that they are a people who have chosen to follow a particular way of life.

The purpose of describing the working lives of Mike and Alton has been to present the timescapes of such island families and their work. As we read next about how Fay, Mark, and Christie respond to schooling, the first two chapters will provide the context for students' descriptions of time in school. The next three chapters will describe how instructional time at different grade levels is organised, and how students respond to the time order of learning to write.

Fay and her friends in grade one.

Chapter Three

FAY: TIME ON THE THRESHOLD OF WRITING

"Takes a long time to say just one sentence."

A few children on the island walk to school but more arrive by car or in the familiar yellow school bus. Fay in grade one, Mark in grade six, and Sherrie in grade seven all ride the bus. Sherrie who lives across the road joins Fay and Mark, and together they wait in the dooryard at 7:15 a.m. Even though Fay cannot tell the time by looking at the clock in the living room, she has heard her mother say that the bus comes at 7:20 a.m. and won't wait. "My mother wakes me up and says, 'Fay, it's six o'clock,' or she shouts, 'Fay, it's six-thirty!'"

Likewise Fay knows the time of her favourite TV shows, "Sesame Street" and "Mr. Rogers." But evening seems a long time away as she skips around at the roadside and watches Mark flip rocks into a stand of silver birch behind their home. Fay likes to go to school and is even more excited than usual because her class is planning to make Halloween masks and costumes for the town parade. The excitement of Halloween runs high among the elementary school children with the big parade only two weeks away.

Fay's only regret on leaving home this morning is saying goodbye to Carrie, her Cabbage Patch doll, a much-cherished birthday present. The bus stops just long enough for the three of them to board. While Sherrie, in grade seven, lugs an armload of books onto the bus, Fay trots behind cradling a huge pumpkin fresh from their garden. Mark pushes in front of the girls and heads for the back seat. Sherrie sits alone in the first empty seat and begins reading *Helter Skelter.* The bus roars off to pick up the next knot of youngsters waiting a couple of hundred yards around the bend.

Fay spots her friend Megan from grade two, and they immediately exchange stories about their weekend. Megan whispers to Fay that her whole family is going to the parade as a swarm of bees with her father as the beekeeper. Fay swears to keep the secret. Megan's father is adding an extension onto their home so she and her baby sister will have their own room. Her father found an old bird's nest under the eaves, and Megan is bringing it to school for show and tell. Fay went up to Milltown for a shopping spree and then to a movie with her sisters and mother. Her new Snoopy T-shirt is proof of her trip off-island. Sherrie spent hours wandering around the Mr. Paperback store. She has discovered the pleasure of owning her own books, like her mother who buys Harlequin Romances at the drugstore.

By 7:30 a.m. the bus is more than half full of elementary, junior high, and high school students. A couple of seniors who board the bus are quickly told, "Leave your ghetto blasters up front. That's the rule of the bus." The rules of the bus prevent students' walking up and down or playing any but the quietest of games. Time spent on the bus is like school time: rules and punishments control behaviour. Yet it is also like time at home since students are usually free to sit where they choose, talk with their friends, finish their homework, or daydream. Riding the bus is a time of transition between being at home and studying in school. The noise of the engine and the bouncing of the bus over the switchback roads encourages loud conversation among those who feel like talking. Others sit with backs to the windows and stare into the aisle. Behind their heads slide by the colours of a New England fall punctuated by occasional glimpses of the sea.

As more students board the bus, talk gets louder and louder until Butch asks students to keep the noise down so he can concentrate on his driving. Butch describes these students as a pretty good group by comparison with others that he has carried to and from school. In the past he has had to park the bus by the roadside until the children settled down enough for him to drive safely to school. At Oceanview Corner, Sherrie is joined by Clayton, a classmate who can do math. Before the bus is back in top gear, she is getting a little help with last night's algebra equations that bothered her no end. They lean together in an effort to steady the bouncing pages of letters and numbers, not long enough for Clayton to explain their mystery but long enough for Sherrie to scribble down the results that she was unable to produce. Clayton gladly shares what he knows, as does Sherrie when Clayton needs help.

At 7:35 a.m. the bus swings into the school yard and parks in front of the elementary school, a single-story building from the 1950s with generous windows stretching from the roof to the brick foundation. The school is set well back from the road and surrounded on three sides by a play area. On fine mornings this provides a gathering place for those who walk to school, who arrive by seven, followed by the bus students who begin to arrive at 7:20 a.m. At the edge of the yard, a small group clusters around the teacher on duty, a familiar and trusted face who greets the students as they arrive from home. She forms a natural centre around which the youngsters come and go. It's already cold enough for their breath to make quick trails above them as they stamp and chatter about her. She listens with interest and patience to countless stories of the weekend and also a few tales of complaints about fellow students. Consoled, the tattlers run off to resume their play while others stand on the edge of the circle as new students join the swirl around her. Tomorrow a different teacher on duty will greet Fay and her friends, but the caring will be the same.

Fay heads straight for her classroom as the school bus carries Sherrie, Mark and their friends off to their school. On her way to class, Fay passes the open door of the school kitchen where her Aunt Kate sits scraping carrots for a hundred students. She waves to Fay and asks her where she pinched the pumpkin that dwarfs her and why it's going to class and not into one of her own famous pies. Fay laughs and dumps the pumpkin on her desk before joining her friends outside.

At the first bell at 8 a.m. all the students line up in front of the bright red swinging doors. The shouts and screams of a minute ago trail off into noisy chatter and then quickly into silence, the signal that everybody is ready to come to class and to start the school day. They walk quietly down the hall and pause outside their room to hang up hats and coats into a wavy line of brightly coloured sleeves and hoods. While trooping down the hallway, they look up at a row of freshly mounted pictures. Fay smiles proudly when she sees her work displayed.

The day starts formally with the Pledge of Allegiance to the flag, followed by the count for lunch and the collection of milk money. Students talk quietly at their tables as Ms. Cole completes her daily clerical work. A mood of quiet expectancy replaces the noisy clamour on the schoolyard a few minutes earlier. Fay and her friends are on the threshold of learning to write.

For us to understand how these young students orient themselves to the temporal aspects of this process, we need to understand first how students understand and respond to the schedule of the school day, a primary context of all learning. Here is the school's schedule:

8:15 a.m.	morning routines and announcements
8:30 a.m.	handwriting practice
8:50 a.m.	math papers
9:20 a.m.	reading groups
9:40 a.m.	spelling
10 a.m.	morning recess
10:10 a.m.	math groups
10:50 a.m.	cleanup for lunch
10:55 a.m.	lunch
11:30 a.m.	second recess
12 noon	afternoon routines and announcements
12:10 p.m.	reading groups
1:15 p.m.	afternoon recess
1:25 p.m.	Monday–Thursday: writing Friday: social studies, science, and health
2:10 p.m.	cleanup
2:20 p.m.	end of the day and arrival of the buses

This schedule for grades one and two appears far more controlled by the clock than is in fact the case. The beginning and ending time of each activity can vary by up to a quarter of an hour to accommodate the students' pace and interest in the work at hand. Ms. Cole has both grades one and two in her class, so it is important to be able to schedule the work assignments as flexibly as possible and to fit in the planned activities for that day. Although Ms. Cole must take her class to recess and to lunch, and have them ready for the bus at the end of the day, she is able to organise the time between these fixed events according to her needs and those of the students. This degree of flexibility is also available to Mark's teacher in grade six, but not to Sherrie's high school teacher in grade seven. At that level, each activity has become organised into periods taught in different rooms by different teachers and allotted a fixed period of fifty minutes. While Ms. Cole schedules activities with one eye on the clock, the young student is unlikely to tell time in this way and more likely to be aware of the passing and length of school activities in a range of different ways.

Telling Time

Some students as young as 5 years old and younger can tell time from the clock. Obviously this ability develops earlier in some students than in others. Ms. Sloan gave me the following estimates for her 4- to 5-year-old students:

> "By the latter part of the spring term, most kindergartners can read the hour when the long hand is on the 12. By October, one-quarter to one-third of the class know when the time for recess is by looking at the clock. Their stomach alarms go off at all times, but most know that when Math is over, it's snack time and then recess."

In first grade, I found few 6-year-old students able to tell the time in the fall. Either they had lost this skill over the summer, when they had few occasions to look at the clock, or Ms. Sloan's estimate of "most kindergartners" was high.

By the time Fay and her friends are 7 or 8 years old, many will be able to tell the time by looking at the clock. Then they will be able to see how long they have been working at one activity and estimate about how much time remains before the next begins. At age 7, Fay is beginning to read the hours correctly, but as yet she makes only a hazy connection between the position of the clock's hands and the occurrence of particular events in the school day.

I ask Fay and her friends about what they do in school and when and for how long they work at particular tasks. "After the morning recess, we come inside and read. Then we do our math and handwriting papers." (She reverses the actual sequence.) I ask Fay how long she works at math, and she replies, twenty minutes. She tells me that she can tell the time a little, but Megan in grade two cannot. Fay says that after the math papers are done she has "free time for as long until the teacher tells us to go to our seats." Megan says that she does her math for eighteen or nineteen minutes, a precision that seems uncharacteristic of youngsters who appear to measure duration more by their own subjective span of interest than by the objective measure of the clock. I ask her how she knows it is eighteen minutes, and she replies that she does not think she works for twenty minutes, a unit that represents to a 7-year-old a long period of time to work at one task.

Bryan joins the conversation by telling us that his math takes six or ten minutes. His attachment of numbers to measures of time appears random, yet perhaps it would not be, if we could understand his system of measurement. In answer to my question about how he knows that it is lunch time, he tells me that Ms. Cole pulls up the curtains. Our conversation now turns to the recess periods that punctuate the different activities. Megan counts five in her day and Bryan counts four, "ten minutes, ten minutes, thirty minutes, ten minutes." Fay quickly interrupts:

> "There ain't no 'just ten minutes, ten minutes, then thirty minutes.' It ain't like that, Bryan. It goes an hour and ten minutes, then twenty minutes, then a half hour, then an hour, half-hour recess, and then ten minutes, and then another hour."

Although Fay's description of the school day most closely approximates the teacher's schedule, it is not the same. Fay sees the day clearly divided into periods of work time and much shorter periods of recess time.

For students in kindergarten through second grade, time is measured less in terms of the duration of an activity than in terms of the daily sequence of activities. Fay and her friends know what they will do each day. Although they are beginning to predict the order of activities, they cannot as yet relate their knowledge of when activities change to the measure of the clock. Ms. Sloan tells me that her kindergarten children tell her if she misses the Flag Song or other opening exercises like doing the calendar or weather chart. "This is because it was his or her job, not because we passed the time for it." Students, however, do understand that clocks are one way of knowing when they will go out for recess, begin writing, eat lunch, and go home.

While these children are learning to tell the time, they rely both on internal or individual and external or social signals for discovering when certain events will occur. In making this distinction, however, I recognise that the child's response to a social signal is a personal interaction, a way of discovering that relies on the child's own experiences, in contrast to ways that depend on information provided by other students and adults. These two ways of time telling thus do not function independently of each other. They interact and can conflict, for example, when a child's "stomach alarm" says it is time to eat, but the clock reads only 9 a.m.

In this dialogue, as teacher interviewer, I try to discover how two of Fay's friends know when it's time for recess.

Teacher:	What time will you go out to recess, Cindy?
Cindy:	After we do our morning work.
Teacher:	Aaron, how do you know when it's time for recess?
Aaron:	When the bell rings.
Teacher:	If the bell didn't ring, how would you know?
Cindy:	When the big hand is on the twelve and the little hand is on the six, we go out to recess.
Aaron:	When the big hand is on the twelve and the little hand is on the ten.
Teacher:	How do you know what you'll study next?
Cindy:	Well, each day we do our pages of study at the same time.
Teacher:	How do you know it's the same time each day?
Cindy:	Because I usually look up at the clock when we are going to do something different, and when we get our work done. Most of the time when I look at the clock, I know what we are going to do, sometimes. In the morning is the only time I look at it. In the afternoon I forget to.
Fay:	I can tell the time, and I don't really need a bell. I know when you are supposed to go out.

Cindy's final remark, "Most of the time when I look at the clock. . . ." suggests that the clock is starting to become an external way of validating what she already knows for much of the time. Her proviso, "sometimes," perhaps indicates an unwillingness to make absolute predictions about her ability to use correctly what to her at this stage is an adult measure of time—a realm of uncertainty for the young child. Since the mornings tend to be more task-oriented than the afternoons, she may watch the clock during the tasks she enjoys the least.

The class ends at 2:15 p.m. in time for the first bus at 2:20 p.m. I tell our small group that it is half-past one now and ask how long before we will be going home. Student answers vary from one to five hours. In the room in which we are sitting, there is no clock, yet at around 2:00 p.m. Fay and Megan become restless, fidget, and tell me that they should be going so that they won't miss their buses. On another occasion the appearance of the bus outside the window sends them scurrying back from our small group to their seats in class. Fay knows that her bus gets her back home at around 2:40 p.m.—the last precise measure of school time before television time begins at home. The first show that Fay watches is "Sesame Street" which begins at four o'clock. She knows the time of this show and that "Little House on the Prairie" comes on at seven o'clock. In contrast, according to Ms. Sloan, less than a quarter of the students in kindergarten knew the time of their favourite shows.

Several students in the first three grades described how they knew when it was time to do certain activities without the use of a clock: They relied on body/mind signals. I discovered this when Leroy in kindergarten told me that writing his book had taken him a long time. I asked him how long was a long time. "Twenty days," he replied. His parents had told him that twenty days was a long time.

Teacher: What makes something feel like a long time?

Leroy: My brain. When I close my eyes, it says, "Leroy, it's a long time."

Teacher: How does your brain tell you it's a long time?

Leroy: It has a mouth in there, in my body. It comes out of my bottom and disappears in my ears. It disappears when I have to poop. It disappears in my belly.

Teacher: When does the voice come back?

Leroy: When you are done pooping and wiping your tail. It's time to go to school if I have to poop before.

Teacher: Do you hear it at any other times?

Leroy: When I'm asleep it says, "Leroy, it's time to get up" and it says, "Leroy, it's time to eat breakfast." When I'm playing, it says, "Leroy, it's a long time. It's time to learn your ABCs. Go to school. Leroy, time to go to school."

Leroy says that he also watches the clock, at the same time as he relies on this inner voice. "Sometimes I forget what the voice says, so I need a clock. When the little hand is at 6, it's time to go to school." Here is an example of how a young child will turn to the external measure of time when his own time sense fails him. A little puzzled by Leroy's account of an inner voice that tells him when to come to school, I casually ask Fay's friends if they have ever heard a voice inside themselves telling that it is time to do certain things. Nervous laughter is the first response of these 7-year-olds. Fay then asks if I mean the voice of God or of Jesus. I ask again if any of them ever hear such voices.

Larry:	Sometimes. It sounds like a low voice. It sounds like this guy up to church. He was singing in this real bass voice.
Teacher:	What did the voice say to you?
Larry:	Once my mind told me it was time to come in for lunch.
Teacher:	Kim, have you ever heard a voice like Larry has?
Kim:	It sounds like . . . I don't know. Like my little brother.
Teacher:	What did your voice say?
Kim:	"Come in and play with me."
Teacher:	Do you ever hear the voice talking to you in school?
Larry:	"It's almost time for recess, Larry." About five minutes later it was recess. Sometimes it says, "time for supper." Sometimes it says "time to salute the flag." But Ms. Cole says that, too. The voice tells all kinds of things. Sometimes it says my Nanna wants me to come up. I hear that pretty often.
Teacher:	When the voice talks to you, do you hear it in your head?
Larry:	It doesn't sound like it, though I know it does. It does it in my head, but it don't sound like it. I can hear it too. It's like my head knows everything.

This internal way of telling the time is the least dependent on the help of other people, bells, or clocks. Knowing when it's time to eat, sleep, and poop can be understood partly in terms of bodily rhythms. When I first talked with Ms. Cole about what Larry had told me, she laughed and told me that Larry was putting me on. Six months later she wrote and told me that she had asked each of her students if they ever heard voices in their heads; sixteen out of eighteen said that they did. As students become progressively more attuned to the public time of the clock, however, they rely less on their private inner time sense. School not only institutionalises clock time and socialises students into its values but minimises the need for students to be responsible for their own management of time.

As we have seen in the descriptions of Fay's home in Chapter Two, mealtimes and bedtimes are regulated less by the clock than by completion of work. Nevertheless, her mother and Christie do decide when meals will be served, a socialising influence on the bodily rhythms that tell Fay when she is hungry and wants to eat. Knowing when it is time for recess or for the bus to come is knowledge learned and reinforced on a daily basis in the school.

Developing a uniformly segmented sense of duration probably develops fully in the junior high school, where the whole day is divided into fifty-minute periods. Activities there are more numerous and structured into separate classes, with a new room and a different teacher for each. But here in grades K–2, the duration of an activity and the transitions between them is less sharply established; for example, the change from math papers to reading groups is not marked by a bell and a change of room and teacher. Children learn that they will go on to the next activity when most of them have completed the ongoing one or when the teacher feels that the class has worked for long enough on a particular task. Ms. Sloan describes her approach to time scheduling. "I will continue tasks and suspend or postpone others if the motivation is high, in order to increase the attention span of the children."

Consequently, the duration of an activity is controlled more by the demands of the task than by the clock, a model for work that is complementary with how people like Mike and Alton work in the community. Morning bell, recess, lunch time, and the afternoon bell do impose time limits on activities within the school day but are markedly less apparent and intrusive than in the seven-period day of the high school. The organisation of activities in the elementary school is closer in structure to the day of the pre-school child for whom broad stretches of time alternate between play, eating, and sleeping.

Fay says that she would prefer not to divide the day into separate divisions for different activities, but rather to work for a whole day on each before going to the next.

"Every day, one thing all day. One day all math, and one day all writin process and one day all recess. I'd like to just spend all day outside playin, and when I was hungry I could go in and eat. Go to Katie's kitchen whenever you wanted to. I'd like to do art and phys ed, too."

Megan agrees. Her reason for this preference is that sometimes she gets mixed up with whether she is supposed to be doing her math papers or her handwriting.

Beyond the reasons that these students give for preferring broad stretches of time for each activity, it appears likely that they would begin to look for an organisation of schoolwork that resembles how they see people work at home and in the community. This observation becomes more true for upper-elementary and secondary-level students. They have more fully internalised communal time than have Fay and her young friends, who say they like to change tasks fairly often in the day.

Those students who watch much television become more accustomed to a complete change of subject at regular intervals than those who do not. Perhaps the latter expect less variety of activities in the school than do avid television watchers, and are less accustomed to an arbitrary segmenting of time. Those who do watch television know the time when their favourite shows will come on, even though they ask parents to tell them when that time has arrived. The sharply segmented blocks of time that frame shows and alternate with the advertisements introduce students to another kind of time that contrasts much more with "natural time" than with the clock time of the school. Given that television has particular ways of temporally framing and representing experience, it would seem likely that these students are influenced by its time schemes. Because I have not explored in detail how television influences students' growing awarenesses of time, I can note only that it probably is an influence.

Fay already has told me that she likes to write a lot, but when asked whether she would like to have more time or less to do her math or English she replies:

"Two minutes. Then I could do it all. Do it all scribbly—heeheehee. Throw it in the waste basket and go outside and play, heh, I like to play. Sometimes I wish I could just go and be all done, and I'd like it, our work to be one second, and then we get to play for ten hours."

From talking with Fay and her friends about time in school, the following themes emerge: Fay's teacher allows for a high degree of flexibility in scheduling learning activities to suit the educational and social needs of the students at different times in the day. This freedom is limited by the school only for recess, lunch, and the arrival of the afternoon buses. From speaking with other lower elementary teachers in this district, however, I sensed that some organised their school day with a greater regularity and uniformity than did Ms. Cole. The temporal contours of learning activities within an individual elementary classroom reflect the time values of individual teachers, and might show a higher degree of uniformity than the school's schedule requires or that which its philosophy supports.

Although Ms. Cole was attentive to her students' pace of learning and motivation, she seldom asked her students to participate in deciding on the sequence or length of activities. Although both Ms. Sloan and Ms. Cole clearly want to provide for their students' needs, they do not recognise the need for students to have some control over their own time in school as a fundamental one that underlies attitudinal responses to being in school. When I discussed this issue with the principal, he questioned whether young students could be responsible, even to a limited degree, for how their time in school was used. This same argument was given also by the high school principal for students between the ages of thirteen and eighteen. Based on this observation, I will argue that the politics of time are related more to issues of authority and the social control of students than to an appraisal of their capacity to be held in part responsible for how they manage their time in school.

By first grade, students are attuned to the school practice of presenting activities in a sequence that shows little variation. Students are beginning to know for how long each activity will last. Those students who cannot use a clock internalise the approximate duration of an activity and begin to predict when an activity will end. Teachers report that some of their students start to put work away or line up for the bus at the appropriate time without any direct instructions to do so.

Students in K–2 tell time in the following ways. These are listed beginning with personal measures, proceeding to the public measures. Students know when it is time for a particular activity:

1. by noting an internal signal that may take the form of an inner voice or a "stomach alarm";

2. by learning the daily series of activities and remembering which comes next;

3. by asking another student or the teacher when it will be time for the next activity;

4. by the teachers telling students that it is time to stop one activity and to begin another;

5. by hearing the bell or seeing school buses arrive;

6. by looking at the clock.

Writing Class

At 1:25 p.m. Fay and her friends come in from the afternoon recess, hang up their coats, and prepare for the class known as "Writing Process." The name of the class suggests the particular approach to writing adopted by this school district. At the invitation of the elementary school principal, this method was introduced for grades K–6 in 1981 by visiting professors from the state university. The method owes much to the work of Donald Graves[1] and his colleagues. The full process of several stages features the production of multiple drafts, peer editing in conference sessions, and "publishing." Once "published" in handwritten book form, each student's writing can then be read by other students, friends, and parents.

In this school district, as in others in New England, the approach has been conspicuously more successful and more widely adopted in elementary schools than in high schools. At the elementary school level, students do not see the task of writing-conferencing-rewriting as an indication that they are being asked to repeat what they have accomplished already. Furthermore, at this age few students have any other models for how writing is produced. Elementary students in kindergarten through second grade are far less likely to see revision as correction of errors than are upper elementary and high school students who, as we shall see in subsequent chapters, tend to regard the process as work being repeated to get it right this time. Part of the resistance of the high school students to this approach was resistance to a pedagogy that was not taught to them in elementary school.

Keeping Track of Students' Writing

Fay sits with her friends around low wooden tables and waits for the writing class to begin. Each group goes up separately to the stand where their individual writing boxes are stored. The boxes contain their completed "books" and working copies of ongoing writing. Before class begins, Ms. Cole goes around and asks each student what they are writing about and how far the work has progressed. The purpose of this accounting, known as "status of the class," is for students and teacher to keep track of what everybody is working on. Students are introduced first to this procedure in kindergarten and continue with it in modified form until grade six. In the context of this "status of the class" session in Ms. Sloan's kindergarten class, the students learn that writing is an activity to which the teacher will allocate a limited amount of time.

Ms. Sloan:	What are you writing about today, Sharon?
Sharon:	My book is about my brother and his cat.
Ms. Sloan:	How are you coming on this? You've been working on it a long time.
Sharon:	Takes a long time to say just one sentence.
Ms. Sloan:	How about you, David?
David:	A book about going out to haul.
Ms. Sloan:	You need to come up with a name for it. Are you almost finished? You've been working on that book a while.

Reading this passage, Ms. Sloan felt that my drawing attention to her time emphasis did not fully represent her practice:

> "In the beginning of the year, I emphasize that thinking and writing take lots of time and writing takes lots of time and encourage much adding of details, re-reading, and thinking more about their topics. But after three or four weeks on one piece, I then begin to let individual students know that words and sentences need to begin to be the main task, as a few students would just continue to add fine details and colors to the pictures instead of writing."

Writing Topics

The range of topics from which these young writers choose represent their current interests. Students choose topics as varied as rabbits, my family, myself, Halloween parties, and Thanksgiving. Ms. Cole tells her class, "It's up to you. You are the writers. You have to decide whether you are going to write about your dog or about Halloween. Think of something that you know a lot about. Put a lot of information in." The emphasis is on writing about what students know and have directly experienced rather than writing about imagined events. Island teachers who follow the Graves model of teaching writing argue in 1984 that when students write imaginatively they lose control of their subject because they are describing what is beyond direct experience. One consequence of this belief is that student writing focuses on the time frames of present and past and tends not to explore futuristic fantasy worlds of what might be. In a "status of the class" session in Ms. Sloan's kindergarten class, Jim tells the class that he is writing about talking sandwiches.

Teacher:	Now do you really know about that?
Jim:	Yes.
Teacher:	But sandwiches don't really talk, do they? (Jim mumbles an inaudible reply)
Teacher:	We want to write what we know and care about. It's OK once in a while to do that, but not very often. It would be silly to write about that.

In these lower grades, talking about students' topics is an integral part of the process. During the conference sessions, students share their ideas on a regular basis. Today, Leland is having difficulty getting started with his work. Ms. Cole asks him why he doesn't write some more about his pet salamander. "'Cause my mother let it go."

Prewriting

In the following dialogue, Fay and Megan describe the time they give to getting started on a piece of writing:

Teacher:	Before you start to write, do you do some thinking?
Fay:	Couple of minutes.
Megan:	Five minutes. My best friend—I'm writing a book about her, so I don't have to think very much. Do you know why I only have to think a minute about her? Because I go to play with her every day.
Teacher:	Do you start to think of things as you start to write?

Fay:	Sometimes.
Teacher:	Does talking help you to think about what you want to write about?
Fay:	Sometimes.
Teacher:	Can you think of a time when it did?
Fay:	Sometimes when the teacher comes and says, 'see what you can write about after we have read what we have in our books.' She asks us some things about it, and we have to give her some answers. Sometimes — I can't believe what I'm doing. Each time I say this, I'm going "sometimes, sometimes, sometimes."

Fay's frequent use of "sometimes" reflects a broad tendency for people in this community to be reluctant to commit themselves to absolute statements about how they will act or what their opinion might be. Answers are tied closely to an individual situation and a particular set of circumstances. Statements are context-specific. "Hard to tell" was a common answer to any questions that I asked that appeared to look for certainty in a place where change was the normal expectation.

Penmanship and Drawing

In the first stages of learning to write using this process approach, students draw pictures of their topics as a rehearsal for writing. Then they write a sentence or two about their illustration. Once students are able to write simple sentences, these are written first and then illustrated. For students who have difficulty reading back their own simple sentences, the drawings serve to remind them of the content of their stories. Although the drawings may not always appear to the teacher to represent or correspond to subjects and experiences described in the story, the illustrations clearly are meaningful to the students, who can usually describe in great detail what the squiggles and curves mean to them. Ms. Cole asked her students why they liked to draw pictures to accompany their writing. Here are some of their replies:

1. They're fun to look at.

2. They help me remember the words to go with your words.

3. They're fun to color in.

4. To show people how I can draw.

5. To decorate up my book.

6. I like pictures for old people.

In kindergarten, drawing figurative representations of the events in a story marks a stage preliminary to learning to write. Next, students are asked to scribble on the page the ideas they have in their minds. At first there is little if any correspondence between the child's marks on the page and the words that they read back to the teacher who patiently prints above the apparently "random" markings the intended words. In kindergarten, some symbol-sound reading-readiness instruction occurs as preparation for both writing and reading.

Spelling

As students learn the correspondence between the sounds that they can hear within a word and the letters that represent those sounds, recognisable words emerge from their marks on the page. In these early grades, teachers constantly encourage their students to sound out words and listen for the sounds that they can hear. "Say it slowly to yourself and write down the sounds that you hear" is advice frequently given. Students use the letter/sound correspondences that they know. When a spelling for a particular word is unknown, they are taught to use two strategies on their own before going to the teacher.

First they can invent a spelling using the sound/letter correspondences already learned in their alphabet work, for example, *fyst, fest* (feast), *uego* (ago), *pakt* (packed), *tot* (taught), *dangrist* (dangerous), *pigrs* (Pilgrims), *tam* (them), *becoz, bekos* (because), *iglend* (England), *heab* (hay). Examples such as *stdr* (water), *tdc* (kite), *eda* (pumpkin), and *eth* (butterfly) are invented spellings that illustrate the earliest stages of trying to represent a sound with a symbol before the student has learned the particular yet arbitrary sound/letter correspondences. Distinguishing between an invented spelling and a spelling that the student believes is "correct" is difficult on the basis of the word on the page. Spellings that look like obvious improvisations to an adult reader represent the student's best approximation of how she hears that word spoken by those around her.

A second strategy for spelling an unknown word is to leave a blank at the place in the word where sounds are heard, for example, *ho_ɔ* (house), *k_ð* (could), *m_t* (met), *ye_r* (year), *fe_ɔ* (feast), *w_lð* (world), *ab_t* (about). Precise letter/sound correspondences are not looked for at this stage. Words produced in this way may show little or no correspondence to our idea of what constitutes standard spelling, but the technique allows students to begin representing their thoughts in writing before they master standard spellings. Spelling slowly approximates standard forms as the teacher prints the intended word above the students' words on the page. By leaving a space or by inventing a spelling, students can continue writing without the aid of the teacher.

Ms. Cole tells the story of one young student who was trying to read to her from one of his first books. When he came to a word that he didn't recognise, he stopped and pondered over what he could have meant by his strange combination of standard letters and invented ones. He cocked his head on one side and laughed telling her that he didn't know what the writing said. Ms. Cole told me that he had written down this sentence ten times. "I like gorls." When she asked him to read back his sentences to her, he couldn't read the word beyond "like." She read the sentence back to him, and he blushed and said, "'Girls,'—I thought it said 'goats'!"

Teachers encourage students to work with whole sentences and blocks of language from the outset rather than to work with words and phonemes, an approach associated with phonic-based methods of teaching reading and writing. Ms. Cole explains her view of how children learn to spell:

> "Kids learn to spell from reading their own writing and not from lists. Reading is like oral language when the teacher reads. They don't learn from my reading to them. They model what they see written down—the reading they do themselves. As they become better readers and able to read more, they become better spellers. Spelling lists memorized for tests are learned and often forgotten after the spelling test. A child learns to spell a word from seeing it over and over and over in print."

Going into this elementary classroom is always a warm experience because the students greet me by bringing up their work and asking if I would like to hear it read. Yet when Larry reads, his delivery is slow, deliberate, and jerky compared to the quick light playfulness of his talk. He is learning a new rhythm for the delivery of his written ideas, one that contrasts markedly with that of his talk.

Writing and Talking

In the early stages of learning to write, students' writing closely follows the continuous unsegmented flow of their talk. In kindergarten and first grade this phenomenon is recognisable in their handwriting. At first, the students' writing is not separated into individual words. They write down a kind of visual transcript of the sounds of their speech. The marks made are represented in a continuous form. (See writing samples at the end of chapter three.) Only later do students learn that when they write, the wave of sounds that they hear must be broken up into separate particles called words. When they begin to write, they see a graphic representation of what previously had been an oral experience of their own language.

Ms. Sloan explained this transition to me by comparing talk with music. "Many of the words in a stream of talk, like the notes in music, are not heard as separate units at first." She explains that in kindergarten she is trying to get from her students a melody, a simple statement of their ideas rather than the elaborations that will come at the end of grade one and in grade two.

Conferences

Once students have written down a few sentences about such topics as their trip to Camp Washington, a visit to relatives off-island, or an Easter Egg hunt, they get together with another student for a conference session. Small cosy spaces are popular places for conference sessions. Megan and Fay like to crawl into the footwell under Ms. Cole's desk. Leland and Martin favour the corner behind the chalkboard while others simply exchange their work at their tables. In these meetings, which last up to fifteen minutes, students read each other's writing, often with the assistance of the author to decipher invented spellings. One purpose of the conference is to discover if the writer has given the reader enough information and explained it clearly or not.

Ms. Cole instructs her students to tell each other a couple of things that they would like to know more about. The emphasis is on encouraging children to share and to receive help with their writing as it is in progress. Before Ms. Cole reads each student's writing, another student has already read it and commented on it. Students enjoy these conference sessions a lot. Much of the enjoyment of learning to write in this way appears to come from writing for friends in a relaxed and safe setting. Fay has made no secret of telling me that writing is her favourite activity. Ms. Cole gives another reason for conferences.

"The purpose of the conference with the teacher is for the writer to practice reading what he has written to help him remember what his invented spelling says. The more he reads it, the better he'll remember it and be able to read it again."

Conferences are not scheduled according to any preconceived routine but are arranged as needed. Their frequency and duration are attuned to the students' needs. Students simply ask a friend to listen to their work, to ask questions and say what the work needs for improvement. Before Megan can help Fay with her story, she must first make sure that she understands what Fay wants to say—the meanings that she has in mind. The writing undoubtedly will have a variety of other meanings for different readers, but at this stage Ms. Cole encourages students to view the writing's meaning as something owned by the author. She believes that her students' writing says, "This is me." For this reason, she shows great respect for the meanings that her young writers are attempting to convey and does not attempt to put her own ideas and interpretations before those of the students.

The reader, whether fellow student or teacher, first puts a major emphasis on the content—what the writer wants to say. The formal conventions of writing are introduced a little at a time, when the teacher believes they are needed. Students first learn to separate words from each other and later learn to mark sentence boundaries with periods. Standard spellings are lightly written over the students' spelling, so they have the "correct" spellings before them. Attention is never primarily on correctness, and students are not afraid to write for fear of making errors.

Revision

Ms. Sloan, who has conducted training sessions for writing teachers in this district and in the state, here explains what she sees as the purpose of revision:

"Upper elementary students already begin to see revision as rewriting, because after they conference and revise, they rewrite the whole thing in a near perfect 'finished' piece. Unfortunately, they do not go first through the process of conference–revise–conference–revise several times, and the teacher often does not look at the piece until this process is 'finished.' The teacher then often will request further revision and sometimes several revisions. After several teacher perusals, each one resulting in a 'rewriting,' the student hopes that this time the work will be satisfactory."

In primary grades, children have from one to five content conferences with the teacher or peers, and one or two editing conferences before publication. However, in kindergarten and first grade, the author does not rewrite the piece but simply adds details, words, phrases, or whole sentences, or adds newly learned punctuation, a title, etc.

After the conference between Megan and Fay, they both return to their desks to make revisions to their respective pieces. Formal revision does not usually start until the end of grade two. First graders revise by choosing to write on the same topic a second or third time after they have talked with their friends and teacher. Further revisions can be made in the future. In this respect, the idea of writing as a finished product receives less emphasis than writing as a continuing process. This emphasis on process rather than product runs counter to the way in which most writing had been taught in this district until the late 1970s.

Fay cradles her head on her hand and labours away carefully on her revision. Her concentration is apparent from her wrinkled brow and lower lip pressed down beneath the tip of her tongue. Classmates write busily, stopping occasionally to share their writing with a friend or to show it to Ms. Cole. Since talk is an essential part of this approach to writing, students seldom are asked to work more quietly, but usually the only noise is that of scratching pencils, quiet talk, and the laughter of delight at what someone has drawn or written. With students facing each other around the low tables, conversation is easy and natural. Students are free to leave their desks and to come up to Ms. Cole for help on how to develop a topic or simply to share their work. She moves around the class offering encouragement and serving as an over-the-shoulder reader. In this workshop setting, because students write at their own pace, each is at a different stage in the whole process, in contrast to the synchrony of writing activities that characterise the upper elementary and high school writing classes. Elementary students conference when they need a reader rather than at a teacher-appointed time. Within the writing class, students are responsible for managing their own time, a challenge that they take seriously.

Sharing Writing with the Class

This pattern of writing activity remains the same Monday through Wednesday. On Thursdays, students volunteer to read their week's writing aloud for the whole class in a group sharing session. The sessions described below are from Ms. Sloan's kindergarten class. Her students sit in a circle around the author's seat. The chosen author today is Martin, who reads his work with pride and confidence to the whole class. His story is about a many coloured house, the home of several cats. Kim asks Martin which part he likes the best. He looks unsure and says he doesn't know. Brenna tells him that she likes the description of Lorraine's cats. He smiles and tells her their names are Tinker Bell, Ralph, and Bandit—additional information he could have included in his story.

The next turn in the author's seat goes to Josh, who has written about a trip to Storyland, an amusement park.

Brenna: I like best where you get trapped in a maze.
Leroy: I like best the shoe ride.
Kim: Is the story true?
Josh: Hmm, kind of.
Kim: Where is Storyland? Is it next to your place?
Josh: Near my friend's house.
Nancy: Does it take a long time to get there?
Josh: Takes four hours.

There is a natural curiosity in the students' questions which Ms. Sloan encourages and carefully focuses by joining in and periodically asking her own questions. From her participation, students learn different ways to comment and to ask questions that will be helpful to them in future writing conferences. As part of the circle around the author's seat, she tries to become a member of the group, one of the several people for whom the student will write. In this way, she encourages students to write for each other and to trust their own responses to their classmates' work. Yet as the teacher it is difficult for her presence not to be seen as the adult authority in the group. When asked for whom they wrote, students in grades K–2 listed friends, parents, students, as well as the teacher. Martin included Bandit, his cat.

A Time to Talk and a Time to Be Quiet

As these children in their first three years of schooling learn to write, they also learn that talk in the school is regulated differently from talk in the home. The degree of difference will vary from one home to another. Taking turns to talk, and not talking until the present speaker pauses or stops, is a practice more familiar to some students than to others. Fay knows that if she interrupts her older brothers, sister, or parents there will be trouble, but her conversation may be interrupted at any time by her family. In school she has learned that holding the floor is not related to the sex, age, or power of the speaker but to a right given by the teacher, after a raised hand has been acknowledged. In school she must wait her turn, but at home she can speak without this ritual. The rule that writing and many other kinds of work in school must be done in silence has to be learned—often through a system of punishments and rewards.

While Ms. Cole neither expects nor insists on silence during any of her classes, this expectation becomes a rule in most classes by third grade and is the rule in Ms. Sloan's class. At the end of one kindergarten class, the teacher's aide arrives. Sam, who has not yet learned or accepted the "No talking" rule, tells Leroy, who looks straight ahead and says nothing. Without saying anything to Sam, Ms. Sloan writes his name on the board and continues the lesson. Sam now turns again to Leroy and asks him why his name is on the board. Leroy looks even more anxious but keeps quiet. He has had experience with "assertive discipline," a behaviourist approach to social control used by this school system, and he knows the next step. Now a check goes against Sam's name and Ms. Sloan explains why. "You will have to stay in during recess and pay back the time that you have taken from the group by talking."

Experiences like this one teach students to regard time, like a commodity, as a limited resource that when taken away must be paid back. The same concept of time drives the detention system used in the high school. This concept underlies this punitive mode of social control commonly found in economic systems where "time is money." I will argue in subsequent chapters that the values underlying this view of time are not only inappropriate for educational systems but are fundamentally at odds with the "naturalistic" view of time held by many people in this community.

Preferences of elementary children for quiet time during writing vary quite markedly. Their preference is influenced probably in part by the noise levels they find in their own homes. I ask Fay if she likes quiet when she writes in class. "If it's quiet, I can't concentrate. I'm used to music at home." At the other extreme, Larry prefers quiet when he writes. "I like it to be quiet 'cause you can't concentrate when it's noisy. At home my brother always has his radio going. And my father always has to talk to somebody. My mother is using the vacuum cleaner."

Publishing

Sharing with the group marks the successful completion of a piece of work. The title of the story is then written onto a record sheet that remains in the writing box. After the teacher has read through each story and carefully written corrected spellings over the invented or omitted spellings, the work is stamped with the date. Students, teachers, and interested parents are thus able to see the progress of each person's writing. Dating the work in this way also introduces students to the practice of locating writing at points on a time line, a strategy that introduces the importance of chronology for written records. Students become accustomed to seeing a date on all written material. In contrast, the time of a conversation can only be retrieved through memory.

Showing to students at the end of the year what they wrote at the beginning often produces embarrassed laughter followed by a great interest in their earlier work. This interest appears to continue throughout their school years. When I returned to their school after three years, several of the graduating seniors asked me privately if I still had copies of the writing they had done in their junior high days.

At the end of the quarter, students select from their writings stories that they would like to see "published." Parent volunteers then neatly copy these selected stories and securely bind the pages with a decorative cover. Presenting students' writing as simply bound and attractively covered books is far more likely to ensure the preservation of the children's work than trying to keep together pages of unbound paper. "Publishing" the writing of these kindergarten children and first and second graders emphasises the value the teacher places on the children's writing, an accomplishment in which most students take great pride. The pride of ownership in work preserved in this way is very evident when the kindergarten students bring up their writing boxes to show me their favourite stories — the first they have ever written.

I ask Larry what "publishing" means to him. "To put a cover on my book and to put new words in so you can read them. Ben's mother changes it so it's neat." Larry doesn't mind that someone else writes down his work neatly, but he doesn't think that his words should be changed in any way:

> "That's not good. If somebody wants to show you about the author, and you look at the book and you didn't know that she did that and it changed, then the person would be mad. We are going to put the books in a case and everybody gets to read them. We read the children's stories."

The excitement of young children on the threshold of writing, their eagerness to write and their openness and willingness to share their work with friends and classroom visitors were in themselves an inducement to write more. Will the excitement of these students about their own writing raise their parents' valuation of literacy in homes where it is not? When Ms. Cole asked her first and second graders how many of their parents read their writing when brought home, she found that fourteen out of seventeen children thought that their parents looked at their papers and read their books.

Time and Story

Young children's writing emerges from a particular lifeworld and expresses how time and language are conceived there. A story by Lindsay in grade one leads me to ask how this young writer's manipulation of the time order of language relates to her own developing concepts of lived time.

MY KITTEN

My kitten is dead.
I'm getting another one.
I love my kitten.
It is different colors.
My kitten plays.
My kitten play with Christmas tree.
My kitten was in my Easter basket.
I play with my dead [sic].

At first reading, readers will note with respect to tense management that the story is "deviant." Our expectation that tense will be consistently managed is not met. We assume from sentences two through seven that Lindsay is describing her new kitten. Then in sentence eight she announces that she plays with her former kitten. We then assume that sentence eight should have been cast in the past tense, which would have radically altered her intended meaning. The effect of Lindsay's narrative, I believe, is to resist the notion of irreversible time that precludes playing with a lost pet. By the last sentence of her narrative, she has created a time frame from memory and imagination in which she can construct a replay of the play she has lost, continues to want, and can achieve in her story. She has done so through what I initially called a "deviant use of tenses."

While I would argue that writers manage the time order of language to express their own psychological needs, it is arguable to what extent Lindsay consciously manipulates the tense system to reflect her wish to play again with her kitten. Throughout the duration of her story, Lindsay does play again with her kitten. In so doing she briefly reverses the opposition of life and death. Although Lindsay was willing to give me her story, she was reluctant to say more about her eight short sentences at the time that she wrote her story.

A year later I showed Lindsay the story, and she looked puzzled by her incomplete ending. I asked her to read the story again and then to tell me which of the two kittens she was referring to after the first two sentences. At first she said the second kitten, but then changed her mind to the first kitten. Then I asked her when we use "is" and when we use "was." She answered that we use "is" for now and "was" for things that are far away. I then asked her why, if this was so, she had used "is" to tell about her lost kitten. Here is her answer:

"My kitten was really pretty. I was still thinking about my kitten, and I was crying that day because I was thinking that she was home. She had green eyes, and my family liked her. It was a girl. I thought she would live longer and have kittens. I still can remember her, and I think she is with me. She got hit with a fish truck. Her name was Magic."

Lindsay's sentence, "I still can remember her, and I think she is with me," suggests that what appears to be a deviant sequence of tenses in this story are not simple errors. Rather, they indicate that Lindsay's use of language to describe the loss of her kitten reveals an experience of time in contrast to that represented in the idea that a life precedes its death. Her use of tense indicates how losing a kitten is an experience framed by her own time and by how she thinks about this event in writing.

In the first part of this chapter, I have described the ways in which Fay and her friends are learning about time in school, followed by a description of how these young students are learning to write. The task now is to look at how these two kinds of learning can be related. Since the following account is based on observations of one particular group of children, I intend to suggest points of similarity rather than to claim definitive conclusions about how learning about time and writing relate. This account will serve its purpose, then, if it prompts teacher researchers to suggest other possible explanations of this relationship.

When a child first learns to speak, his or her sense impressions and emerging concepts of the world are shaped by the talk heard at home. In part, learning to talk is a process of differentiation in which the flow of the child's early experiences and perceptions of the world begin to be segmented into discrete elements. Naming elements in the flow allows them to be abstracted and considered separately. For example, before Fay learned to talk, she would have perceived the colours in a rainbow differently from how she distinguishes them now that she has learned the names. The language that Fay has learned has given her the power to contrast its bands with words like *yellow, green,* and *blue.* Naming the world began her process of dividing it into parts that she can consider both in isolation and in relationship to the whole of what she perceives. We should note here that the process of differentiation that occurs as the world is named is itself culturally determined. The contrastive features that we recognise, for example, between *yellow* and *brown* will be marked differently in other languages; language and culture shape our perceptions.

In learning to talk, the words that refer to the child's mental concepts of named objects and experiences are combined into the continuous wave of sounds we call speech. In contrast, learning to write is in part learning how to separate out from the acquired stream of oral language individual words that provide meaning in themselves and in combination form larger units of meaning. The complexity of the process is illustrated by the difficulty that one of Ms. Cole's students had. "I've got one kid this year who says sentences, but he can't yet say the words separately to help himself write them down. I have to say them one at a time for him. I don't think he has the concept that what he is saying is a stream of separate words."

As the child learns to write, he will soon discover that within his oral language there exist separate units of meaning. Initially, however, writing is often, although not always, a continuous smear of marks on the page in which individual letters and words are fused together. One way in which students learn to recognise, for example, word and sentence boundaries is by reading their writing aloud to others. The child's ability to recognise the larger units of discourse such as paragraph, section and chapter is acquired during the elementary years. And although the child is already managing large units of language in talk, he does not mark distinctions between the parts within the early stages of writing.

The movement from undifferentiated to differentiated, of learning the relationships between the parts and wholes of writing, is at the same time being experienced by the child in learning to tell time. The child learns that a whole day can be divided into periods of varying duration: hours, minutes and seconds and a year broken into seasons, months and weeks. The child's concept of time will vary, however, from home to home. For example, the child who has experienced set routines of clock-governed nap, meal, play and bed times will have different expectations about time and its management than the child whose day is a seamless web of flexibly scheduled activities. The sense of time that the child has acquired at home and now brings to school is modified and extended by how the teacher organises learning and schedules time for writing activities.

Whether we are considering time or language, the structures of each system segment or organize our experience according to socially sanctioned conventions; between words and referents and time and its measures, the connections are neither natural[2] nor essential ones. The measures and expressions of time and the forms and uses of language are shaped according to the cultural values and practices of particular communities. For teachers to observe both continuities in and divergences between how the time and language of home and school relate will enable us not only to respect differences but to avoid significant conflicts for young learners. For example, the child who has not internalised a quiet-time rule, whose biologic rhythms are out of synchronisation with recess time, or whose attention span does not coincide with that of his peers is likely to be punished because she or he did not understand or accept the logic of time in school. Similarly, the child who has learned a different set of practices for taking turns in a conversation at home in contrast to one in school is likely to encounter problems.

A Critique of the Writing Process

On the basis of this discussion on how these kindergarten through second grade students learn to write, the key aspects of instruction in composition can now be summarised. This summary will be the first of my critiques of the writing process. It critiques the approach to writing that the school has adopted, and not the teachers who practice it. Individual teachers interpret any pedagogical approach within the larger context of his or her own philosophy, and emphasise or de-emphasise particular aspects. I recognise that this particular approach to teaching writing has been very successful in elementary schools and represents a marked improvement over earlier approaches to writing instruction.

In the following chapters, I will make further critiques; the purpose will be to examine how appropriate the process approach to writing is for the youngsters in this particular community. My assumption is that modes of instruction are likely to be most successful when they fit the existing patterns of social and cultural behaviour of the students. This observation, however, does not obviate the obligation for these schools to provide an education that meets the perceived needs of those who live there—an increasingly diverse group of people—and to develop a curriculum that will enable students to live and work in other communities with different educational expectations and concepts of literacy.

In learning to write, students in kindergarten encounter two different kinds of time: social time and quiet time. During social time, students are encouraged to discuss what they want to write about, to read their writing to other students in conference sessions, and to present their finished work before the whole class. One of the greatest values of these activities is that students are learning a new way of talking and listening to each other; when students relate to each other in this way, writing becomes an occasion for close social contact. Students learn that writing, like talk, occurs within a social context. This kind of social time has the potential to build a community of young writers as they share their ideas and help each other with their work. However, the process of understanding the young writers' world, their ideas and values, takes time and cannot be rushed.

In the class sessions, students hear the other students describe the progress of their work. Teachers comment on how much students have written and how long each has been working on a particular piece. When a student is told in front of his friends that he needs to hurry up and to finish a piece or to get started on a new one, the writer's self-esteem and motivation to write more are negatively affected. Students are not learning how to become responsible for the use of their own time if the teacher always decides when students have had enough time to complete a task.

During quiet time, students are encouraged to write on their own. The contrast between social and quiet time was most sharply drawn in the kindergarten class, when talking at the wrong time often led to punishment. Quiet time has the potential to allow students to concentrate on their writing and to focus on the new skills of forming letters into words. Quiet time also can isolate students from each other and prevent them from using their resources as talkers. When students are punished for talking at those times when we want them to be writing, do we risk discouraging them from wanting to learn this new form of silent communication?

Students are free to choose topics provided that they are part of what teachers judge to be the student's own experience and not something imagined in the sense of being fantastic. If fantasy occurs within a dimension of time beyond the one in which students physically live, we risk inhibiting students from exploring and developing fictive time frames by insisting that students write about actual rather than imagined experience—a problematic distinction, especially for a young child.

Despite students' obvious interest and engagement in school work, they appear to value "free time" or "recess time" more highly than the times for school activities. Free time is a time when students can let off steam and be in a less restricted space with comparatively few teacher-imposed constraints. If students prefer time in which they themselves organise their activities to time in which teachers make these decisions, can we avoid this problem by teaching them how to become responsible for the organisation of their own time? How can we make them active partners in determining the time frames of work and play?

I am playing at airplanes.

Me playing in the dirt.

Kindergarten writing.

Help Someone I am
on a little Island
I am lonely and
hungy Help oh Help
oh Help I don't like
it here oh Help
I Want to go home
oh Help

Grade one writing.

on The varey First Thanksgiving
the pilgrimms Movet to
A Now jentrey. (country) 364
yeras (years) uego (ago) the pilgrimms
livde. if i Livde pi wade (j)
be 364 yeras old but i
wase Not (364) theere. But the
Pilgremms ware (j)
with The inDiyins tha MaP frends
a Beg (Big) Fyst (feast). Tha tod At the First
thanKsgiving. The pigremms
salo on a boeted (sailed) (boat). And Its Name
is the May Flawer.

By melissa

Grade one writing.

DearMiss5

ToDay we Ho D.HoTDoDG
^and QODBRKL ^broccoli aod ^and Oranges I MisstYOU
I Miss you A Lot WAn you ^when owad Kome ^would Eon ^came ^in
IRRom ^our toom I tnIt ^thought wos ^was niso ^nice y ^of ou ^you to TAO the ^take
Thr ta QODDOPI+Fourthr ^teacher's tray and dump it for her I opy ^hope you Go+B2 ^get ^bet
tai+Mi ^ter. toth ^My. Kamot ^tooth came out I Kint ^can't WAt ^wait to
TALmimom and I Ko NOt ^tell WAtto ^can ^wait
TALyouethr ^tell I Loke ^either + ^like WAv ^(the) you Kamento ^Came ^iNto ro ^toom

Love   Emmi

Mark and his friends.

Chapter Four

MARK: WRITING IN GRADE SIX

"Once you know what happens, get all you can into a sentence."

Woodsmoke curls slowly upward from their chimney on this morning in late October as Mark and Fay wait for the school bus. Mark wanders over to the log pile left by Mike from the previous evening's cutting and looks at his prospective task of stacking the logs into cords to start drying for next year's fires. Mark starts to complain to Sherrie, his neighbour, about the good clam tide that he will miss today and the seventy-five dollars that he could make if he wasn't there in school being taught what he claims to know already. Sherrie laughs and reminds him of the "gold mine" he had planned to dig last month.

Instead of going to school, Mark had boarded the bus but on arriving at school had pulled on his boots and hit the flats for a morning's digging. At two he caught the returning bus and came home at the usual time of 2:20 p.m. He probably would have cut school successfully if the dealer to whom he sold his three bushels hadn't told his father that Mark was growing up to be as good a digger as any he knew. Proud as this made Mark's father feel, he knew that the days when one could make a good living on the clam flats were going by. As Mark pitched rocks and kicked idly at the logs representing that evening's work, he was still irked at being grounded and losing his day's money.

The long yellow school bus swings to a halt in front of Mark's yard. The flashing red lights of the bus bring to a standstill a short straggle of motorists on their way to town. Mark waves to a friend behind the wheel of a pick-up truck loaded down with lobster gear and then boards the bus. Impatient to start this day that he has not chosen for himself, Mark pushes in front of Fay with her pumpkin and Sherrie with her books and heads straight for the back seat. Butch, the driver, asks him to sit in his assigned seat up front and to keep him company. Butch still remembers when Mike and Tony were in junior high. They slid a loose back seat out of the emergency back door into the road. The story has the seat landing in the homeward-bound path of the school superintendent in his car.

Every few hundred yards, the bus stops to pick up a few more youngsters. Mark wipes the condensation off the cold window and peers out to look for his friends. He catches a glimpse of three hunters dressed in fluorescent vests heading into the mist behind Steven's house and stares after them enviously. Steven clatters up the bus stairs, grunts hello to Butch, and sits down next to Mark. Steven asks him if he wants to go this afternoon in his boat over to a nearby island where he has found some mussel beds that haven't been picked over for a while. Mark agrees immediately; already he is anticipating the sweet sound of the last bell of the day.

The bus stops at the elementary school to drop off Fay and her classmates and to pick up students going with Mark to the upper elementary school. In a bright flutter of red, Fay disappears into a knot of friends gathered around the teacher on duty. The bus swings back onto the highway and heads south for the junior high school five miles away. Once they are on the bus, the noise of their talking is too much for Butch: "Come on now. You've been very good so far. Don't spoil yourselves." Later in class I ask Judy, one of Mark's classmates, how she feels about riding the bus. "It's loud, very loud, oh my, when my mother drives me to school, it's so quiet." Mark likes to ride into school on a wave of chatter that brings him up to date on what has happened since last night.

The bus turns into the school yard at 8:20 a.m. A stream of cars and trucks go by, and several park across the street next to the restaurant. A group of mothers and tradespeople gather here every morning for a slow breakfast and a chance to catch up on the previous day's news. Over the dull buzz of early morning talk, a Citizens' Band radio crackles its messages from a truck parked outside. Somewhere off-shore Mike is out hauling pots with Dave who handles the boat and talks on the CB with other fishermen about such topics as why the lobsters aren't moving much yet. The restaurant is a good place to hear news on the school budget, or to listen to the arguments about what should be done with the Volunteer Fire Department's vintage engine.

News items like these are likely to become a part of what everybody knows in this small island community. Tall stories and more "factual" information are relayed swiftly from one group to another in person, on the telephone, or over the CB. News about a lobster boat going aground or an ice storm breaking the power lines to the island's homes will first be heard through the network of talk and later read in the newspaper. Mark and his friends do read the island newspaper, but at age thirteen they rely more on what they hear. Frequently they claim that the newspaper has misrepresented what actually happened. "They've got it wrong again."

Students straggle into school from the different directions of their homes. The students on the bus pour into the lobby, up the broad wooden stairs, and past the superintendent's office into the school. Built early this century when architects remembered that teachers and students need to look outside once in a while, white clapboard rises above a base of massive granite blocks hauled from the quarry. The school creaks comfortably as Mark and his friends hurry in.

The noise of the bus riders tapers off as Mark and his friends climb the bannistered stairs and cross the top landing to Mr. Eaton's sixth-grade class. I ask Mark what coming into school from home feels like. "Bad, oh no, another day, a waste of time. I dread going inside." At 8:15 a.m. the first bell of the school day rings. The students who have walked to school or have been dropped off by parents now come in from the schoolyard to their classroom and head straight to their writing folders.

Writing Class

Every day in sixth grade starts out with the unvarying routine of the writing process. Mr. Eaton is already sitting at his own desk writing. Instructions on the board read:

Please take out your writing folders and begin writing 8:15–8:40 a.m. Conferences at 8:40–8:55 a.m. Each student will use this time to work on his or her chosen topic.

At 8:40 a.m. Mr. Eaton meets for a few minutes with those who are ready for a reading of their work. He gives suggestions for revision, and lots of encouragement and support.

Mr. Eaton has clearly laid out his expectations for how the class will proceed.

GUIDELINES FOR THE WRITING CLASS

1. Begin writing as soon as you come. Get out folders and begin.

2. Do not disturb me until 8:45 a.m.

3. Use the bathroom, get drinks, etc., before coming to class. (No bathroom breaks during writing.)

4. If you need an encyclopedia, sign yourself out one quietly.

5. If you are stuck on one piece, go on to another until I am free.

6. Work independently and quietly.

7. Writing does not mean sitting doing nothing at all.

The no-talking rule is well observed. I am struck by the stark contrast between the mood and sounds of youthful conversation on the bus and the silence in the classroom. Mark goes to his folder, takes out some papers, and then attempts to catch the eyes of the students in adjacent rows who arrived earlier and are already at work. Encouraged by a smile from Steven, Mark whispers across the row to him. Mr. Eaton speaks Mark's name and points to the boy's work. This school day has now officially started. Later I ask students how they feel about not being allowed to talk. Laura sees the no-talking rule as unreasonable. "I think we should be able to get up when we want to; no, not all the time. I think we should be able to get up and go over there and talk with our friends." Although Laura occasionally shares her writing with other students around a table at the back of the room, usually she has to wait until 8:40 a.m. for a conference with Mr. Eaton when he will read her work.

At 8:30 a.m. the last bus arrives and several more students come to class. The temptation to greet classmates is too great for Mark, and this time his name is written on the board. In the adjacent row sits Steven who has been idly thumbing his folder since he arrived with

Mark. He gazes across the room and from time to time looks up at the wall clock or smiles sheepishly at his neighbours. He looks glumly at the same few sentences that he wrote about volcanoes last week. When he tells me about Vesuvius and the other volcanoes that he has tried to read about in the encyclopedia, he gets excited and wants to show me the pictures of molten lava in his books. When he tries to write, however, the words flow slowly, and he worries continually about the accuracy of his statements and the correctness of his spelling.

Mr. Eaton gets up and closes the door behind the last students who are now seated and writing away. The outside hallway is silent and the loudest noise in the room is the heater unit humming. Mark has told me many times that sometimes it's just too quiet to think clearly. He would at least like to hear the sound of a radio or television in the background. At home there is a constant stream of noise—the talk of his family, the television, a chain saw outside, or Mike building something. The only times when Mark is silent are when he is sleeping or out hunting. Chris, on the other hand, goes to write in his room where it is quiet and where he cannot hear the sound of the television. Otherwise, "I start writing what they are saying instead of what I'm saying."

Topics

Mr. Eaton does not prescribe the topics that Mark, Steven, Jody, and Tim will write about. This approach to the subject matter of writing is based on the teacher's belief that students can write most successfully about what they know and care about. Students turn to the following sources for material about which to write: personal experiences and topics about which they are knowledgeable, books, television shows, and the stories they have heard. These sources are used singly and in combination. Freedom to choose a topic frequently leads students to draw first on their own experiences and knowledge. What has happened to them becomes a rich source of material for writing, which is often either a factual narrative or a relaying of events experienced, as in the following account.

BAITING MANIA

I bait pockets for money in the summer I usually bait 800–900 a day. I made 1,000 dollars this summer. I get five cents a pocket. I usally make

$130 a week. I can make $300 a week, but that's a lot of pockets. I stoped baiting pockets because of school. Some other kids do it now. They are Troy and Brien. The only thing I dont like about baiting pockets, is that we get the bait from the factory. The women that pack sardines get a bad can then throw it down the shoot. The cans are very sharp. I got cut by one. I will be back next summer doing the same old thing, baiting pockets.

Knowledge of what has happened to friends and family and other people in the community supplements personal experience as a source of writing material. Although some of this information will be recorded as news in the local paper, most of it will be stored only in the individual's memory. Mark explains to me the kinds of events he remembers:

> "We remember the exciting things, the things that we like to do, like going mackereling, going lobstering, and catching dogfish. Going to Florida and going to Walt Disney World, traveling and seeing a lot of things, going on rides. Getting to drive, important things, something that's popular that you just have to do. Watching a funny movie. Trying a big ride, being scared. I remember being sick. I remember the first time I see people."

Chris joins our conversation by adding what he remembers:

> "I remember exciting things, like we went to this restaurant in Florida. They had a big band right in the middle of it. I remember just about everybody I met at camp. I had a whole bunch of friends, and I had to leave. It's the first time you do something. It doesn't have to be exciting. I remember the first time I rode my bike. I ended up with two black eyes and a broken arm."

Memories such as these become the starting point for student writing. Serendipity plays a large part in influencing which events in the students' lives, on reflection, will seem worth writing up as a story. The following example from Mark suggests that the moment of inspiration is unplanned but favoured by living in a world of rich experiences:

> "Sometimes when you are out in the bay, it just might come to your mind. You might write a story about this. And you just forget about it and say, 'It will never happen.' You will never be able to do it, 'cause

nothing happens. But when you get back in, and you sit there at your desk and go, 'You know, I could write a story about that,' and it's different."

Students fashion their writing from the language they hear at home, on the waterfront and from their teachers. Students appropriate these prior texts into the language game[1] of writing in school. From personal experience, observation, and memory of tales told, they weave stories with scant regard for the conventions, for example, of a narrative having a formally delineated beginning, middle, and end. In school, students express who they are and want to become as they attempt to manage both time and writing.[2] In a six-sentence story by Cortinee from grade six, her four-sentence orientation suggests that the time and familial setting of her narrative interest her as much as the single run-on sentence that narrates what actually happened.

STORM

Before my sister was born, when I was two years old, Dad, Mom and I lived downtown, upstairs over the liquor store. There was a small building on a rock where the bricks are near the new peer. Where there is "like" old gray boards on the top is where a little building used to be "at one time or another." I don't know anyone that knows where it is, but I do know somebody who knows what happened to it, my mother. It was a very stormy day, my father had gone out to haul lobster traps and Mom looked out to see if she could possibly see Dad but he had already come in so of course she couldn't see him but what she did see was the little building I was talking about that was once on the rock floating down the bay. That was almost nine years ago so I don't think it's floating down the bay or farther out to sea.

In fisherman's style, Cortinee weaves her story from remembering what her mother has told her about the event, from playing in this setting, and from knowing how island people tell stories. The presence of the old gray boards and logs are an occasion for a written narrative by which Cortinee inscribes herself in local history. She assumes authority and creates a personal identity by narrating an event from the town's past and her family's place within it. Part of her identity as a writer emerges in managing time in ways consonant with the islanders' practice of interweaving their past and present personal experiences.

But Mr. Eaton's well-intended suggestions for revision instruct Cortinee that acceptable stories move in linear fashion from past to present and maintain a consistent temporal viewpoint. In addition, he suggests that the compounded narrative action should be separated now into several sentences. The present shape of her story creates legitimate concerns for him, yet his suggestions, if followed, would edit out modes of expression and techniques of invention that characterise her lifeworld and are fundamental to how these students use writing and time to shape their identities. As helpful as Mr. Eaton's comments are intended to be, students like Cortinee resent them:

> "The teacher will have you write stories, but you have to write them like he wants. Write the way they are supposed to be. Write them in correct English: Maine people use words like 'ain't.' Got to have correct punctuation."

Imaginative Writing

Stories are usually started without warning. A long pause between exchanges is enough time to allow the introduction of a story illustrating the particular theme of the conversation. Requesting a story usually produces silence or a promise to try and remember a good one later. This is a form of talk that one accepts as given freely but not available for close analysis in terms of the factual accuracy of the content. A listener knows not to challenge a storyteller, for example, about the precise size and location of the whale that surfaced directly beneath the *Mary-Ellen* and carried her clean past Green Island before the whale was any the wiser. Everyone knows, including the teller, that this is a tall story, but the group nods yes at the end. The story is challenged not by pointing to the unlikeliness of events but by telling another story that to be credible requires an even greater stretch of the imagination.

We see here that both personal experience and stories told by friends and family contribute to memory, a major source of what students write about. The telling of stories in everyday talk deserves a brief comment. The audience of these stories accepts and to a degree expects an imaginative recounting of the events. Yet this expectation changes in school, and, as we have seen with Fay and her friends, such writing tends to be discouraged. Yet Mr. Eaton accepts the value of imaginative writing more than many of the elementary school teachers.

Students have various reactions to the school's unwritten policy of discouraging imaginative or fantastic narratives. Mark and his friend Chris believe that, if a story is realistic, it should represent only the events that actually occurred:

"If you write something that you know probably didn't happen, then it's not going to be a good story. A good story tells exactly what happened at the time. It might just go on and get more fictional. It would be a problem, because you know it's not the truth. If you die, it would just keep on going until you did fool people [for example, into believing that] you were flying through the air. You say, 'I'm pretending I'm flying through the air. . . . I was playing Superman, and I jumped up and flew through the air and stopped a speeding train, jumped in front of the cars, threw them out of the way.' If you write a story that's really stretching the truth, people are not going to like it. They are going to say, 'Come on and be realistic.' If you write a make-believe story, that's all right. But if you write, 'This is what happens to me,' you should do it as much as you can, because if you write it real fictional, they'll say, 'This story. . . .' They want realism."

In this discussion Mark and Chris distinguish between "realistic" or "what happened" kind of stories and stories that are wholly or in part fictional. Clearly these two students, in contrast to Judy, Laura, and Tim, value the former more highly than the latter.

Judy and Laura's story about the cat and mouse represents a type of narrative that makes no pretense at mirroring the physical world in which they live. They create a fantasy world in which animals talk. The story, more in the genre of a fable, is written expressly for children younger than themselves who will suspend willingly the reality that is so important to Mark and Chris. Judy has clear ideas on why she prefers to write fantasies:

"I hate factual writing, more guidelines. It's easier when you make it up. Don't have to do what other people say. I guess I'm just lazy. If you write it on your own, you don't have to keep going up to the teacher."

Although Mark and his friends live in a remote corner of the United States, television and mass media bring news of a technology with a potential for destruction quite unlike anything in this setting to which they can relate. Many students say that they fully expect a nuclear war will occur during their lifetime; how they envision the outcome of such a war is expressed in this student's gruesome story.

PROLOGUE

10–9–7–6–5–4–3–2–1 . . .

All nuclear missiles are launched. Cities and U.S. Army and Navy bases are destroyed. Corruption, caos, and death are everywhere. Bloody bodies fill the streets. There is a raw stench lingering in the air. Radiation clouds seem to dance along the horizon. Violent sun rays beam down and torch all matter into flame. Stirred ashes slowly glide to the ground. Over all, the whole earth now looks like an uncovered grave yard.

SIX YEARS LATER: TUSCON ARIZONA

A dust blown wood and earth hatch built into the ground pops open. Two hands appear, then a head, and soon two male figures stand outside the hole inspecting the area sadly.

"Nothing, nothing left. But just when we were kids it was all here. There was Mr. Stevenson's house, And Hooper's gas station sat right there," one of them said pointing to a certain place.

"But it all gone now. Why? Why couldn't we just die like the rest of them? You don't like it anymore than I do, do you?" Before the other guy had time to answer, Erik continued, "if it wasn't for this stupid hole, we wouldn't have to suffer like this!" and with that, he ripped the cover off the shelter and threw it as far as he could. Dust that was stirred by the landing seemed to taunt his efforts.

"Come on, Erik," Steve said soothingly. "We're gonna make it. For a little while anyway," he said, realizing the odds. "We can plant foods, and heat is no problem, I learned in school that when the nuclear bomb goes off, it will brake what they call the ozone layer and heat rays will constantly beam down. And, ahem, water, ahem," he started to choke. Thrashing back and forth violently, a gurgled sound came from his throat. Then he keeled over and fell to the ground on his stomach.

"Oh quit it." Erik said. "It's a nice joke, but you can't fool me. Steve? Steve?"

Erik turned him over and the sight he saw was hideous indeed. His brother's eyes were closed but his mouth was open, and most of his throat was on the ground.

"The radiation must have gotten to him!" Erik screamed. "But it's not going to get to me!" With that he dashed for the hole. But just before he got to it, his eyes rolled back into his head.

As gruesome and stylised in terms of outcome this story might be, it does reveal the kinds of fears that haunt the minds of these young students. Even though these students live over fifty miles from the nearest traffic light, yet television, books, and visitors bring them knowledge of a potential future quite unlike any situation anticipated by their everyday experience.

Several students rely heavily on books as the main source of information for their writing. Mark's classroom has access to a small but well-stocked library, in addition to reference books and encyclopedias housed at the back of the classroom. At home Mark can read through old copies of *Maine Life, National Geographic,* and *Down East,* and Mike and his father's assorted collection of manuals and books on fixing and making things. The town library periodically gives away back numbers of these periodicals, which Mike collects.

Reading reinforces the idea that students can find information independently of the teacher and is to be valued for that reason. Yet for some students it has led to an overdependence on written sources of information to the detriment of drawing on personal experiences as a source of knowledge. Judy writes about camels but has never seen a live one, only pictures and perhaps a film in which they have appeared. Her first story is about camels. For the past few classes, she has been sitting at the back of the room in the library. She has looked up information in the encyclopedias and yearbooks just as she did for a previous report about unicorns. She shows me the camel report and asks if I would like her to read a section:

> "One of the most useful of all animals is the camel. It has helped man live in the deserts of Africa and Asia. It can travel great distances over hot sands and go for days without water. There are two kinds of camels. The Arabian or single humped camel is found in North Africa, Arabia, and Western Asia. The bactrian or two-humped camel is found in Asia."

I ask Judy how she uses the information that she finds in the encyclopedias and the *World Books.* She says that sometimes she will take words out or put words in to make it sound more like her own words. This section appears to follow closely her reference source. Consequently, the possibility for Judy's being able to feel her piece as her own is much less likely than for Cortinee, who wrote about her experience within a familiar part of her own known world.

Steven's problems as a writer are similar to Judy's in that his writing draws not from the richness of his own experiences but on the knowledge that he finds in books and cannot as yet handle. Part of his frustration comes directly from trying to write about material and information that are not his own. Reluctant to show me his writing, he agrees to read to me from his work:

> Volcanoes are made of ash and lava. Volcanoes are very powerful and make a lot of mess and kill a lot of lives. There is a volcano in a lake. The name of the lake is crater lake. There are forty active volcanoes in the world. There are three active volcanoes in the United States, and there are two in Hawaii and one in Alaska. There are fifty inactive volcanoes in the United States. After a hundred and twenty years at rest, Mt. St. Helen has erupted. It had the power of six atomic bombs. It was eight thirty nine a.m., May 18th, 1980.

Although Steven is excited to read about towns being swallowed up in rivers of lava, he has had no direct experience of this subject and consequently concentrates on trying to report faithfully what he has read but never seen. He does not yet possess the vocabulary and direct experience that would make writing about this topic a less daunting task. He struggles for weeks to write one paper, and by the end of the quarter is very anxious about his grade.

On the other hand, Steven has an expressive vocabulary for talking about the kinds of spruce and fir that surround his house; he knows their smells, and spends hours climbing and making tree houses. At home he builds small model gardens from rocks, moss, and cut twigs. He talks a lot about how his next paper will describe how these gardens are made—what materials have to be collected and how they are arranged and constructed. He knows his subject in detail and loves to talk to anyone who shares an interest in his world. He describes for me with excited gestures how he and his friend Christian like to climb in the trees behind their home:

> "Sometimes he comes down to my house. I got one tree that is good to flip on. It's got a bunch of branches hanging off of it, and we stand on this branch here. There's a little branch comes off this. We put our hands on, and there's a third tree here. It's got a one like that, a couple of others. We go onto this and get our feet on that and flip. We are three feet, four feet off the ground. I've got another tree that is bigger around

because it's two trees together. One tree's got hundreds of branches coming off it. Do hundreds of tricks on it."

Steven and his family live in a white clapboard farmhouse built by his grandfather from wide pine boards cut on his own land. Wood from the forest around their home provides their winter heat. His father's boat and traps were built from oak and pine felled in the Maine woods. The paper on which Steven now struggles to write came also from Maine land owned by the huge paper companies up North. For students like Steven, wood is a beautiful and familiar material, yet he has not been encouraged to write about it from his own experience and perspective.

I ask him where he finds information. "I look it up in a dictionary [an alphabetical encyclopedia]." Sydney, a friend of Steven, adds, "If we run out of ideas in our heads, we can always go down to the library and look up *Trees*"; Judy mentions the thirteen books she has consulted in order to write four stories. But after his long pause, Steven replies, "Going in the forest and looking at the trees."

A third source of material is television (and radio to a much lesser degree). The students' capacity to create fantastic situations draws considerably on what they see on television or in film. All the sources of material for a composition may be used singly but more likely will be used in combination. Each source contributes a distinctive kind of language that the student attempts to synthesise into his or her own stories.

Audience

In answer to my question, Who are you writing this story for? Mark's answer represents his class mates: "For the class, the teacher, and for student teacher conferences." Judy and Laura have been writing together on a children's story called "The Cat and Mouse." Judy plans to make several copies and give them, perhaps sell them, to younger children in the school who she thinks will enjoy reading the story. Before these authors know how their story will be accepted, they explain that they will have to wait for their readers to respond: "You'd have to wait till they bought it. You'd have to wait till they read it. If they hated it, then you'd have to wait for them to give you the end." Judy explains that telling this same story would be different from writing it down: "People would sit here going, 'I don't care.'"

This group of readers is separated in her mind from her own classmates and marks a notable exception to the general rule of teacher as audience. Although Mr. Eaton will read her story and make comments and help her, finally she has to meet the judgments of her younger friends. Through writing stories, she has discovered that readers can be hard to please and to persuade that a story is worth buying and reading.

I ask Judy if she would rather tell her story to her friends or write it down for them. "Tell 'em — I like writing, but it takes a long time, you know." Judy recognizes that through talk she can immediately tell her story, whereas with writing she must ask the reader to defer immediate gratification. In so doing she believes that she will risk losing her audience. Writing takes more time not only to produce, but also to reach its intended readers.

These young writers asked for their writing to be read as soon as it had been written, and did not want to wait for a response to their work at some remote time in the future. Their experience of receiving immediate replies to oral messages led them to expect that written communication could work within the same time frames. That it did not proved a constant source of frustration about the utility and value for them of learning to write.

Planning the Writing

I ask Mark when he will start thinking about his next topic for a story. "I think about it at home — before I go to bed and when you come home from school." The two topics that interest Mark the most right now are hunting and clamming. I know little about either of them. After Mark is satisfied that he really is the expert, he starts to tell me how he goes about planning his story:

> "Write down the highlights. Plan it in your mind. Think what happens first. Once you know what happens first, get all you can into a sentence. Then go to the next and the next. You just think of what you did first, and what you did on the way. And you get on the boat, and you haul the buoys. You just think of a beginning, a middle, and an end. You just think of ways you do things."

Thus the temporal organisation of Mark's stories frequently follows the chronology of the experience as it happened or habitually happens. An example of this is found in Mark's description of planning to write about a clamming trip and embedding the stages of shucking a clam—a task that he has already done many times:

> "I usually think it out, then go right to the first draft. Just go one step at a time. Start out where I went, get that in my head, and go on to where the tide was that day, who went with me, and what I got. I write down some of the facts, the main ones, and then I'll put them into a story, like setting it to sentences, setting it down, then into paragraphs, stuff like that. I'll keep going through it."

I ask Mark how he learned to plan his stories in this three-part structure. He claims that he learned himself. In answer to the same question, Judy explains that her teacher last year told her to think about these divisions when she wrote papers. Judy equates the three-part structure with putting paragraph divisions into her work:

> "You had to see, you put paragraphs yourself, he'd tell you. When there was a break, and if you don't break, back to the start, and if you didn't get it right the second time, you'd have to stay in at recess and do it."

Judy's account suggests that the division into beginning-middle-end is taught to the students by the teachers and is not a segmenting that originates in their own thinking. Cortinee's storm narrative offers strong evidence, however, that other students import into their narrative structures a very different configuration of time than that represented in the simple three-part structure of beginning, middle, and end.

Mark continues to describe his own process of composition:

> "If I'm starting a sentence, I finish out the sentence, and when I get done with the sentence, I think of the next. After I get it all down there, with my sheet of what I'm gonna write and everything, then I go and edit it."

Tim, who has said very little up to this point in our conversation, waits for Judy to finish her explanation and then offers his own. "I think ahead. I think ahead what I'm gonna think, how I'm gonna put, what I did on the vacation, and I don't think about the beginning." I ask him if he thinks about the order of his story in terms of time at all. "Well, once in a while I'll think about what I did after that happened in time—that happened at twelve o'clock, something like that."

These students prefer to write drafts of their papers at one sitting without being interrupted to begin another activity. Mr. Eaton follows the clock quite closely and likes to begin math class by 9.15 a.m. each day. His students react against having to stop writing, to turn to math and warm up to that. When Judy returns to her writing the next day, she finds it initially difficult to start again. "'Cause you gotta redo what you were doing the other day, y'know." She would like it better if she were allowed to get at least half the project completed before being asked to work on a different activity:

"I wouldn't care, as long as I could get the paragraphs done. So you can start on the book, so you can write it, in page to page, like you get a paragraph here, and you wanna write that paragraph in the book. You write the paragraph there, and you wanna turn the page and get on with the other paragraphs, you know what I mean?"

Students are not allowed to continue working beyond the time Mr. Eaton assigns. Yet Judy and her friends have not been told why he decides to go on to the next activity at the time that he does. "I mean, you're busy working away in your book about the cat and the mouse, and then the teacher says, 'Okay, time to do math now.' I don't like it. You get into writing, and you wanna get it done."

Tim, who loves to write, is frustrated by having only about an hour a day for his writing:

"I like writing process. I start writing a story and then writing process is over. I have to do my assignments, so I can't do writing process. When I get home, I'm usually so tired I just lay in bed and read and listen to the radio. I keep thinking about my ideas while I'm outside or laying in bed reading. I can't wait until I start writing."

Judy and Laura tell me that they would love to sit and write all day if their teachers would let them. These two girls take more pleasure in writing than do Mark and his friends, with the exception of Tim. Mark claims that writing is a waste of time and serves no useful purpose. This perception becomes a dominant issue for many of the senior high students.

Waiting for a Conference

I ask Mark how long it takes before he has a conference with the teacher to discuss his writing:

"Before you write a story, you go through the steps, have a final draft, and you show it to Mr. Eaton, and he approves it. It takes about two days to write the first draft. I don't like waitin that long. You are sittin there writin, you ask for a conference. You raise your hand, and he picks someone else. You keep raisin your hand, and then when writin is over, you are not picked."

Mark thinks that he waits for about a week before the teacher reads his work. "It takes about a week before the teacher gets to my work. I don't like waitin that long." To an adult, a week may not seem like a long time to wait, but for students who still do not understand fully why the teacher cannot read their writing immediately, it is a long time to wait.

Judy is called on next while Steven waits patiently to get some help with his description of volcanoes. To a greater or lesser degree waiting for a teacher conference poses a problem for all students. Judy has solved this by writing on two or more pieces at the same time. This practice of starting a second piece of writing before completing the first solves the problem of waiting. "He's in conference so you say, 'Okay, now, what am I gonna do next?' And you sit, and you think for a minute, and you just get in a different piece of work and start working on it."

Judy's approach is still sequential in that she writes on one story until she has completed a first draft. Then she begins to write a second story while she is waiting for a conference about the first. After the conference, she goes back and makes a revision of the first draft of story number one before writing more on the second story. Yet this recursive pattern of writing contrasts with the tendency of most other schoolwork to be taught in a strictly linear fashion. New work starts after the previous piece is completed, the one-at-a-time task method.

The Writing Conference

By 8:40 a.m. most of the class is still writing, but now it's time for conferences with Mr. Eaton, and three hands are already up. After the first working draft is completed, students meet with Mr. Eaton to discuss their work and to hear suggestions for revisions. Whereas students in Fay's class freely share their writing with classmates, Mark and his friends seldom do this. They show their work mainly to the teacher. His major objective is to encourage students to expand and develop the ideas already written down. This aim is accomplished by asking for more information, more explanation and greater detail than most students are likely to offer on a first draft. His responses at this stage are primarily to the content of a piece.

Talk about the students' writing is conducted informally at Mr. Eaton's desk. Mark shows his working draft about deer hunting to Mr. Eaton, who reads through it and slowly nods his approval at certain parts. At the end, Mr. Eaton asks Mark to write more about the kinds of places where he goes to hunt. Mark immediately starts to tell him in great detail the finer points of choosing a place to wait. His explanations are cut short since other hands are asking for help. Within five minutes of arriving at Mr. Eaton's desk, Mark has returned to his seat with the request to write down all that he has started to tell his teacher. For Mark, one sentence does it. His finished draft is a shadowy resemblance of what he had told me about hunting for rabbit, moose, pheasant, partridge, and duck.

DEER HUNTING

On the first day of hunting season my father and I went hunting. I was real excited. We went in a secret field. I bought a .44 Magnum and my father bought a 308. We left real early. We stayed for about three hours. Nothing came out. When you are in a field you have to be very quiet and cant move. If you wait long enough you may get a deer. A good field is one away from the road good apples on the trees and some green grass. In about three hours we left with nothing. Well better luck next time.

Writing about hunting allows Mark to think about the trips he makes with his father and uncle. Sometimes Mark goes up to the northern woods for deer, at other times to the scattered islands off the coast in search of sea duck:

"We get up at four-thirty in the morning up there, and we get down there around five probably. And we have to walk all the way over to the end of the point. And we'll set our decoys, and get the guns ready and loaded, sit there. And my uncle watches the middle, George watches the right, and I watch the left. We spread apart. George and my uncle would be in the middle and I'd be about right here, so far you'd be spread apart. If I see one coming to the left, I'll call real low, so then they will look over there. If one or two just sort of left, then the flock comes in: You say, 'Flock to the left.' Flock of coots came in. There were about ten of them. We brought down eight."

When I read stories like "Deer Hunting," I am struck by a thinness of description in contrast to the spoken recounting of these kinds of experiences. Mark and Chris were irrepressible in wanting to tell me stories about their various exploits in the woods and out on the water. Yet when they came to write about these experiences, they gave spare, minimal accounts compared to the richness and life of their oral stories. Part of this difference lies in these students' lack of experience and attendant inability to find and express their ideas in writing. Part of this difference lies in students' seeing no real need nor occasion to write about what they would prefer to tell.

Steven waits patiently to show his work to Mr. Eaton. Talking with Steven about his work will take more than the five minutes his teacher can reasonably give to each student conference. Steven's answers to my own question come after long pauses and promptings. Responses when they do come are scarcely more than a whisper. Steven does get help from a special education teacher for about one hour a week. Despite her caring for and understanding of Steven, by the end of the quarter he has fallen way behind his peers. They will have produced six stories and he only two, and he is worried about his progress compared to that of his friends. Mr. Eaton, who is aware of his rate of writing, accepts what Steven produces—a meager amount compared to what he might be able to write, if someone could find just a few minutes a day to talk with him about his ideas before he tries to write them down. But in a large class, time is at a premium, and it is hard for any classroom teacher to give enough attention to students like Steven.

Mr. Eaton's students often ask him to read their work immediately, while they are there to see his reaction. Since there is a limited amount of conference time available, he must tell students that he will read the whole piece as soon as he has time. This imposes a double jeopardy on students like Mark. First, he would have preferred to tell about the hunting trip rather than to write about it. "After all, I was right there with Mr. Eaton when I could answer his questions about hunting." Second, now he is told that he must wait for an unspecified length of time before he will know how satisfactory his account has been judged to be. Waiting for writing to be read is an experience that all students react against. Students learn that even though the person for whom the writing is intended may be physically present, writing requires time to be read.

Mr. Eaton tries hard to return work as soon as possible, but with a class of twenty-five students writing four days a week, delays inevitably occur. Some students like Mark and Steven will find themselves waiting several days. Although students cannot control how long they will have to wait for a conference or for their completed work to be returned to them, they are responsible for deciding how much time they will allocate to each paper. In Mark's words, "It's kinda like I'm choosing [when to complete the work]."

Revision

In theory, working copies go through as many revisions as necessary until a "near-perfect" finished copy is produced for the writing folder. In practice this may mean writing two or even three drafts. Mr. Eaton's comments on these working drafts focus on content and organisation. By attending to such features of form as, for example, spelling, punctuation, and grammar only at the end of the revision cycle, he claims that the students' attention focuses on discovering and working with content. Formal corrections become a priority only when the piece is presented in its final form.

After the rough draft has been revised several times, a final draft is kept in the writing folder along with the copies of previous essays. At the end of the quarter, a period of about ten weeks, these are evaluated and awarded a grade. Less sharing of writing occurs in the sixth grade than was the case for Fay and her friends in kindergarten through second grade. There students read each other's writing on a daily basis. In contrast, the writing of sixth-grade students is read most often by the teacher. Less written work is displayed on the walls, and the idea of sharing work through "publishing" is less common.

Tim's attitude toward revision represents that of many students in his grade level and certainly that of most of the older high school students, who take less pleasure and see less value in the task than do Fay and her friends in first grade. Tim confides. "I like writing first drafts, but I hate revision, having to correct everything, write it over. I don't write another draft. I just do it on the paper, and I do the final story." Mark immediately agrees. "You have to write it over and over. You might want to get into another story and keep going."

Much of the resistance to revision comes from the procedure of working between an original draft and the new revision. Tim's explanation is one that I encountered both in his class and in talking with older students:

"I don't like to look at my working copy. I look at comments, this is what I have to watch out for. I have to put in more periods, make paragraphs more often. Sometimes I get content comments. You will look at the copy to remember and then work from memory. I could work out the stories in my mind. I don't like to copy. I like to go from my mind."

I encountered this practice both in upper elementary students and in high school seniors. Since multiple-draft revision is a major aspect of the writing process, students' resistance to working from a draft rather than from memory poses a problem until students learn and accept the value of this approach, which many do not. That high school seniors offer the same argument for resisting revision as do these sixth-grade students suggests that this resistance has its origin, in part, on the reliance of this culture on oral ways of knowing and remembering. Students react to the amount of time and effort it takes to write and revise a single piece to the stage when the teacher accepts it as completed. Many if not most students see revision as a waste of time, a carrying to perfection of something that is already adequate by their own standards.

A Critique of the Writing Process: "Why Write?"

Although many of these students clearly enjoy writing, they are starting to ask, "Why write?" Part of this questioning can be attributed to the students' belief that talk serves more easily and more effectively to communicate information than does writing. Students look for the same kind of immediate expressive response to their writing as they receive from talk. Students have learned that stories travel quickly in this community, but they are still learning to accept the fact that writing and waiting for a reader's response take much longer. In this respect, writing entails deferred gratification for the writer, and for the reader, deferred knowledge about the writer's topic. Not only the teacher faces the problem of insufficient time for student-teacher conferences — a task that Mark's teacher clearly enjoyed and took seriously — but in turn, students were very frustrated by having to wait for a conference with the teacher.

Students confer less frequently with each other in Mr. Eaton's class than in Fay's class, and they are often unwilling to critique each other's work. Tim is clearly concerned about hurting other people's feelings and about making comments on what he sees as the ideas of another person. "I don't like to conference on fiction. It came out of his head, came out of his mind. It's his idea, and it's strange that we'd criticize what's his." Tim's commentary suggests that as we teach students to revise papers on the basis of comments from friends, we need to be aware of how students perceive the identification between an idea and the person who is writing about it.

The contrast between the talk outside the school and the silence within is sharply drawn and strongly enforced by the teacher: Writing means not talking; time for social talk and talk about writing is discouraged during much of Mark's writing class, for example. Yet although students require periods of quiet time in which to write, they also need time in which to talk with readers other than the teacher. They need to talk before, during, and after periods of writing. Learning how to write in silence frustrates students who have not yet learned or accepted that while writing and talking are communicative acts, they have both shared and contrasting features of form and modes of functioning. In a community that places such strong emphasis on social contact, a form of communication that is performed alone and then circulates among a limited number of people is likely to be of questionable value for serious communication. Where writing is not shared frequently in student publications, the isolation of the writer from her fellow writers is emphasised.

Although it is not always the case, if a boy establishes the identity of his father as a fisherman, then he will give little time to writing. Few boys reported seeing their fathers write anything at work or at home. In comparison, more girls told me that their mothers would sometimes write letters, notes, and occasionally something for the newspaper. Many of the girls live in homes where the mothers read a great deal. More students might see the potential of literacy to play a valuable role in their adult lives if we could bring students into contact with a greater number of local adults who valued literacy.

Time Management and the Quarter System

An account of how students respond to being taught to write in school will need to consider the broader temporal framework of the activity and how it affects the students. In school, students discover a much more uniform system of measuring time and the work produced within it than at home. We have seen that the writing class begins and ends at just about the same time every day and that many students are disturbed by having to start and stop their writing by the clock rather than in accordance with their interest in writing and their motivation to do it. Although Mr. Eaton has the flexibility to schedule his classes as he chooses, as was the case in Ms. Cole's and Ms. Sloane's classes in grades K–2, he follows the clock more closely than they do. He explains that next year his students will be in the junior high school where each period will start and stop with a bell. And the uniform structure of time found in the length of these class periods is found also in the larger units of time dividing the school year into four quarters of approximately ten weeks each.

How individual students manage this time period is left to their discretion, a strategy that encourages them to take responsibility for how they use class time. At the end of each quarter, each student should have six stories in the writing folder, with working drafts completed and ready for evaluation. Mr. Eaton has access to their writing folders and can see how many pieces are completed as the quarter progresses. Mark tells me, "The teacher would know before the end of the quarter if the work wasn't done. He'd know because he conferences with me. He'll look in the folder to see what I've done." Judy, Mark, and Steven are all concerned about how much they have left to complete with only two weeks remaining. Mark has two stories finished and a working copy of his third. He knows that he can and will write three more acceptable stories by the end of their first quarter. Judy has only three stories completed by the eighth week, but her children's book is acceptable in place of three stories. Steven has still not finished his volcano story. He tells me now. "It takes me years to finish anything and get it right." The quality of Steven's finished work reflects the time and effort that he puts into his writing, and he worries more about his rate of progress than does his teacher.

All of Mark's friends say that they do not like the deadlines at the end of each quarter. They generally agree that they would prefer to have all twenty-four stories collected at once at the end of the school year before the summer vacation. Judy tells me. "Having a deadline makes you feel like you are hurrying." She feels that she would get just as much work done if she were allowed to organise her own time throughout the school year. She believes that the work she missed in the first quarter would be completed by her in the next. Judy doesn't think that she would fall any further behind working in this way than when she has to submit work each quarter. In fact, she thinks the present system of dividing up the school year into quarters is too lenient for the students.

Homework

Students' concern about homework emerged in a group discussion about how students felt about doing English work at home. As we talked, I remembered how Mike and Alton thought that assigning homework to people who had to work was very unfair; it took their time away from making a living. At thirteen Mark now has an attitude similar to his elder brother's:

> "I don't think it's fair, 'cause our time at home is our time. That's why they don't call it 'school.' At school it's called 'school,' and we do schoolwork. If the teacher gives you an assignment, 'Here, you're gonna get this for homework,' well, you're not going to do it. But you know if he gives you an assignment in the middle of the day, you're probably gonna do it. You know if you don't get it done, you'll probably bring it home."

Unlike many of his male friends, Tim is perhaps atypical in this group in that he likes to write at home as well as in school. His mother is a teacher, which in part explains a commitment to schooling that he has heard at home. But even he thinks end-of-the-day schoolwork assignments are unfair:

> "It's your responsibility, if you don't get it done. If he assigns you work at the beginning of the day, and you can't get it done in the time he gives it to you, it's your responsibility. So you have to bring it home, but if he assigns you something at the end of the day, I don't think that's really fair."

Learning at Home and in School

At age thirteen, Mark and Chris are already looking critically at the whole school system and making their own judgments about what they will need to know in order to survive, if not to thrive and prosper, in this community. Attitudes toward the value of learning to write are influenced by a broad set of attitudes toward the value of what is learned at home and its relationship to school learning. As a teacher, I ask students whether it's possible for them to learn all they need to know during school hours. Whereas Tim believes that he is learning all day long, Mark immediately disagrees. "No, really, I don't learn anythin at school." I ask him where he feels that he does learn:

"Out in the woods, huntin. You learn somethin there for sure. You learn a lot of skills. I know a lot of things about the weather. My father has taught me a lot about the weather. I didn't know much about guns, until I'd hunted for a bit. Now I know just about everythin. We learn more at home. The stuff we learn at school we don't really need to learn that to live around here. So the stuff we learn at home, we can get along with. We could make it in this town right now."

Part of the issue here is how people are taught at home and in school. At home, children learn by watching an activity in progress and asking questions. In elementary school there is not a set of ongoing activities performed by teachers that students want to imitate. They look forward to high school because they have heard that there they can watch people at work in the shop and in craft rooms on practical projects they can identify with and want to replicate. Watching a teacher go through a math problem or outline an essay on the board is a demonstration of what appears abstract compared to the present interests and immediate needs of students. When I ask Chris how he sees the experiences of learning in school and what is learned at home fitting together and helping each other, he replies, "a little but not much." This sentiment is expressed by many of his classmates. As Tim explains:

"At home you learn different things than you do at school 'cause at home, your parents don't give you a book and say, 'This is spelling.' They don't give you a lesson, an assignment. It's not like, 'Do page fifty-six.' At home you learn stuff you need, but at school you just learn options [sic]. You don't have much of a choice at school. Don't do that work and you've got to stay in. Don't do that work and you're in trouble. And there's no choice about not going to elementary school."

Chris picks up the theme of learning at home:

"Like around here you just watch someone do something, and you learn — we don't need to go to college. You learn about simple things. I know how to work on my father's boat right now. I've seen him do it, and I sit there and say, 'What's that?' He'll just tell me what it is, and I'll go, 'Where does that go?' He'll say, 'Right there.' When I didn't know much about fishing, I'd say, 'Heh, how do you plug a lobster?'"

Chris says that he has learned how to build a house and how to fish from his father, not from what he has learned in books.

Again Tim balances Mark's perspective:

"I don't want to go against school 'cause I like school. I learn a lot from the teachers. School teaches you how to use your mind and how to use your mind in a job, so you won't be so dumb that you can't do a job. That's what I like about school."

For students to be able to ask questions freely plays a large part in this issue because questioning is at the basis of learning in this community. Asking a question in school is more difficult than at home, even for students like Tim who are articulate and motivated to learn. Tim explains his frustration:

"You have to wait your turn in school and wait until the other people get done. You might forget what you are going to ask. School is made up differently than home. There aren't many people at home. It's easier to ask questions at home, because you are used to your father or your mother. You don't have a million kids around having their hands up, yelling out. You keep forgetting your questions. Just come right out at home, don't have to raise your hand. Keep your mind on that question. Minute I come up with a question at home I go up to my father or mother and ask it."

So at home, students are accustomed to having their questions answered immediately face-to-face. The questions they ask there arise out of their own particular interests rather than out of a set of activities devised by the teacher to further their education.

The students only learn with great difficulty that the rules for school-talk and home-talk are not the same. Often students will either forget their question or stubbornly refuse to ask it, when they have to wait to ask the teacher to answer their questions. This kind of waiting bothers Mark a lot. "Students keep raising their hands and someone else gets called on. Hands up. It's a piece of junk. It's a pain." On a winter's morning Mark will sit patiently for hours in a cold duck blind until he is numb, but he will seldom keep his hand raised for five minutes in class.

As a teacher here, I recall asking parents to come in to school because their children were failing courses and/or causing discipline problems. It was common for a student's mother to come without the father, and when both parents did come in, more often than not it was the mother who did most of the talking. Those fathers who did speak often appeared genuinely surprised at my descriptions of their sons' behaviour. (I cite the example of boys here rather than girls, because in my experience the mothers were more likely to agree that their daughters could be uncooperative and "smart in the mouth.") Fathers' replies were often in the form of anecdotes illustrating how cooperative and attentive their boys were when they were being shown how to do things on the boat, in the shop, or around the home. We might argue that this response is predictable given most of these boys' high interest in machinery. Furthermore, there is a different kind of relationship between father and son than between teacher and student. Despite these differences, I think part of the boys' cooperation at home and non-cooperation at school was elicited by different modes of instruction.

By sixth grade, classes are organised far more by the clock than in grades K–2. Students now know the approximate time limits of each activity and can confirm these by the clock. Mark's teacher knows that next year his students will be on a fixed schedule, and believes that he should prepare them now for that adjustment. This leads to a schedule that, while still responsive, for example, to students' motivation or the teacher's need for more time for an activity, is less flexible than the schedule of the lower elementary school.

There is little choice in school about how the students will use their time compared to the relatively high number of choices students can make at home. Mark's sense of the passing of time in school is often measured by the clock; at home, duration is measured by his interest in what he is doing, by his motivation to learn. When these students have little if any participation in deciding on the frequency, time of day, and duration of activities, they see less reason to devote themselves to the activity than when they are engaged in activities about which they have made such decisions.

By sixth grade, students strongly believe that schoolwork should be confined to the school day and not infringe in the form of homework on time at home, "our time." School time and home time are sharply contrasted by now in the minds of students. In school, students have little choice in how their time is used compared to the greater freedom they have at home. Consequently, in school students seldom invest themselves in the ongoing activities to the extent that they do at home, where they are learning in the here and now. Students often felt that their time in school might be used more profitably for work at home on activities with an immediate pay-off. In contrast, in school the value of present work was projected into a future that often seemed remote. While Mr. Eaton, aware of this problem, occasionally involved students in planning activities and offered them choices, he was working within a school system that assumes that the teacher should make all major decisions on behalf of but not in cooperation with the students.

Literacy and the Future

Tim is caught between two worlds. His mother's influence as a teacher is apparent in his attitude toward the school and his work. But Tim's father is a lobster fisherman whose work and life style pull strongly on Tim even though his ambition is clearly to teach:

"I need my school 'cause I'm gonna be a teacher when I grow up, so that's why I'm gonna go to college. I might do a little bit of fishing on the side. Fishing isn't going to last the way it's going now, so I want to get an education. If they have any common sense, look at how many pounds people get a day, like forty. You know, that's low."

By sixth grade, many students on this island know that a change in their life-style is inevitable and imminent. The failing of the fishing is a constant theme in our conversations, and a popular topic for students to write about. Tim writes:

LOBSTERING IN MAINE

Lobstering is a dying industry in Maine. The fishermen feel that there should be a closed season. The reason the lobsters are going is not just because of over fishing. About five live when there are about twenty thousand eggs hatched by a lobster. A closed season would be good the fishermen feel, but they can't afford to miss a season of lobstering. A lot of traps are on the coast of Maine. Surveys say too many. I don't know, I'll leave it up to the fisherman.

Mark does not want to accept the fact that he will be unlikely to make a living in the manner of his father and of his father before him:

"If fishin now was like it was when my father was a kid my age, I would go definitely any second. My parents just beg me all the time, 'Go to college, go to college.' I don't wanna go to college, but I don't know what I wanna be. I wanna stay around here and fish. I don't wanna go, even though there is nothing here. I like it here. It's just got woods you can go out and hunt in. Or you got the shore. It's got everything, I guess. No cars zooming about at two o'clock in the morning."

In conversations like these, one feels the tension that male youngsters experience as they are pulled between wanting to follow the traditional work of their fathers and elder brothers while realising that when it is time for them to leave school, fishing may no longer be an option. Many students who now remain in school until graduation at eighteen will be more literate than those adults who had to leave school and begin work at fourteen—their own parents who now encourage their sons and daughters to stay in school until they have a high school diploma. Yet students like Mark and Chris are still drawn toward identifying themselves as prospective fishermen.

These boys mistakenly believe that fishing demands little more than a grade school education. Their parents, however, frequently tell me that to be successful at fishing, in an industry becoming progressively more competitive, one will need familiarity with sophisticated navigational equipment and knowledge about running a small business. Now it is often the wives who handle the bookkeeping and year-end tax returns. So even fishing now requires more than minimum levels of literacy and math.

By sixth grade, the conflict between time for school and time when money could be made is apparent. This conflict is especially strong for boys who may have begun already what they hope will be their life's work. At this age, male students tend to have less ambition to go on to college than girls. Girls who already believe that any work related to fishing offers poor monetary prospects are considering now both the prospects of college and becoming a young bride and mother. When some of the young women tried to embrace both of these options six years later in their senior year, they had to deal with young men whose career plans led in different directions. The lives of these students we shall see in the next chapter.

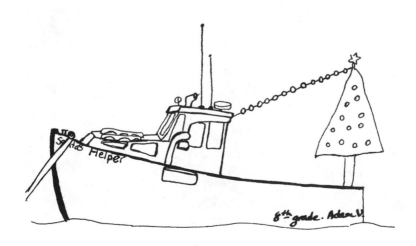

8th grade. Adam V.

Space for living and learning.

Chapter Five

CHRISTIE: WRITING AND THE FUTURE

"As a high school student, I very much resented anyone's control over me and my time."

While Fay, Mark, and Sherrie wait in the dooryard for the schoolbus to arrive at 7:20 a.m., Christie enjoys an extra half hour to get ready for school without the clamour of her younger brother and sisters fighting to get into the bathroom. She is the proud owner of a 1979 Camaro bought this past summer to gain a little more independence during her last year at home. For the luxury of owning a car, she pays a high price at the end of a school day. By 3 p.m. she is serving customers in a local store, a job many of her friends would like.

A few minutes before eight she leaves home and heads for the high school to arrive before the warning bell at 8:10 a.m. Her first class is at 8:15 a.m. By the time Christie reaches her homeroom, most of her friends are already sitting quietly at their desks talking with each other. Snatches of conversation bring her up to date on the weekend's news. The boy's basketball team beat Jonesport 90–78 at Friday night's game; Ann was seen riding around town with Dana on Saturday night; the state police had to chase Kevin ten miles before they could catch him for speeding. . . .

Christie has heard it all before and is anxious to start her day. Skimming over her math homework, she checks the answers she calculated after checking groceries for six hours. In the few minutes remaining before the first bell, her homeroom teacher sits at his desk patiently explaining a chemistry problem to Ann. Overhead strip lights glare harshly over the rows of red, yellow, and blue desks at which Christie and her friends sit. After twelve years of school, she has her own special group of friends: Ann, Jeff, Dave, Andrea, and Glen.[1]

The High School Daily Schedule

As these young adults prepare to begin their school day, I want to understand how the shape of the schedule and the time values on which it is based influence their responses to literacy instruction. We have seen in previous chapters that the sociotemporal context of schooling informs both how students approach learning to write and more broadly, how they come to value literacy. I first ask Christie to describe the rhythm of her day in school:

> "My day is almost in a cycle. When I first come to school, I'm half awake and really not pleased unless something good is happening that day. Then I'm sort of awake. By one o'clock, I get really tired. Then with just about ten minutes for the bell to ring, I really wake up. I could almost be falling asleep, but just as soon as I get home, I could stay up till one, and it wouldn't bother me. School just wears you right out. It's the constant monotony, the constant having to do the same thing."

In looking back over his years in school, Nathan agrees with Christie's response to the monotony of the routine:

> "School was second nature for me. I could say that it was comparable to mowing a lawn. When you're doing it, you either think of something else, or just don't think at all. Unlike mowing a lawn, however, when I finished a day of school I would be tired and have no sense of accomplishment."

Christie gazes through the glass door onto the frozen sports field and the stands of silver birches beyond. In January it is hard to imagine that in five months she'll be able to sit beneath the trees and watch the teams practicing. This is Christie's last year in school before she goes away to business college. She is planning how often she can come home to see Dan, who wants her to stay on the island while he fishes for a living. He accepts, however, that further years of schooling are important to her right now.

The morning announcements interrupt her daydreams:

> "Period two will be an assembly to listen to the stage band. Students interested in talking with an Army recruitment officer should report

now to the Guidance Office. All students please note that until further notice. . . . "

Christie picks up her bag and prepares for first-period class. This morning it is English, and tomorrow it will be business math. When I ask Christie to explain the rotating schedule to me, she laughs:

"I love the way it rotates, but you go from seven to three to five and they jump around, and it doesn't make any sense at all. I'd like to have it the way they had it before, where one day you didn't have one class. You would come to school looking forward to not having algebra. I like a rotating schedule much better than having the same time every day."

The high school class schedule is as follows:

	Periods
Monday	1–7
Tuesday	2–1
Wednesday	3–2
Thursday	4–3
Friday	5–4

The bell rings, and Christie is caught up in the rush of three hundred students heading for lockers and first-period class. Students who are repeatedly late are required to "pay back lost time" in detention, a punishment compounded for Christie by lost pay at work.

In the high school schedule, the times remain the same but the periods change sequence.

First bell	8:00 a.m.
Warning bell	8:10
Period 1 begins	8:15
Period 1 ends	9:00
Period 2 begins	9:03
Period 2 ends — break	9:45
Warning to end break	9:49
Period 3 begins	9:50
Period 3 ends	10:32
Supervised study block begins	10:35
Supervised study block ends	11:05
Period 4 begins — first lunch	11:08
First lunch ends	11:28

First lunch students to class	11:31
Period four ends for second lunch students	11:50
Second lunch begins	11:53
Second lunch ends—end of block four	12:13 p.m.
Period five begins	12:16
Period five ends—break	12:58
Warning to end break	1:02
Period six begins	1:03
Period six ends	1:45
Period seven begins	1:48
Period seven ends	2:30
Office detention begins	2:35
Office detention ends	3:35

Students' Attitudes Toward the High School Schedule

Attitudes toward the length, frequency, sequence, and time between classes vary among Christie and her friends. Many students respond negatively to its setting limits and resent the lack of opportunity to have any control over their own time. When I ask Christie how she feels about having to follow the schedule, she answers:

"It sucks. I don't like it. At school I'd like to have work done when I can get it done, like with the elementary school. There we did the work until we got it done, and then we went to another thing. Now, if you don't get everything done, it's more like your tough luck. There's nothin that we can do about it."

Christie does enjoy her English class and for her its periods are too short:

"I don't think the periods are long enough. I think it flies by wicked fast. The teachers don't get in half the stuff they want to, you know. Some students disturb it, so that means she has to go back and start over again. Then the ones that have listened and paid attention, they get bored and sick of it—tired of her saying things over and over. But I don't hardly look at the clock. I mean, I figure the more I look at it the longer it's gonna drag. We have it forty-two minutes. Some people can't handle it, but I could handle it for an hour. I mean I love to read, and I love writing, that's me. When we get into grammar, that's when I'm likely to walk out, looking at the clock."

Christie thinks that students' minds cannot be programmed to learn fully or to practice adequately any topic in only forty-two minutes. She notes that because teachers need to take attendance and to deal with office announcements, the amount of time for uninterrupted learning is often much less. Many of the girls responded favourably to the idea of longer periods of activity unbroken by bells moving them to a new location, activity, and teacher. Christie, however, would prefer longer classes for only some subjects, but not for others.

> "It depends on what class you are talkin about. Accountin, a half hour is long enough. If you're talkin about readin, you might read for a couple of hours, because once I get into somethin, I don't want to put it down."

Christie is least aware of the passing of time when she is reading, something that she does well:

> "I liked it when we had silent reading one day a week, a whole period for silent reading. I loved it. It's just that people get interested in it, and they don't care if anyone comes in the room. It don't bug 'em, you know."

Many of the boys in the high school, however, would not like longer class periods. Jeff wants frequent social contact and physical movement to break up the daily monotony of schooling:

> "When you're workin, you don't wanna do the same thing all the time. You want something different all the time—break it up. It makes it seem a little bit better. If you are in the boat for just six hours, and you are in school for six hours, I think probably the boat would pass time away faster 'cause you are movin all the time, always doin something, keepin yourself occupied."

Many of his friends regard the senior year as little more than a review of "the same old thing." Unlike several of the women in this group, they would not want to take all of their classes in the same room as they did in the elementary school.

Students like Glen and Steven, who is now in college, are exceptional in that they would have liked longer classes. Steven wrote, "In my English literature class, (my favorite) there was hardly a day that passed when I wasn't interrupted by the bell, often I was reading or in the middle of an assignment."

In tenth grade, Glen was so disenchanted with the high school that he dropped out. With the help of his parents, Glen found himself a retired schoolteacher on a nearby island to tutor him in math, science, and language arts. After a year of spending his mornings and afternoons in a very different kind of learning situation, he came to this conclusion:

> "Cramming all those classes into one little short day is too much. In the elementary school, I don't think they had that many classes in one day. I know I didn't. I might have had three subjects, and we worked on those for a couple of hours, and I think that was more comfortable. You'd have a lot longer time to work on a specific thing, and you could get it really embedded in your head, so you wouldn't forget it."

I ask Glen if he sees this as a possible model for a high school schedule. "Instead of forty minutes you have two-, two-and-a-half-hour classes. Some people might find it boring. Class would meet twice a week at the most."

Learning the Schedule

Many students who have had five years of a highly regimented schedule are now inured to the way in which learning is parcelled out in discrete experiences. When elementary students come into the junior high school, they change from being in the same classroom all day to switching teachers and subjects every forty-two minutes. Many of the boys like this because they can move around more. They do not feel rushed between classes, as John explains: "You got freedom to walk around. You got plenty of time—all the time you need."

The transition between elementary and junior high, however, is significantly more difficult for many of the girls, as Sherrie points out:

> "At the elementary, you start on something, and they usually give you almost an hour to finish it. We usually get it done in that time. Here, when it's English, 'Do your English,' math, 'Do your math,' science, 'Do your science,' social studies, 'Do your social studies.' Then just cut right off in the middle of it, finished or not. And then you do it again, and you cover it up, and then you go home, and you do the other half of everything. It's like cut everything in half. When I'm at school, I feel like I'm bein forced."

As we talk, Sherrie doodles on her pad and draws a series of little boxes strung together to represent how time passes for her in junior high. Next she draws a line rising and falling into a series of peaks and valleys, her time in elementary school. A straight line shows her time at home:

"You just smoothly go along, and you can go as you're done. It's like you walk a path, and you don't stop until you want. If you're sittin down in English and the bell rings, there's no choice, you have got to leave. But at our house, if you're sittin down at your house, and you're in the middle of your English, and supper is done, you could just say, 'Well could you please wait?' But you can't up here. It's just bang, the bell rings, and you've gotta go, that minute, and you're all done."

Sherrie describes the shift each day from school to home:

"Like bang, bang, bang, and then all of a sudden bang, and you're home. Like all of a sudden you ain't got freedom and all of a sudden you do. It's just like bein tooken out of a jail, and stayin at home for a while, and then you go back into jail. They take you back there."

When I ask Sherrie how time in school and time at home might come together more easily for her, she replies:

"If you like maybe furthered school out, so it connected. If the rules didn't go bang, bang, bang, maybe they'd just sort of go smoothly, like in the elementary. But if they went really slow, they let you finish English, didn't have you go on to your science, on to your math."

Transitions between Classes

Putting work down every forty-two minutes and starting on another new and unrelated subject creates problems for students in all ability ranges. Christie, who is taking college-level courses, describes her disorientation as she turns from thinking about one subject to studying another:

"In high school now, you go from one thing, you are thinking of that, and you've got a test tomorrow, and you've got to think of that. You go to another class and you think, 'Heh, where am I? I've got to think of what I'm doing now.'"

I next ask Ann if she sees connections between subjects, if their sequence is conducive to students' relating them to each other in some kind of educational whole:

"Algebra and English, you'd never think of them helping each other out. It seems weird to go from one world to another, one boring class to another. I think in elementary school, they hoped you'd forget it [the former subject] a little bit, so you'd push it back a little, so you wouldn't mix it in with the next thing you were taking. It's almost like you had to do that to push it out the way, so you wouldn't get the kids all mixed up."

The high school principal recognises the problem of students being disoriented because of the frequent transitions between classes. He sees a need for the teachers to set the stage at the start of the period by establishing objectives. "Activities that are student-centered during those first few minutes are perhaps more helpful in easing this disorientation than teacher talk."

The change-over time between classes is three minutes. All students claim that three minutes is insufficient time to go to their lockers, pick up books, and walk to the next class before the bell. Without time for sustained conversation between students and teachers, many students find school learning to be impersonal. Students note also that their teachers have problems getting to their next classes on time.

By this time in his schooling, Jeff does not question why the schedule is organised in this way:

"The change in classes isn't really that much of a bother, just something you get used to. It's a way of life, I guess. You set your mind to it, and you do it. It doesn't bother me. I'd rather do that than I would sit still — get a little pat and pound in the hallway. Say 'Hi,' change the scenery. Some of the kids get in fights."

School Time and Personal Time

Students like Jeff and Christie, who turn to non-school activities once at home, appear less likely to accept the time values of the school than college-bound students and those engaged actively in extracurricular activities. Using home time for school work, and planning assignments to get them in on time, are habitual behaviours for the latter. Steve is a good example of a student whose life at home continued to be strongly influenced by his activities in school:

"At home, for me, things are not so different from school. Often throughout the school year I am involved with basketball, soccer, student government, academic decathlon, and many other projects as well. These things can make for a very hectic schedule, and so I have to be responsible enough to set aside enough time for each activity. For me, the organization of time from school to home is quite similar."

Our conversations on the control of time in school prompts Suzette to reflect on her own need to plan closely her time at home, and to plan her time around the more flexible schedule of her father.

"You have to regulate your time. You have to know what you're gonna be goin durin the day, 'cause if you don't, you're goin to be disorganized. You have to really regulate your time, so you can get everything in that you need to. If you're a woman, you have to make your husband's supper at a certain time. If you know when he's comin in, you have supper on the table, and you go to bed at a certain time, if you're workin. When I work, I have to go to bed at a certain time 'cause I can't work the next day. I'm tired."

In school, when students are allowed to work on individual projects in study hall, few of them use this time for schoolwork. Many prefer to talk or read a magazine. Teachers often describe these activities as time wasting, arguing that this is a good time to get schoolwork done. In contrast, students reply that this is the only time in the day when they are free from classes and have even a modicum of choice over how they will use their time. Students' attempts to create personal time within school time are likely to result in punishment, for example, when students talk during class, come to class late, or attempt to leave school during the school day. Daydreaming is a way students can create private time by exploring their own imaginative space within the confines of class.

Time and Being in School

As Christie and her friends discussed their attitudes toward time in school, the following themes emerged. Being in school has been the experience of living and studying within an institution that allows students few opportunities to be responsible for their own uses of time. As young adults, students argued that they deserved to have the same freedom and responsibility to manage their time accorded to adults in the community. But teachers declared that many students had "little sense of time," and therefore should not be given the opportunity to negotiate the time needs of particular activities. When Christie's English teacher nevertheless invited her students to participate in deciding on course content, procedures, and sequence of writing activities, she was disappointed that they did not respond with greater initiative. Although her students appreciated that she sought their opinions, by their senior year it appeared too late for this group to be motivated to think for themselves; they had become programmed to follow the teacher's plans.

Many senior high students take the daily schedule for granted. The walls of time that partition the school day are largely invisible. Inured to the schedule's demands, few students can now conceive of school time being structured any differently. Yet that the current forms of school time create problems for education is evident, for example, in students' reports that they find learning a fragmenting experience, have difficulty establishing intellectual rhythms, and find so little private time with friends and teachers that school fails to meet the basic need for sustained personal contact.

By the senior year, students frequently work in part-time jobs and plan seriously for their future livelihood. Consequently, this is the time when many students would like to begin their careers and now evaluate their time spent in the senior high school in terms of the extent to which they believe it can prepare them for the future. Students who are not planning on a college education often conclude that further education is of questionable value at this stage in their lives. These attitudes toward both present and future time bear directly on how students approach and value literacy.

As students talk about their English studies, their attitudes toward the institutional time frames of their schooling surface again in their approach to writing. To provide a context for our discussions of writing, students described first what they saw as the different parts of their English course: study of grammar and usage, reading literature and writing. The teachers' emphasis on each component has changed over the past three years largely as a result of an intensive K–6 writing programme and because the high school's English teachers now increasingly recognise that more attention needs to be given to writing. Before 1984, teaching grammar and mechanical skills took up much of the time, with only a secondary emphasis on reading and writing about literature.

Grammar Review

Each year continues to feature several weeks of review of grammar and mechanical literacy skills. Even the brightest students see much of their English course as a review of skills and material learned in previous years. But the only portion of the course that is substantially the same from one year to the next is the grammar section, which introduces increasingly complex accounts of the structure of sentences. The grammar component of the senior high school programme is the part of the work that students claim they neither understand nor see the value in studying. When I ask Christie if she likes to write, she answers in terms of her attitude towards grammar:

> "I feel like I get better grades when I write than when I do grammar and stuff like that, 'cause I don't understand why I'm doin it. I mean, I can use the right punctuation and words, but I don't understand why I'm doin it. I just know what's right."

Jeff, who occasionally enjoys the stories that he writes, strongly resents the grammar section of the course:

> "It's boring, 'cause it's like teachers will say, 'Well, you have to learn this, or you're not goin to pass the class.' Well, why should you have to learn it, if you're never goin to use it after that class? You ain't going to go around after school diagrammin sentences for the hell of it, y'know."

Jeff grudgingly admits that, "proper punctuation 'n stuff like that might be useful for applications."

His phrase, "stuff like that," again suggests that what for the teachers are separate areas of study are all part of "grammar" for the students. Few if any students distinguish between grammatical descriptions of the language and the conventions governing its usage. In this community, what a person knows is not abstracted and codified in isolation from the active practice and application of that knowledge. Although many American students resist the formal study of grammar in their English classes, the reaction of these particular students surfaces as part of a general resistance in the community to establishing a "knowing that" separate from a "knowing how." People soon reach the point beyond which to describe rather than to perform an activity is seen as deferral and a poor use of one's time.

Many of these students say that in talking and writing they use the conventions of usage appropriate to their community. They know the locutions more acceptable to teachers but readily admit that they don't care about using these formal locutions. Since students' major concern lies in getting the work done, in this case producing their writing, they regard the study of grammar as a waste of their time. If these students had found that studying grammar actually helped them to write more easily in less time prose that they liked better, then they might have been persuaded that studying grammar was a productive use of class time.

Students also resist the study of grammar for social reasons. They believe that the grammar that they learn in school accounts for the structure of school-based writing but not of island talk. The rules that emerge from grammar texts and manuals of usage frequently do not account for their talk or any writing of theirs that has a strong oral base. For example, rules that tell students to maintain consistency of tense in their writing appear to conflict with their actual talk in which tense shifts are common.

Time Frame for Composing: "Due Monday; I'll Do It on Sunday"

Most of the major writing assignments in senior-high English are written at home. This practice contrasts sharply with the situation in grades K–2 and 6, where students have a writing class every day. Although teachers at the high school are aware of their students' need to develop their writing skills, teachers continue to place a major emphasis on the study of literature, especially in the precollege classes. For the next paper, college-bound students will write on a topic of interest from their readings of Old English literature. They have been given three weeks in which to write their next paper. To understand the value that students attach to each stage of the writing process they have been taught, we discuss how they will use this time to write their papers. The teacher would like to see students use the three weeks to research the topic in the library, make an outline, write a working draft, and turn in an edited finished copy. With this model in mind, I ask these seniors how they would use a three-week period to write their papers.

Answers varied, from the majority who would write the paper the night it was due to the very small minority who would start the paper the week before and write a working draft. These students told me that their English teacher had surveyed her class to see how many students had started the paper a week before it was due; only three out of the twenty-five students had begun. In the following discussion, David, one of the brightest college-bound students in his class, explains to me how he writes a paper, using an approach most frequently found among his friends.

Teacher: When you have a paper due in three weeks, how would you use that time?

David: I don't know. I've done things over a long time, and I lose all my information, 'cause I keep most of it in my head. I write on paper some page numbers for references.

Teacher: Do you make a working copy that you revise before writing your finished draft?

David: No, I don't. When I do my book report, I have two things to do in two days. So one night I just do all the research, 'cause I speed read. I take three or four books home, and I can read them all that night, take my notes, then any page numbers I want. The next night I'll make the finished copy.

At this stage, Todd joins the conversation.

Todd: I spend five or six hours on the whole paper—due Monday, I'll do it on Sunday. I don't care to do papers. I read plenty and stuff like that.

Teacher: Do you ever make a working copy as a way to think about the topic, to look at what you can say—like a dry run?

David: Well, my notes are a dry run, 'cause I make complete paragraphs and sentences as I'm goin through, and I'll draw little arrows.

Todd: I've got another book report due in two weeks. I haven't even chosen a topic—worry about it then.

Kim notes that "Todd's last comment, 'worry about it then,' symbolizes Island life. People carry this attitude into academic matters."

The next student to join the conversation is Ann. Although in the college-bound set, Ann has no plans for college. She wants to get married soon and raise a family. She is not prepared to defer this goal

until after college. High in ability and one of the most thoughtful students that I taught in junior high, she welcomes the chance to talk
about how she writes her papers:

> "If it's due on the Monday, I usually do it on the Sunday before it's due,
> because like last year I had a teacher that we had to hand in our bibliog-
> raphy cards, hand in our note cards, and we got graded on every single
> thing. Rough draft and every single thing we had to hand in. So we had
> to do it her way. I got an 86 on that, and the papers that I always do at
> the last minute, I usually get like a 97 or a 98."

When I ask her why she thinks this was the case, she replies, "I
don't know. I must just work well under pressure, you know. I'm not
sure. Because I know I have to get it done, I really pay more attention
to what I'm doing." Given the similarities between how this group
describes writing, I next ask Ann if she thinks that her answers represent how most students in her class compose. "I think everybody does
it about the same way, just wait until the last minute. I mean you ask
somebody, 'Have you got your paper done?' 'No, I haven't started it
yet.' I mean everybody is the same."

We continue to explore the temporal aspects of composition by
discussing how students would use a three-week period to complete a
research paper assignment. Andrea, who plans on going to college next
year to study for a diploma in nursing, leads the discussion. I ask
Andrea about how she plans her papers:

> "When I do mine, I just read over the material, and then I write it. I
> usually do it on vacation, like next quarter we'll have Christmas vaca-
> tion, and I'll do my paper then. When Christmas vacation comes, I'll
> stay in bed all day and work. I do it like that. I stay in bed until the last
> minute, then I'll get up and get ready and go to work. It's quiet up there,
> and there's nobody else. So I just write for school. February vacation
> and April vacation, that's when I do mine. Well, we didn't have a vaca-
> tion this quarter, so I stayed out from school [to write the paper at
> home]."

Andrea keeps a tally of the times that she takes as unscheduled vacation weighed against the work that she will do in return. When she
doesn't get a vacation, she takes one anyway, but does work on the day
she skips school, an indication of the degree to which school time can
penetrate time at home.

In our conversations, I became increasingly aware of students' attitude toward the teacher's control of their time. Andrea's irritation at my continued questioning of when she would start her next paper and how she would use her time was apparent both in the tone and content of her comments. "I start it when I feel like it. If I feel like Monday I wanna take the day off from school, that's how I work, whenever I feel like it." Kim picks up on Andrea's rebellious tone and comments, "It's very true. As a high school student, I very much resented anyone's control over me and my time."

Andrea does not regard the assignment as immediately valuable for herself. Apart from the grade, she does not invest her self in the writing, yet the teacher requires her to put her time into it. To assert her independence she must control her time. She does so by giving as little as possible and at her own convenience. When Andrea does write, she does so intensely, to complete the work in a short period. Then she will go for long stretches without writing.

Rhythm of Writing

For these students, both talk and writing are activities that tolerate few interruptions. As Andrea explains, "When I get talkin, I don't stop that easy. If you're gonna do it, do it and get it over with. Do it all at once. Do it right, no more." Similarly, once her writing is in progress, the rhythm sustains the writing until it is finished:

> "I don't wanna stop when I get started writin a paper. I couldn't do it any other way, 'cause if I kept stoppin, I'd like lose my train of thought, and I'd have all these sentences and paragraphs and pages flowin in my mind, and then I'd just lose them, if I don't do it all at once."

I ask Andrea if a working copy would not be a way to save her ideas so that she could return to them later. Her instant reply, "It wouldn't work. I don't write that way," suggests the problem that teachers face when they introduce ways of composing that conflict with students' preferred practices.

Although most teachers probably would not see the approach that Andrea and her friends practice as equivalent to a full writing process, her method is broken into the stages of gathering material, making notes, and then writing the paper. Writing time, however, is unlikely to extend beyond a week and is more likely to be crammed into an intensive few hours.

Jeff in General English reported the least amount of writing time:

"I can sit down in an hour and write a story, no problem. Got one right there I wrote Sunday night, before I came to school the next mornin. That hour writin that story is spread out quite a lot. That's the way I write the story. That way it don't take me no time."

For this quarter, the students in Jeff's general class have to write seven pieces that they describe as stories. The term "story" is used very broadly to include a fiction, a book report, or a description. The term is used less often by college-bound students whose writing is usually based on readings from literature.

Jeff knows that Mike has been reading about diving and plans to write about what he sees on his dives:

"Like Mike was readin how to dive 'cause he wanted to dive. That's somethin he wanted to do, and if he wanted to be a writer, then you ain't gonna learn how to write stories all these different ways. I already know how to write. 'I can sign my name.' Lot of people like that. They don't care."

Jeff goes on to describe how he wrote his last paper:

"We had to write a couple-of-page story about war. That's what our test was on, and it had to be a fiction story. Somethin like that where it's your own ideas, and it can be anythin. So you just think about it, and it starts comin to you. You think back about the movies you watch about war and stuff like that, and start putting them together. What I do is like once I started writin it, I wouldn't stop until it was done 'cause then I'd lose the idea of what I was doin it on. If the first copy was good, I'd probably hand that one in, but if it was all full of scribble marks and stuff, I'd do it over."

I next ask Jeff how he plans his writing:

"I get like an idea and go from there. On that war story, you think of a topic or somethin that you can get a lot from, like break it down into different paragraphs, somethin like that. Usually I'm plannin as I'm doing it, 'cause it comes to you as you are doing it."

Jeff's teacher requires a working draft for each story. All of these students resist drafting, as Jeff explains:

"The way the stories are written, you have to go through all kinds of study. You just can't write the story. You have to have a draft and all that stuff. Takes quite a bit of time. If we could write them our way, it would be all right."

Jeff's objection to writing a draft runs deeper than the by-now-familiar theme of its taking too much time:

"What the teacher wants you to do is discuss a topic on somebody and then write down all you know about that topic. And then have somebody ask you four questions about it, and then you go from there. But the way I write a story is, I figure it's my idea. I'm the one who will write about it."

Jeff does not like to share his writing with a reader while it is being written because it interrupts the flow of his ideas. His need to complete the draft at one sitting precludes the possibility of anyone else's responding. In the senior high school, students often refuse to write more than one draft. "Do it once and get it right," expresses a common belief and practice. Students believe that to revise what is adequate for their purposes is a poor use of time and does not produce better writing or a higher grade, the final issue for some of the college-bound students. By grade twelve, most students resisted showing their writing to readers other than the teacher.

Gail is not from the island, and until recently has been educated in the public schools of Massachusetts:

"I've taken out books from the library. That's as far as I've gotten, and I've sort of looked over the books a little bit. But, basically, probably the Sunday before it's due, I'll probably write down notes on it in my notebook, and then during the week, I'll probably use the typewriter at school to type it out."

Gail did not mention showing her work to either other students or the teacher before handing it in. Compared to the other students' accounts, she starts her paper far in advance of the due date. Yet she does not describe anything like the full composing process that Mark and his classmates go through in sixth grade. Teachers often claim that students do not understand the value of what they are learning at the time it is taught, an argument supported by the testimony of resistant students who return to thank their teachers.

Three students who have completed high school now give their viewpoints on the value of drafting to complement the opinions of students currently in school. From her perspective as a college student,

Kim now sees value in writing a working draft, which eluded her while in school. Steven, who is about to begin college as an English major, makes the rare admission that he finds a draft useful. "A rough draft always helps me to discover new viewpoints and fresh ideas when writing. The rough draft really is essential to a good paper."

Nathan, one of the most successful writers to graduate from the high school, presents an attitude that would characterise most students in the college-bound group, if not all in the General English class:

> "The only time I wrote rough drafts for my essays was when the English teacher counted the drafts as assignments. Otherwise, I never bothered to write rough drafts at all. If I discovered something I wanted to change while writing, I would go back and rewrite that small section."

Naomi has one more year of schooling before she can leave the island to prepare to become an English teacher. For her,

> "Yes, there is definite value in writing a rough working draft. Without one I could not take chances or make improvements. Drafting also helps me put all the pieces of knowledge together that I've acquired through researching. I would spend the first two weeks researching and writing and revising a first draft. The final week would be revising and creating a final copy."

Rhythm of the Quarter and Due Dates

For the students in Christie's group, the quarterly grading period has a definite rhythm to it, a momentum experienced as an ebb and flow of study and writing activity. Christie has just received her report card and has done well enough to justify her plans for college next year. "I'm just glad it's over. I just don't like working under all that pressure—term papers done overnight." I ask her if she sees her pace varying much over the quarter:

> "At the end of the quarter, I work real hard, and at the beginnin, 'cause I'm tryin to do well. It's like you are at a high right at the beginnin 'cause you have done good and want to keep doin good, or you have done bad and want to do better. In the middle you are kind of bored with the whole thing, and you don't want to really do it. Then at the end you are tryin to get good grades. You are goin crazy to get all the long-range things done quickly—tests and things like that. I don't even know they exist until she tells me I don't have them."

As a teacher here, I found few of my students concerned themselves about their grades until the final two weeks of the quarter. Much of their grade was dependent on writing that was usually started in school but completed at home. While many students cooperated, a significant number never handed in work on time. Instead, they would promise to get it to me by the end of the quarter. If papers were not in on time, students forfeited part or whole grades—a regular occurrence for some students, despite my explanations and demands for work on time. The concept of "on time" appeared to have little immediate value in terms of their own lives.

About two weeks before the quarter was over, these students would crowd my desk and ask to see their grades. Running their fingers along the rows empty of grades, they scowled and asked for their grade at this point. My guesses of usually below a "C" brought urgent requests to tell them the missing assignments. Once they heard the paper topic, they invariably claimed to remember writing the paper. "Yes, I remember doing that one, honest, I know I handed it in. You must have a hole in that old briefcase of yours."

The next nearest student would prove to be the staunchest ally in having seen the paper go into my hands along with his or her own missing work. Even the grade of the missing paper could be recalled. "I think it was either a 'B' or a 'B+.' I know it wasn't an 'A' 'cause you asked me to add more information and use quotations. I took it home to revise it, like you said." Once I learned the scam, students would write those papers that I could still accept. This situation was frustrating for student and teacher alike. I wanted to read papers at regular intervals, but some students wanted to produce the better part of a term's worth of composition at the end of the term. Both the more and the less able students followed this pattern. We would talk over the problem that late papers created for the student as writer and the teacher as reader. Even when students agreed that allowing time to revise was desirable, their agreement seldom changed their writing habits.

Repeatedly asking a student for late work or reminding students when it was due was regarded as a breach of trust and even an insult. A student would say, "Don't keep buggin me. I told you I'd get it to you just as soon as I could, didn't I? Don't worry, it's comin." The writing usually did arrive, often when least expected, and sometimes not even in the same quarter period. If I protested that it was now too late to count for that term, the reply was, "I thought you wanted this. Here, take it. You better read it." When I became frustrated, students advised me that in time I would get over not always getting work in on time. Experience teaches students how strictly their individual teachers will keep to the due date. Trying to negotiate an extension with a teacher is common practice. The only absolute deadline that students accept as unnegotiable is the end of the quarter, when the report cards go home. Jeff explains:

> "Everything has gotta be done by the end of the quarter. I haven't got any done yet, so I've got to make a few up, kind of go along and do them. And that way you ain't got so much to do at the end."

Rhythm of the Year

The rhythm of the quarter has a larger counterpart in the rhythm of the year, which follows a movement from times of slow writing activity to times of peak productivity. Linda takes over the explanation for this next section:

> "At the beginning of the year, I'm high, and at the middle of the year I'm dropping down. It goes like a letter 'U.' Whenever I come back to school in the year, you think, 'I've got four or five months to bring my grades up,' so maybe in the winter time I work harder—seems like if you do good, you have earned a Christmas vacation. If I miss two days of school before a weekend, I don't feel like I've earned a weekend. You've got, like, so much work to do. You've got so much work backed up, and you think there's no way you can do it, and it really bums you out."

For students who want to play on the sports teams, the rhythm of their written work follows the sports season; Linda continues:

> "I think the patterns go mostly around sports. Basketball season is now, and the kids have to do good, above a 'C' in order to play. They are going to be doin good, and that's in the winter. In the spring they are goin to have baseball, and they have to do good to stay on the team, too. So I think that's what this school revolves around, their sports. For a lot of the other kids, it doesn't matter what they do."

In these conversations on how students use their time, gender differences became apparent in attitudes towards writing and reading at home, a place where students have greater freedom than in school to decide about their use of time. Andrea leads the discussion:

> "I think they'll spend more time. Girls care more about their grades, or they're more interested. They find more time to do things. Guys would rather go out and play with cars and ride on their three-wheelers or some things like that. I think girls spend more time. More guys hate to write, anyhow. Most guys, they say, 'You can't read my handwriting, or I don't want to write this, y'know. I guess I just won't do it.' Then they'll go off and play outdoors or something."

Waiting for the Return of Papers

Students' attitudes toward waiting to get their papers back from the teacher provide insight into another dimension of how time and writing relate. Students on the island appeared far less concerned about the fate of their papers than students in other schools where I have taught. In our conversations about waiting for a paper to be returned, students shift between talking about waiting and their attitudes toward their teacher as reader. As I talked with this group, their answers sometimes appeared unrelated to the questions that I had asked, because when students discuss waiting, I learned, they do so in close reference to how they and others evaluate the writing itself. Students like Andrea and Jeff, who evaluate their own work and then forget about it, are not waiting in the same way as Christie and David, who are much more concerned to hear the teacher's response. Andrea and Jeff wait only for the grade.

For her recent paper, Andrea was asked to write a modern-day version of one of the Canterbury Tales:

> "The teacher wasn't happy with mine, doin it in the first person. She said that wasn't right—took fifteen points off for it. So I guess she didn't like that, huh? I like to write in first person: I think it makes the story more realistic. I liked it and was happy with it. She said it wasn't right—that's all! Whatever I think is good, nobody else is impressed with. She said I wrote it in the wrong style. I liked it, but she wasn't impressed."

When I ask Jeff if he looks for his papers to be returned quickly, his answer reflects Andrea's comments on the difference between the student's and the teacher's evaluation of the student's writing:

"The way I really see it is, I write the paper, and I read it, and I think it's good. All that really matters is that I think it's good. So I don't care what anybody else thinks about it, 'cause it ain't theirs, it's mine."

Although the teachers want to encourage and support their students' writing, the "mine—theirs" theme emerges throughout these conversations.

Students like Jeff and Andrea decide if they like their own work, but the teacher decides on the grade. The two evaluations are not equal, in these students' eyes. By contrast, David and Christie do value the teacher's judgment of their work. They have just handed in a term paper and expect to get it back in a week; Christie says,

"I'm usually worried that they won't like it, worried that they think I've copied it out of a book. All the teachers have liked everything I've written. They see it the way I do. It's expressing feeling."

When David waits for a paper to be returned, he wonders if the teacher is picking his paper apart:

"You wonder if the teacher is tryin to break it up and see how much you're thinkin. I wonder if she's tryin to break up what my character is, what he's gonna be like, if what he says his tale is would fit his personality."

When David has to wait a long time for the return of his paper, he worries that the teacher has lost interest in it and will not return it, which annoys him:

"It's kinda irritatin if somebody doesn't pay any attention at all. I don't mind if they think it's bad. That's not like a reason not to return it. But if there's just no reply at all. . . . "

According to the students, the time it takes for teachers to read, respond, grade, and return papers ranges from days to weeks. "Ms. Brown sometimes passes a paper back at the end of the quarter and some of them she returns quickly." Since the teaching of writing has not so prominent an emphasis in the high school curriculum as in the elementary school, students expect a somewhat longer turn-around time. Most of the students think that the waiting time is reasonable, given that their teachers have up to 120 papers to read, compared to the twenty to thirty in the elementary grades. The longest that Ann remembers waiting for a paper is a month. She forgets about it, turns to her next assignment, and dismisses my questions about waiting with, "Not as if I'm gonna die or somethin!"

Her response is very different from that of my junior high students, who would ask me to read their writing as soon as the ink was dry. The younger students expected their teachers to respond almost as immediately to a piece of writing as to conversational exchanges. Waiting for a reply to a spoken question and a response to a written paper both require time, but the former is given usually in seconds while the latter is likely to take from days to weeks. In the elementary school, waiting for teachers to respond to writing takes less time than in the junior and senior high school, where the writing component of English courses receives less emphasis.

Grades and Comments

When I taught in this school, I was dismayed and annoyed to see many students discard writing into which both student and teacher had invested time as writer and reader. One reason for throwing away narrative, descriptive, and expressive pieces of writing is that, for some students, the writing is only a copy, a transcription of the original memory version.

Mike claimed that he knew what he wanted to write before he wrote it down for his teacher to read. When he made revisions, he set aside the draft bearing his teacher's comments and worked from what he remembered from the conference:

> "You've already got the story in your head. If you write a story, you know everything you've written because it comes from your own knowledge—one way or another. So if you've got it all in your head and know the mistakes you've made, you can erase it while you are going over it with that person, on the paper. Then the paper's thrown aside, and you are ready to write the story."

This explanation would account more for personal writing than for material found in books and then reported. A comparable explanation was given also by sixth-grade writers.

When the papers are returned, many senior-high students are more concerned with their grade than with the comments. As long as the grade is above a seventy, many are satisfied, and, after noting the grade, students often throw away the paper. Other students, however, have saved their papers and can recall the pieces that they wrote in our class seven years ago. Both the most and least able writers saved or threw away their work.

David, in contrast to many of his friends, claims much interest in his teacher's comments: "They understand your work. You're gonna get a grade. Most teachers, if they put comments on it, at least you know that they've understood your work along the way." David is unusual in admitting publicly that he wants his teachers to understand his work.

In contrast, Todd ties the value of his teacher's comments back to the grade:

> "I like to have comments because, y' know, work on them things. You can see where they're takin off points and stuff. If you get a grade, that's a comment too, really a grade. You gotta be told why you're given an extra point there, why you lost one here."

Naomi and Steven also find their teacher's comments helpful to them, as first Naomi and then Steven report:

> "The teacher's comment is very important to me because it shows me the teacher has put some time and thought and consideration into my very hard labor, and the comments help with future essays as well."

> "The meaning behind the grade and comment is what is important to me. I am willing to listen if it will improve my work, always."

The girls in this group believe that they care more about grades than do the boys:

> "Girls care more about themselves and the image that they project. The grade shows something about yourself. It shows that you're organized, that you're with it, that you're not lagging behind. The grade shows that you care."

Discussion of grades and comments again opens up the perceived differences between the projected future roles of young men and women on the island. David speculates:

> "I suppose if she's a homemaker, she's gonna be at home teaching the kids, more likely. Most girls here won't go to college. Some will go, but some will just be homemakers afterwards. You'll probably go out and get a job, but most people here won't."

Ann sums up the young women's reactions to David's observations: "Well, you can go out and get a college diploma, or get a nice job and still be a homemaker, too, you know!"

Through conversation about students' attitudes towards waiting for a paper to be returned for its grade and comments, I discovered that the different aspects of writing in school were thematically interconnected in students' minds to the extent that we could not talk for very long on one issue before students introduced a second and then a third. For these seniors, conversation invariably turned finally to their view of the future and the role that literacy and education would play.

In the discussions about writing, time, and identity, the following themes emerged. Most students start their writing as close to the due date as possible and claim that their one-shot approach encourages the flow of their thoughts, unlike the distracting interruptions of writing in stages. Almost all students regard revision as a time-consuming process that does not lead to better work. Students often refuse to hand in their work on time as a reaction to their teacher's reluctance to negotiate due dates. To understand this resistance to their teachers' expectations, we need to consider explanations grounded in the students' life world and more broadly in the community. We will look next at prewriting, revision, and meeting assignment due dates.

Prewriting

Students' approach to writing parallels the "fisherman's style" of making, a poesis driven by the pragmatics of necessity, the aesthetics of improvisation, and limited time. For example, a quilt maker will assemble different squares of any available material and the builder of a small rowing skiff will recycle wood and fastenings from previous projects. The maker will piece and patch a new project together from what fits and will work with little concern for the intended purpose or formal qualities of the old pieces.

A phrase that island people frequently use to describe their approach toward work is, "Do it until it's done." Whenever possible, labour is not consciously organised into stages, with reflection and preparation for each successive step. The stages of designing and carrying out a project usually evolve together, as Jeff explains here in his comments about building a barn:

"If I'd done it before, I'd probably just do it. If it's somethin that I ain't never done before, I would talk about it. If it was somethin simple that didn't take much, just do it in your head. Some people would have to draw everythin out right to start with. Other people wouldn't have to draw nothin. An island person would be more likely to just go ahead and do it."

When I asked Andrea, a former student now in her senior year, how she and her mother made a quilt together, she told me, "I did it all at once. We stayed up real late one night; my mother and I finished it. We just started it and did it all day. That's the way I am. When I get started, I never stop." Whether the work, for example, is making a quilt, cutting wood, or writing a paper, activities once started are followed through until completed. This model requires closure and completion—in Todd's words, "Get it off, get it over with."

My students wrote their papers in similar fashion. I wanted to teach them different ways to start writing, such as listing possible ideas and topics to develop, free writing, and provisional outlining. Arguing that they knew already what they wanted to write, students preferred to write one finished copy. This argument is grounded in their culture-based experience of whenever possible completing an activity and not prolonging its duration by interrupting its progress.

Revision

The reasons for the students' reluctance to revise in grade six and for their full-scale resistance by twelfth grade are complex and deserve full explanation. Resistance to revision is by no means unique to students here on the island, but their resistance becomes more intelligible in the light of local practices than when dismissed as "typical student laziness." To write and rewrite within a short period of time is a fundamental feature of revision. But this aspect of production is seldom found in how the islanders tell stories, give directions, or provide explanations, nor, in the realm of the material texts, of how they construct their houses, boats, and fishing gear. Islanders will say, "If it works, leave it alone. This is good enough—finest kind."

Minor changes in the forms of cultural artifacts will occur in subsequent versions, but these variations will evolve over a period of years. The maker and user of familiar objects locates a creation within a far greater stretch of time than does the teacher whose temporal perspective anticipates a cycle of making and remaking within a very short time period. Islanders tend to see events within a cycle of natural recurrence, in contrast to a linear stream of unretrievable opportunities. Consequently, students are more willing to produce a stronger subsequent paper than to go back in order to revise what they see as completed writing.

When teachers ask their students to revise their writing until it's acceptable, students see this request as leniency, a weakness on the teacher's part, rather than as how writing is produced using a process approach. Students believe that a request to rewrite indicates that because they have failed in their writing the first time around, they are being asked to do it again. The request for multiple drafts can reinforce a student's belief that writing is an activity at which he or she consistently fails, a realisation that must surely challenge the student's self-worth. Students will ask occasionally to rewrite a paper but usually with the major purpose of raising a low grade.

Forgiveness is a human quality that few fishermen attribute to the sea. As superstitious and mystical as they can sometimes be, they assume that the sea will offer few opportunities to learn from mistakes. Fishermen do not routinely expect to get second chances but assume that they will need to get important tasks done right the first time around. Children inherit this attitude and expect that they too should be able to get their work right the first time or live with the imperfections in their writing until the next time.

Writing is one way to establish and maintain the self, but for students like Jeff and Andrea, their identities as writers are challenged by the peer-editing stage of revision. Recall Jeff's argument that to involve another person takes away or shares ownership of the writing. This belief is related to how he establishes his own identity in time. His sense of self is in part dependent on having full control of the temporal organisation of how past experiences become a present written account. The infusion of ideas from the mind of another reader is perceived often as an intrusion that can take away his own story. The temporal unity of his paper is broken when he tries to include comments from readers who have their own stories.

Due Dates

Students often react to their teacher's perceived inflexibility and unwillingness to cooperate with them by not handing in work on time. Teachers who rigidly enforce due dates motivate many students to assert the time needs that they associate with being independent young adults. Teachers' reluctance to negotiate deadlines runs counter to the students' need for and expectation of negotiable due dates in their community. The attempt to negotiate deadlines in school is paralleled by the widely held community attitude of, "Pay when you can, and don't worry in the meantime." Local banks and stores give extended credit, knowing that customers will settle their accounts when they can. This deferred system of payment is based on trust and the belief that a lack of funds in the winter will be followed by ready cash in the spring, summer, and fall, when lobster fishing is fully under way. Temporal flexibility on the part of small businesses toward the fishermen is essential for the survival of both industry and community.

By twelfth grade, many students see the teacher in the adversarial role of assigner of work and pronouncer of grades. Many students react to this role by producing minimal amounts of work and claiming to write for themselves and for nobody else. Although not true for all students, the sharp separation between the roles of teacher as reader and student as writer discourages the kinds of cooperation that could change the dispirited manner in which many students approach writing.

As a teacher here, I asked myself what could be done to make learning to write a more useful and valued activity, a question that the teachers ask when they meet with their students and read their papers. When students resisted instruction and refused to produce work adequate to the assignment and their abilities, I became frustrated. Their response was often a shrug that told me not to worry. On the days when I followed their advice, I allowed the attitudes of the least motivated and often most troubled students to determine my expectations.

On those days I tacitly accepted the judgment of some students that literacy had little or nothing to offer them. If we allow students to make this decision, then we equip them poorly to make future decisions that will demand more than a grade-school level of literacy. Because some students will try to make a decision that teachers, parents, and finally the students themselves cannot accept, we need to make visible key elements such as those discussed above that begin to account for students' resistance to writing.

Homework and Schoolwork: Time for You and Time for Me

The need students feel to make a living is prominent in all our conversations about written homework and about the future. Because many parents need their children's support by ninth grade, the school's demands for homework take time away from the essential tasks of making money to help pay for clothes, transport and in some homes putting food on the table. As already noted students will say, "Time in school belongs to the teachers, but time at home should be ours." The need and ability to earn a living exerts a powerful influence on the students' notion of self. This concern shapes how students value their time in school, which in turn influences how they respond to becoming literate. One major consequence of this attitude is that students allocate only sufficient time to write one draft at the last minute and will revise only if a paper receives a failing grade.

Economic Realities

For many students, the economic demands of the present eclipse the more distant concern of the future. Attending school every day is a luxury that not all students can afford. One evening I stopped by Alton and Sylvia's mobile home where I met Arno, a student that I hadn't seen for a couple of years. He asked me what I was doing back on the island, and then we talked about what he and his friends were up to. When I was about to leave, he stopped me by asking, "Do you know why they kicked me out of school?" My retelling of his story follows as closely as I can recall his actual words:

"My mother's boyfriend wasn't workin last winter. I had to do somethin — couldn't let us all starve, you know. So I dug clams for a few tides and didn't go to school. When I went back, they told me I wouldn't get any credit for the courses I'd taken that winter. And I'd been fightin to get my grades back up. It was somethin about a new attendance policy, and missin ten days of school. They said I could never come back. I told the principal where he could shove his credits, and I haven't been back since. No, I didn't tell him why I was out of school 'cause I was embarrassed to say, 'You know, not everybody's got money round here.' But I wanted my high school diploma. Do you think it's right what they did to me? I might go back and try again in the adult ed course. I don't know."

Situations like these seldom have single villains. The high school principal had tried hard to keep Arno in school. The school board instituted the attendance policy in an attempt to reduce the high rate of absenteeism. In this case, the policy punished a student who at that time in his life felt a stronger loyalty to his family than to the school. Students regard policies that legislate school attendance as a very basic imposition on the freedom to be responsible for their own time both in and out of school. Kim's response to Arno's story suggests the need for schools to recognise and respect students' time needs as they make such policies:

"School is not always and can't always be the most important issue for someone. And this story relays so much pride really. Maybe foolish pride, but pride nonetheless. I skipped school much more after the attendance policy was in effect, it annoyed me so much."

Homework

If we look at the importance of homework from the students' viewpoint, we see how the relationship between time in school and time at home influences students' responses to literacy. When I asked students whether they thought homework was necessary, Janet responds:

"I think a good teacher should be able to explain something in school. There's hardly any time for me, 'cause when I get home it's four o'clock. I do my homework, can't go outside 'cause it's dark. I do my homework for a while and watch TV for an hour. The weekends are the only times I can do what I want to do. Then on Sunday I have to do all my homework. Being at home is like being in school all the time."

David regards schoolwork as work done for someone else, a viewpoint shared by many students:

"It doesn't seem like you have enough time. When I get home from school, I don't like to do homework. I try to do it in school because I do other things at home. I read other things, you know, and I study other stuff."

In conversations about homework, students claim repeatedly that they need more time for themselves.

I ask Jeff if he has a special time to do his English homework:

"If I've got a lot of homework, I'll start on it. Like I'll go home and get somethin to eat and then start doin it. If there ain't that much, I'll watch TV or somethin. Do my homework durin the news, not much goin on around that time and get the rest of the night to yourself."

News time is one of the least popular TV viewing times, in part because the events described appear so remote and unrelated to life on the island.

By contrast, during weekdays, all of Susan's time is given to schoolwork that appears to interest and motivate her. But even for her the weekend marks the beginning of her own time:

"On the weekends I forget that school even exists. I just blank it right out. If I don't have to, I don't take my books home. I usually go down to my sister's house. I've got my two nieces down there. They help me forget about school. The only time I really start to think about it is Sunday. I've hated school since I was really young."

A few students acknowledge the teacher's problem of finding enough time to include all the work necessary to their present schooling and to prepare them for college. Most students, however, believe that by the time they have reached senior high, homework should be an elective.

If we recall the difficulty that Mike had finding time for homework in eighth and ninth grades, then we can see why the need to make a living now raises an even greater concern among students about homework. Although Mike took pride in always doing his classwork, he believed that his failure in school was because he never did any homework.

As these seniors talk about the difficulty of finding time for homework and their reluctance to use home time for schoolwork, their anxieties emerge about the immediate future. Their concern surfaced in part as criticism of a school curriculum that did not appear to prepare them for their anticipated future needs. Students in General English did not see the practical relevance of the kinds of English being studied, and strongly criticised an academic education. College-bound students were more inclined to trust that their English course was preparing them for a future in college.

The Future: A Time to Leave School

Students' concerns around how well prepared they were to begin their future work surfaced both in conversation and in writings, as in the example below by Anita.

> Well, I am finally writing to you at last. We the class of 86 graduated in June. It was a wonderful day in my life. I feel as if my life has just begun. All of those years are over and now I have to decide what to do with my life, such a decision. Where do I begin? As you know I am still working at the Nursing Home. Somedays I feel as if I can't handle it. I always wanted to be a nurse. As I told you in July [1985], I was going to go right on to college. Well, I have changed my mind. As you have probably figured out I am always changing my mind. Well I guess I'm just being a normal seventeen year old.

Anita wrote this letter in response to a class assignment given in March asked her to describe herself to a friend who she had met recently and to present those experiences that had contributed toward shaping the person she is today. Yet Anita writes as if she has graduated already in June; in actuality, she is describing events still in her future. When I ask her why she has written as though she is looking back on the past, Anita explains that she has established this perspective because she wanted to be done with school and to be in the next phase of her life. The temporal orientation of the first sentence indicates that Anita has reached the end of the exhausting business of schooling. "At last" and "finally" emphasise the exhaustion and relief that she now feels.

Graduation and what will come next is the focal event both in Anita's letter and in the lives of many of her friends. What schooling has meant to Anita is represented in sentences that progress from the past tense of sentence three, to the present of sentence four and into the future reference of sentence five: "All of those years are over and now I have to decide what to do with my life, such a decision." Here Anita turns from her years in school to the future that she will shape. Her following question, "Where do I begin?" suggests that she has reached the end of her high-school education without clarity or confidence and without being able or allowed to make decisions about her future. As that narrator of her own life story, she sees herself three months from now having graduated but not yet having decided on what to do next.

Eight of Anita's thirteen sentences evaluate or reflect on her life at this juncture. The other sentences serve the narrative function of explaining what has happened or is happening now, as in "I am still working. . . . " Evaluations such as "I feel as if my life has just begun" and "Where do I begin?" introduce us to a story on the threshold of an as yet obscure future. Anita uses stock phrases that we might assume she has heard other young people use at the transition time between school and work. By reworking old language to make meaning of a new situation, writing begins to move her toward the future. Recognising her present uncertainty starts that process.

The anxiety that Anita feels at this stage of her life emerges in her admission that once she had actually tried working as a nurse she discovered that the reality of caring for sick people was very different from how she had imagined it as a child. In our conversation about her work, Anita wondered if she had the ability to care for the elderly and for those who would not recover—doubts that have led her to question her whole future. When she talks about nursing, the descriptions are copious in contrast to a story in which the reader must imagine the details. In her story, Anita next shifts her time of reference back to the previous summer when she had told the friend of her plans "to go right on to [nursing] college." Her current change of mind anticipates the decision that she is now trying to make.

Anita defers telling us what she might do next and instead anticipates her reader's hunch that she continues to change her mind. Her need to accept uncertainty is apparent here. Anita attempts to normalise her situation by appealing to what we can suppose friends and family have told her, that what she is going through is quite usual. This belief, however, more precisely reflects mainstream schooling in cultures where uncertain futures are more common than in this community where many young girls can still predict their careers on the basis of their mothers' lives.

I have introduced this chapter section with Anita's writing about the future because her writing is emblematic of the time when students must decide not only what to do next and how to do it, but also whether they will stay on the island or leave for college. We see this writer attempting to engage her future by alternating between describing past events and hopes and her present situation. Such temporal movements point toward a future that she is as yet unable to occupy except by projecting the viewpoint of her letter to the time after graduation. A teacher might reasonably encourage Anita to develop her piece further by exploring the future in writing. To do so would be to assume that she is ready and willing to extend the movements beyond her own closing sentences on the state of "changing" and of "being."

To understand how life beyond the classroom informs the responses of young men and women to their last year of secondary school, we need to consider the futures for which they are preparing themselves. The question, "Why do we need to write?" was put to me many times by my junior high students. Now in their final year, the senior students continue to ask what literacy, and more broadly, education, will contribute to their future lives. By the end of tenth grade, many students—aware that their educational attainment already exceeds that of successful parents—believe that their present level of literacy will be adequate to meet their future needs. As young adults about to leave school, their economic and social needs now become insistent.

From their junior high school years, many students have provided their own clothes and any luxuries, such as a car. Any activity that is time-consuming, does not earn money, and is not always pleasurable is unlikely to be engaged in willingly. For many students who do not plan on going to college, school is just such an activity.

By this stage, these students have looked critically at their work prospects. One of the first signs that students are getting ready to leave school is their attempt to make enough money to gain some measure of economic freedom from living at home. Glen has had his own boat since tenth grade, and Christie now owns a car:

"I was talkin to my mother on the phone, and I told her that I was gonna be movin out, and she said, 'But you're just a little girl.' It's like, 'I'm sixteen years old. I have a job, y' know. I'm just gettin ready to go to college in a year or so.'"

Glen knows exactly what he wants after he graduates:

"I've got these goals set. I always do that, and my father says I dream and wish too much. I wanted to buy a boat this last summer. So I worked and I worked, and bought a boat, not much, wooden, six feet wide, got an outboard, nice outboard—twenty-five horsepower. I'd do anything to make money. Like now, I'm making wreaths. I don't care. I'm not ashamed of making wreaths."

Discussions around the topic of leaving school and finding work lead us into questions about the future prospects for fishing and for alternative careers for both young men and women. The present decline in fish catch size causes high uncertainty for everybody. Those who have fished these waters for over fifty years tell of boats that used to return loaded down to the deck with fish. They describe also the frustration of seeing their scallop gear yellow with rust behind the barn. Fishing goes in cycles of plenty followed by scarcity, they explain. Experienced fishermen have seen the cycles and say that even the best times now are never as good. Even the most optimistic say the catch is worse than ever before. Others remain silent; some sell their boats and look for other work.

According to Christie's English teacher, the island men have an almost mystical faith in the sea, a deity who gives up her bounty in the fullness of time but cannot be rushed. This attitude is interpreted by some as passivity or a stubborn refusal to recognise the present reality of fewer fish than ever before. Behind these attitudes lies the conviction that although the sea is now a killer, she will provide again for those patient enough to wait.

Young fishermen have not experienced the long-term ebb and flow of catch size, and tend to see today's catch as what it has always been, enough to get by on but not enough to get ahead to save for the future. Their relative optimism rarely heeds the warnings of fishermen who have seen much better times and foresee the prospects of worse. When a boy wants to fish like his father and grandfather, he is proudly deaf to advice not to buy a boat but work ashore instead.

Fewer graduating seniors, however, now choose fishing as a career than did so seven years ago. More of the young men are choosing different careers. Some have gone into military service, while others have chosen vocational education. A few such as Nathan plan to leave the island and take up mainstream jobs. "I plan to work as a computer engineer or as a business administrator. Currently I don't see much opportunity for myself on the island."

In 1981, twenty four percent of the senior class went on to either two- or four-year colleges. If we compare this figure with the twenty-eight percent who did so in 1984, forty-six percent in 1987, and forty-eight percent in 1991, we see an increasing number of youngsters actively seeking further education to enhance their prospects for careers other than fishing. (Graduating class size has varied from between thirty-one and fifty-nine students over the decade.) By comparison with students in other counties, however, island students are less likely to pursue further education away from home. Out of the nine male students enrolled in Jeff's General English class, six who are currently working in the Co-op programme now plan on full-time fishing next year. Two days a week, Co-op students go out fishing with experienced captains. Jeff tells me:

> "Co-op is the only thing that's changed for me. It works pretty good. I think the idea is to give kids a chance to go out and learn a job. If you didn't do it through school, you'd try it after school. It gives you a chance to know what you might want to do and prepare yourself."

These male students tend to be far more optimistic about the prospects of fishing than do the female students, who know what it means when the lobsters aren't trapping, when the weather is too bad to go out, and when the choice is between starving and welfare. Being raised in a home where money ebbs and flows affects young women somewhat differently than young men. Both recognise the economic uncertainty, but students like Andrea and Christie now see some very real alternative futures for women.

Until recently, work prospects for island women were to pack fish or work in a restaurant, store, or service business. Such traditional jobs for women often do not require a high school diploma. With more small businesses opening in the area, secretarial and business skills are now in higher demand. In addition, the new nursing home requires professionally trained nursing staff and administrators. Students in their junior or senior year can take a course to become a certified nursing aid. One result of a wider range of work for women in this region and a very active guidance programme is that far more young women consider a non-traditional future than was the case even five years ago. Fewer women used to consider any formal schooling beyond the diploma, whether it was in college or adult education. Naomi writes:

> I'm still in school, but I have always known I wanted a four-year college education and a life away from the time-warped island I've been forced to live on for seventeen years. . . . The majority of the residents haven't

changed their life style from their great-grandparents'. They seem to have no concept [of] or ignore the technology of life in the 1980s. Many residents don't even know what MTV is or that successful heart transplants exist!

The traditional plan for many island women after school is to raise a family. This has led to financial dependency in the past. Now an increasing number of women find jobs they can do during school hours or in the home, such as picking crab meat, making wreaths, and child care. Some women dig clams along with their men, or work on the boats.

Many young women now see options other than a pattern of home life and local work which until recently was accepted as normal for island women. Instead they can continue their education at a state college or in training programmes, from beauty school to veterinary medicine. To continue her education beyond high school means leaving the island, family, and friends. Such leave-takings and living away from the island are not easy, since they often bring with them new ways of thinking that contrast sharply with the attitudes and values of those at home. Many of the women who leave plan to return and adopt a family-oriented life style after completing further education. But others plan on an off-island career.

While many adults rightly fear the loss of their young people, students often tend not to see this as a problem because they believe that many will return after living away for a number of years. In Kim's words:

"So many people come back! I don't understand it. I don't see the loss of local people as a problem, because frankly, they usually come back."

Nathan disagrees:

"I can only see people returning to the island after they're retired. Otherwise their jobs will keep them away. If they couldn't handle the business world, then they might return rather quickly. The loss of local people is a problem, because it's a loss of culture. Unfortunately, I don't see any solution."

The changes in life style that alternative futures bring to these men and women are felt deeply when friendship and family relationships tie those who choose to stay and those who study and work "away." (See MacLeod's literary handling of this theme in "The Boat," 1988). Such situations are likely to raise conflicts around issues of loyalty and between the expectations of a traditional way of life and a woman's hope for a career beyond the home. For example, over the last three years, Ann has been going steady with Glen and wants to marry him. Encouraged by her teachers, she also wants to go to college, but Glen wants her here with him. If she goes to college, she stands to lose him. If she stays, she will forego continuing her education at least for the moment.

The relationship in which Andrea and Mike find themselves is less clear cut. They have known each other since grade school and have been close friends for the past three years. In ninth grade, Mike dropped out of school to go fishing. Andrea's view of his prospects and of her own goals dramatises the conflict that can occur between people with different degrees of exposure to the tradition of literacy and, more broadly, to formal education (Goody and Watt, 1968). Andrea has stayed with Mike through his struggles to establish himself. She respects deeply his strength and pride in following a difficult way of life. Her love for him, however, does not blind her to what she sees as the limits of his schooling:

> "He was working as a man at age fourteen. He is still age fourteen, 'cause he didn't have these other things. He didn't go to school. He's not really well-rounded. I mean he can't even spell my name."

I point out that Mike has had a very different kind of education, one that in certain respects is broader in scope than the education she is receiving. She replies:

> "I tried to get Mike to go back to school, right? So he went to night school and he took a medical class there, an ambulance class. He got some little card, and he's certified to do something, and he likes to do that because that wasn't a lot of bookwork and stuff. He took an English class, and he liked the teacher and everything, but he didn't like the readin, and he didn't like the writin. So I said, 'All right you can drop out of this one, but you're goin to take somethin else.' So we did. We took this U.S. history course. I don't know if it was my fault or what, but you know, I read it all to him, and I think maybe I pushed him too hard, but he didn't really listen to any of it. I thought that if I helped him it'd be better for him, if he had my support."

In this next conversation Andrea describes her efforts to encourage Mike to take enough adult education courses to qualify him for his high school diploma:

"It's like, 'Mike, why don't you get your diploma and maybe take a year or two at vocational school?' And it's like, 'No, I don't wanna do anything else. There's nothin wrong with fishin,' and I'll say, 'Mike look at your slips. Average it out.' Last year he made more than he made this year, and it's like, 'Mike!' You can tell it's slowly going down hill, and his uncle's one of the best fishermen. And it's like, 'Well, you know, we'll always be lobsterin, there'll always be lobsterin.' What would he do in ten years if he had a wife, and he had kids, and he had a house to pay for, and he had a boat to pay for, and he had a car to pay for, and he had a truck to pay for?"

David, who has been listening intently, answers without hesitation, "Social security, unemployment." But the pride of supporting self and family without the help of anyone else makes his answer unacceptable to many fishermen. Ann now joins the conversation with an example of one of her own friends:

"I know this one guy. He quit fishin and got a job workin as a carpenter, right? This winter, instead of a little carpentry work, they were gonna haul wood, right? I mean they bought his clothes; he gets four sets of clothes a year. They buy his shirts, pants with his name on it, and he gets his social security. All that's taken out of it, and so I mean he's got it great, and he quit to go scallopin. And he knows scallopin is gonna be bad just like it was last year."

I argue that the desire to go fishing is so powerful that it is part of fishermen's thinking and feeling. Andrea listens politely before laughing at the words of one who has not grown up in a fishing village and does not know what poverty means. "Well, it may be powerfully part of their thinkin and feelin, but they're gonna be feelin somethin else — like hunger — if they don't get their thumbs out."

For a moment Ann sees both sides of the situation: "It might not be logical, but they love it. This whole island is like that. If you tell 'em they're not gonna make anything this year, Jeff said he'd still go fishin." Ann is caught between frustration and sympathy for her friends who seldom consider alternative work. She shows her own values, however, when she remarks,

"My brother the other day, I was really proud of him. He was watchin a lineman out working on a farm, and he said, 'You know, I'd really like to see if I could go in Co-op and work with him or something for a week.'"

As we talk further about why fishing is such a compelling lifestyle, Ann begins to push harder on her own observations that her friends and family love to fish. She returns to the example of her friend who quit his secure job for the uncertain rewards of scallop fishing:

"It's not because he likes the water, I don't think. Fishin is what they've always done, and it's sort of secure. They're just afraid to try other things 'cause they're afraid that they won't be able to do it."

Ann's comments support teachers' observations that some students are afraid to learn new ways of doing things or to think about the possibility of needing to work and live in another place. If fear of failing is part of what makes students resist change, then another aspect is fear of losing what is valued. Kim explains, "Often fear of the unknown keeps fishermen going."

From talking with Mike about what school meant to him and why he left school, I understand his viewpoint. Now as we talk about the future of students who plan to attend college, Andrea gives her account of how Mike quit:

"He started skipping school, and he started just not showing up for school. Nobody pushed him to go, nobody said, 'You have to go.' It's like, 'Well, so what, kid's missed a couple of days of school.' Pretty soon he's missed a month, and then he started not comin home. Well, all right, so he's moved out, and then pretty soon he was working on a boat. And he just quit school when he was in seventh grade, y' know, and they put him through the eighth grade 'cause he was such a troublemaker. They said he passed through, but he didn't go at all. His parents didn't push him.

My father has told us that as long as we live at home, we will go to school. I believe that way, too. My kids will go to school as long as they live at my house. It's very important that a kid should have an education. My kids will at least have an education, at least as far as I can make them go. I wouldn't want someone to end up like Mike. What if fishin does go? He knows nothin else. He doesn't know anythin."

But sooner or later students no longer see themselves learning anything new in school. For some, this time is reached as early as sixth

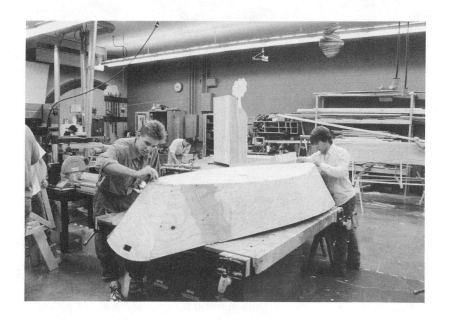

Dory building in school.

and seventh grade; Mike and Alton dropped out in grade nine. Other students don't express this feeling until their last years in school, as with Jeff:

"Like now I ain't learnin nothin in school. You don't really learn anything in your twelfth year. It's just a rerun of grade eleven. It's just a 'goodbye and what are you gonna do, and what am I gonna do?'"

David believes his education was completed in his junior year, and he would have left if his parents had let him. He tells me that he hates schooling and does not see its value.

But Andrea has the last word. "I hate it too, but I realize the need for it." In fact, college-bound students are more likely to be skeptical about the future of the island's fishing industry than students like Jeff, Mike, and Alton who do not want to pursue any other work.

Nathan, however, argues for the pragmatic need of a diploma:

As time goes on, I think fewer and fewer students will drop out. The opportunities for good jobs that don't require diplomas are getting scarce. The trend over the last few years has been for fewer students to drop out.

Yet although fewer students now quit school before graduating than did so a decade ago, many continue to drop out for the reasons that Steve writes here, although he too recognises the need for more education:

> Students become disenchanted with school, failing grades, they can't play sports or those the school offers, they must support a family and often to give birth. Maybe more kids will finish school and go on to a form of higher education, and branch out. Hopefully they will bring something home and give a little to the school and the people that gave them their chance, just give a little back and say thanks.

The words of Andrea and David present a picture of some lives in school that would appear more bleak than I believe is the case. My optimism is based on the present effort of the teaching staff to develop alternative programmes for those students who are not college-bound at this stage in their lives. These programmes both address the immediate needs and concerns of students and attempt to equip them to succeed in different kinds of future careers.

Recently the school has received two grants to develop innovative teaching programmes. The first will fund a course in marine education designed to prepare students to work in a broad range of activities, from in-shore fisheries to sea-related occupations such as boat building and repair, the Coast Guard, and management of marine resources. The second grant will be used to develop a programme to provide a range of support services for young mothers who plan on completing their high school education. This programme should reduce the number of students who in the past have left school to take care of their children. Now these students will be able to continue in school and receive instruction in a wide range of skills, including child care, nutrition, problem solving, and planning their futures. Such programmes attempt to communicate the school's concern that education address areas that include what is regarded as basic both by students and teachers.

Adult education also provides a wide range of courses for young adults who want to continue their education. For some, this means gaining a high school diploma by resuming the schooling that they left in ninth grade. For others it means learning new skills that their present work requires. Last year saw the introduction of a course in computers, a tool that several small businesses are beginning to use. Other classes include instruction in emergency medical care, preparation for college, and a course in adult literacy. The high number of people who choose to continue their education in a school setting suggests that while school appears to alienate a significant number of students during their high school years, many will return to learn much of value.

In several of the English and social studies classes, students have begun to write about the people and events in island history that interest them. This approach has taken students out of their classrooms and into the community, where they have interviewed local residents and published stories and descriptions about familiar places. The information collected has then been revised and published for other students and parents to read. This approach enables students to make connections between the uses and kinds of language they learn at home and those taught and valued in school.

The story of these students' lives in school began for me when Mike pulled out of his pocket a tattered scrap of paper that entitled him to fish for lobster at age thirteen. This license represented—and allowed access to—the world that Mike valued. Shortly before I left the island in 1986, one of Mike's classmates, Tom, who had also quit school in grade nine stopped by to say "Hello." Tom had been rebuilding cars and trucks in a local garage and liked the work very much. After we had caught up on each other's lives over the past five years, Tom proudly pulled out of his wallet a high school diploma that he had gained through a correspondence course. I asked him why he had wanted to get a diploma after he left school. First telling me that the course had been "something to do," he then went on to explain that although most students resist schooling and often quit, many island people value a diploma because "it shows that they went through school. They stuck it out." Viewed in this light, school becomes another setting in which people can meet the community's expectation to complete what has been started.

Christie and Tom both value their diplomas, but for very different reasons. As much as Christie and Kim resist schooling now, it holds out the possibility of a future that is appealing. They defer their immediate needs because their time perspective extends beyond the present moment into a future very different from the one their parents faced at their graduation. In contrast, Mike has found in the present moment of fishing a potential for fulfillment that sustains him but frustrates Andrea to the point where she can only turn away. Each student has seen a very different outcome from the investment of time in school.

Chapter Six

TIMESCAPES FOR LITERACY

On the basis of students' responses to time in school in this one small community, I cannot generalise about the behaviour of students in other schools. Whether teaching in small country schools or in large urban communities, however, teachers can watch how the concepts of time embedded in school and classroom life influence students' responses to education and specifically to becoming literate. Such observations can form the basis for teachers' design of their own timescapes, a term that suggests a shape both spatial and temporal, a form of time whose rhythms and extensions influence the quality of classroom life. Viewed from the present moment, the contours of a timescape will appear static, if not unchangeable. Viewed over time, however—from what Young, Becker, and Pike (1970) describe as a "wave perspective"—timescapes will be seen to change as we attune them to each project. In the first part of this chapter, I will review the different timescapes found in one small rural community and suggest how their differences influenced the students' education. In the second part, I will broaden the discussion to look at how professional writers think about time, one way to see how teachers might design appropriate timescapes for literacy in school.

In describing life in this community, I have noted that people here conceive of time in terms of the events and activities to which they assign significance. We have seen how people's cultural values are expressed by and realised within the various forms of time. Represented in many different ways, time is the movements of the tides, the clock on the wall, students' progression through school, a view of the future, and most broadly, a person's relationship to the world. As time is measured against different referents, so too it is valued according to the particular needs of each activity. Making a living, establishing an identity, and organising the work of students in school each demands different temporal values and carries different imperatives for action.

To characterise and compare the external dimensions of the timescapes below, I have described the temporal contours of each of them using the framework and terms of reference of Eviatar Zerubavel:

> Let me delineate the major dimensions of the temporal profile of any situation or event. One fundamental parameter of situations and events is their sequential structure, which tells us in what order they take place. A second major parameter, their duration, tells us how long they last. A third parameter, their temporal location, tells us when they take place, whereas a fourth parameter, their rate of recurrence, tells us how often they do. (1981, p. 1)

Zerubavel uses these four temporal regularities to describe the patterns of time use in social life, the profiles of different kinds of events and situations. I will use these parameters to describe what might be called the external or public dimensions of each timescape. The meanings that individuals assign to time, however, depend on their subjective experience. We have seen in previous chapters that the internal contours of temporal experience emerge in conversation and in action. In everyday language, we often speak of time as though it had an existence as objective as the clock on the wall. It is easy to forget that time does not exist independently of the language that we use to talk about it. (Berger and Luckman, 1967, pp. 34–36)

Timescapes in a Maine Fishing Community

Activity Time

Offshore fishing is the only example of a form of time that exists almost independently from the other timescapes to be described. Fishermen offshore give scant attention in their work to the hour, to whether it is day or night, or to the day of the week. Hauling pots or setting nets is the framework around which all other activities revolve. Although short breaks are taken for meals and rest, these are scheduled more on an as-needed basis than by the clock. Only after the boat's hold is full or severe weather forces an early return to shore will the captain consider the day of the week for the purpose of selling the catch and refueling. Otherwise, the activity proceeds with minimal reference either to clock or calendar.

Natural Time

The term "natural" is used here to show that there is a cyclical or rhythmic constraint in nature that people recognise as a basis for measuring their time. People in this community recognise three kinds of natural time: daylight, tidal, and seasonal. Although each form may influence the temporal shape of a given activity, for each of the activities described, one or another of the kinds of natural time will exert primary influence.

Since lobstering is legally allowed only between sunrise and sunset, inshore lobster fishermen restrict their work to the daylight hours. As we have seen in Chapter Two, the duration of each workday will vary from one boat to the next according to such factors as: the distance from shore to the fishing ground, the number of traps hauled each day, their distance apart and depth set, and the pace at which each fishermen hauls, picks, and resets his traps.

The second kind of natural time is controlled by the tides. The time of day for clam digging is determined by the time of low water, and only to a lesser degree by available light. (In the past, clammers have worked at night using lanterns when the digging was good.) The duration of digging varies with the range of the tide, influenced primarily by the phases of the moon. On some days a clammer will dig for only a couple of hours, while with other tides close to six hours might be possible. Other clammers will dig to make enough money to meet that day's needs and then quit until the next tide.

The third kind of natural time is seasonal time, for example, the times to harvest the garden, rake blueberries, cut firewood, and collect greens for Christmas wreaths. This particular approximate sequence of seasonal activities is determined by the time when each crop is ready, which varies from one year to the next. Harvesting, collecting greens, or cutting wood continue on a daily basis until the work is done. Inshore lobstermen fish most actively between early spring and late fall. The goal of seasonal work is to make and save as much money as possible in a relatively short period. Since the work must be done immediately or be lost for that season, other work is postponed until this work, which has a short-term urgency to it, is completed for that day.

In each of the three kinds of natural time, we observe a high degree of variation in terms of the temporal location, duration, and frequency of the activities concerned. Although participants can make approximate predictions, these vary from day to day. I have heard people argue that they choose to organise their work according to natural rhythms because this enables them to achieve harmony between the work and the world in which it is done. While this harmony certainly does occur, the need to adapt one's work schedule to the natural time order in fact requires it, a demand further reinforced by economic imperatives.

Yet people clearly value working in this way, whether chosen or determined, because of the change of activities and their variety over a cycle of time. With obvious pride, people will say, "My work is never the same." To work in this way is to accept that natural elements will shape when and how the work is done. For many fishermen, natural agents, sometimes regarded animistically, are preferred to the human ones who control workers in a business or on the shop floor.

Clock Time

In discussing clock time, I will describe first its occurrence in work in the community before examining how it controls school life. Work in small businesses and shift work at the fish packing plant are both organised around an eight-hour workday. The factory, however, schedules shifts in relation to the amount of fish brought in by the skippers of the sardine carriers. When the supply and demand for sardines is high enough to work around the clock, the plant runs three shifts beginning at 7 a.m., 3 p.m., and 11 p.m., and still needs more packers. At other times it runs only one shift with a skeleton crew.

Although the work always means packing fish that come down the conveyor belt, the packers find challenge in variations, for example, whether they are packing tail sections or steaks, and the number of sections to be packed into each can. The sequence of operations changes such that the packers experience variety in the work. The rate of packing is controlled by the piece-rate set by the plant manager and by how fast the packer can work.

In contrast to the piece-work cannery packers, day-workers find employment in community stores, garages, boatyards, banks, or schools, and work at an agreed hourly rate. The duration of the day and the starting and finishing time do not vary except when overtime is available. This kind of work offers a secure income that rarely is found in the community. Yet despite what might appear to be attractive work because of its economic predictability, many islanders prefer to make a less certain living in work controlled by natural time.

School Time

As the school year is controlled by the calendar, so the school day is controlled by the clock. School begins at 8 a.m. and finishes at 2:20 p.m. The arrival and departure of the schoolbuses mark the limits of a day that will vary only in bad weather. In the elementary schools, the only school-wide time markers are for morning recess, lunch, and afternoon recess. Teachers have a high degree of flexibility within the day to determine the location, sequence, and duration of class activities. The extent to which teachers take advantage of this freedom varies widely among classes and grade levels.

Some teachers in the elementary school believe that students need to become accustomed to a sequence of activities that is consistently scheduled such that the timescape of activities remains relatively uniform. In contrast, others believe that students are served better if the signal for a change of activities is the progress and motivation of students rather than the measure of the clock. Factors such as the teacher's own need for planning and prediction in contrast to the need for spontaneity will also determine the teacher's degree of temporal rigidity. For students in the upper elementary school, scheduling tends to be less flexible than in the lower school, as teachers prepare students for the fixed periods of the junior high school.

In the previous chapter, we heard students say that time in elementary school was more conducive to learning than the multiple-period day first encountered in junior high school. We have also heard students, boys in particular, state their need to physically move around at frequent intervals. The possibility for a student to find his or her own personal rhythm in talking, reading, and writing is facilitated by the teacher who, valuing individualised learning, takes advantage of flexible instruction time. Transition between activities would appear easier to create without bells and class changes.

From grades seven through twelve, all learning and social activities are organised within a rigid clock schedule. The day is divided into seven forty-two-minute periods. The exact measurement of time periods is as precisely implemented as in shift work where production is the focus. One major consequence of this pattern of temporal organisation is that information and activities are packaged less in terms of their complexity and the students' time needs than in terms of the available time itself. Students become accustomed to the rhetoric of a class period, so that the scope of their own thinking is influenced by the limits of school time rather than by the possibilities of the material or the activity. We see here one way in which the time values of the "corporate state" have shaped the temporality of school life (Spring, 1972).

The schedule itself functions as a structure within which teachers measure the extent to which the curricular goals for each subject are being met. In meeting these objectives, many teachers plan to cover a certain amount of work in each period, week, quarter, and year. At the end of each grading period, teachers frequently talk of "being behind" in terms of the material that they had hoped to teach. The relationship between time and productivity becomes problematic when teachers attempt to assess the value of those activities that are not product-oriented. For example, in the lower elementary school more value is placed on social talk and social time than in the upper elementary school; kindergarten through second-grade students enjoy a fair amount of time not only to write but to talk with others about their writing. Their teachers see great value in using time in this way to establish a community of writers, a goal that requires different kinds of time use.

The relationship between economic reward and the return for time in school becomes an uneasy one for many students in their last years in school. As we saw in Chapter Five, the time comes when students ask what is the best possible use of time at this stage in their life. The question assumes a greater urgency when students are required to work alone and with little freedom to socialise with fellow students during classes. For some students, playing on a basketball team, working in the shop, or going to the art class are major incentives to attend school. When the personal reward for being in school is indeterminate, students are likely to leave, if their parents consent.

Within the schools' workday, time to talk is seldom encouraged, offered as a reward, and if taken without permission likely to result in punishment. Students often resent waiting until recess, lunch, or the end of the day to talk with friends. The times that students can call their own are either transitions between classes or times when, by law, breaks must be given. This observation holds equally true for many other schools, but deserves qualifying. In the elementary school, especially in the lower grades, the need for social time within the context of work time is recognised and is partially met by activities such as writing that involve collaboration, the sharing of written work, and discussion. By the time students reach the upper elementary and junior and senior high school, private time for social talk or to think one's own thoughts is at a very high premium.

Social Time

For those whose work is controlled by natural time, socialising is set not by the clock but by factors as varied as the weather, the season, and the personal need to set work aside to be with friends and family. Fishermen gather at the dock to talk in the mornings and at the end of the day. Women meet in restaurants and in each other's homes before their day begins. When the weather is bad or in the wintertime, fishermen will visit at the Co-op even though they cannot go fishing that day. Similarly, women come together to make wreaths, quilt, or pick crab meat, activities that while making money also create social time within work time. Since the beginning and end of the workday vary in those jobs controlled by natural time, social timescapes follow the serpentine contours of the work itself.

Social time that occurs outside of work is planned with much latitude. Scheduling as open as "I'll see you before noon," "sometime tomorrow," or "catch up with you soon" is of course not particular to this community, but it does reflect many people's need to plan flexibly and be responsive to needs that people cannot predict beforehand. Public gatherings and meal-time invitations are likely to be set at clock time initially, but then adjusted when the day arrives, if other events take priority. Regular time for talk is highly valued, but when and for how long is hard to predict.

Television Time

Although I have not studied the form of time set by television viewing, it is becoming increasingly significant in the lives of students and adults as they watch more hours of television each day. The presence of television-related items in students' talk is evident as early as kindergarten. As we have seen, students know the times of their favourite shows before they can read the clock, and much of their social time at home is actually spent viewing television with friends and family. Older students, like Jeff, often attempt to do homework within the time frames of the news or before prime viewing.

Events on television are organised within time frames that are rigidly controlled by the clock. Viewers are not surprised to see people cut off in mid-sentence because it is time for a commercial. As is the case with school time, the available time determines both the form and content of information packaged in a continuous flow of discrete units. As viewers, they do not expect one unit to relate to the next. A series of shows follow each other in linear sequence without any pretence at coherence. Any kind of thematic transition between one show and the next is likely to be accidental. Time is fragmented into units of short duration; the content may change several times within the hour. The transitory handling of time on television is accentuated further by the short-lived nature of much of the material presented. It is rare to find a show like "Mr. Rogers" that parents can watch with their children and recall having watched also with their own parents. Students' experience of time and the values that they learn to associate with it are influenced by this technologically structured form of time that many students now encounter several hours each day. Television time is becoming as influential on some of these students' lives as is natural time on others.

Sacred Time

The degree and kinds of influence that sacred time exerts varies from one family to the next within the smaller sub-communities situated around the island. The most apparent public acknowledgment of sacred time is to observe the Sabbath as a day of rest. Few inshore fishermen go out to haul their traps on a Sunday. Although the seven-day workweek is unexceptional in other places, here a day of rest that is calendrically rather than naturally determined is significant. Most fishermen need to haul every day to make their living. To stay at home voluntarily when they could be out on the water suggests the continuing importance of the Sabbath to many islanders. Economic factors, however, may cause an encroachment of what Zerubavel (1981, pp. 101–138) calls "profane time" on sacred time, if the fishing becomes uncertain to the point where fishermen have to decide whether to observe the Sabbath or to fish on Sundays.

Observing the Sabbath and more broadly the weekend gives a social rhythm to life on the island that contrasts with the natural rhythms that control so many daily activities. As the Sabbath punctuates the week, sacred time also establishes religious holidays throughout the year to prepare for and celebrate in school and community. Advent is a time when island people give food and clothing to those in need, a time when work slows down and people recognise both the fullness and limits of human resources. Christmas is celebrated in both secular and religious terms as the time of year when islanders come closest together to prepare body and spirit for the new year.

Existential Time [1]

Because what I refer to as existential or personal time can last for moments or hours, can occur at any stage of the activities described above, and can be a frequent or an almost non-existent experience of time and being, it is the hardest to characterise by formal description. On a daily basis, this time of intense concentration occurs for broad stretches for Mike and Dave as they haul, pick, and set traps, and for Janet and Laurie as their swiftly moving hands cut and pack fish. Slim told me that he could think with greater awareness and focus as he dug for clams than in his years as a university professor. On occasion I observed those times when island students were intensely absorbed in their writing and reading to the point where until the teacher or bell stopped them they were unaware of other activities around them. Each of these examples suggests that an existential experience of time is available under the right conditions.

Chapter Two suggested that personal time was essential for people to establish the kind of identity valued in this community. While "personal time" does emphasise privacy in contrast to the more public or shared forms of time, the term might suggest that the other forms of time can be experienced without mediation by language and culture. Furthermore, "personal time" often connotes recreational or relaxing time. In contrast to these current meanings, I use personal or existential time in this context to suggest a time of extreme concentration and engagement in the activity at hand, whether in school or at home. This is a time when the individual is working out how to become a particular person within the bounds of natural, economic, and social constraints. The fisherman needs to make money but must plan to work in relation to the natural cycles. Students need to define themselves within a school that often requires them to follow practices and values sometimes different and distant from their own. Existential time describes the experience of reaching toward the full potentials of being.

To understand the emergence of existential time in school, we need to observe briefly how students encounter school first as a young child and then through a series of re-entries throughout their school lives. Students' initial entry into the school world is abrupt and for the most part unanticipated in the forms of life at home. Students are introduced into a world made by others on their behalf. While many students like it and adapt quickly to its demands, others are thrown by the differences between time at home and in school. Young students' first project is to discover how they can be at home in school. This process becomes increasingly more difficult for older students as they discover the rigidity of temporal boundaries around every meaningful activity.

Although the teachers do not intend for their students to forfeit the traditions of their home, school often anticipates a series of outcomes and possibilities different from those that many of the students see themselves as moving toward. The school regards itself as an agent of change, a means by which students can escape the determinism of a traditional way of life with an uncertain future. Given a tension that to a degree is inevitable and even productive, if schools are to equip students to move toward a range of possible futures, they will need to ask how they can enable students to establish their identities within a setting that endorses some different notions of time and being.

For students to experience their time in school as authentic and meaningful, they need to see that what is important in their daily lives can be part of the ethos and programme of the school. Students need to feel that their teachers understand the future work that many students have chosen, but that teachers can offer also the means by which students can exceed a traditional life style, if they so choose. When students enter an institution that does not recognise the contours of their own lives and values, their time in this setting becomes inauthentic and alienating.

Island Time

In the preceding pages, I have discussed eight timescapes that while having aspects in common show contrastive features. To present each timescape separately might suggest that people in this community experience time in discrete ways. When I first came to this community, I heard people speak often jokingly but affectionately about "island time." The phrase occurred most frequently in situations where someone from off-island did not understand the temporal contours of a procedure or of an event. For example, a business would close during the day, guests would arrive hours before or after the arranged time, and events would come about in their own good time.

What first appeared to be a single form of time, on closer scrutiny proved to be a multi-layered mosaic of the time forms already described. In this composite form of time, the balance of the other forms varies among the individuals who organise their lives by island time. Each of the forms influences to a greater or lesser degree the composition of this timescape. For example, for those who work around the water or in the woods, island time is likely to be composed largely of frames of natural time, while the island time of those who work in small businesses will be shaped more by the clock. In 1986, the majority of people were in the former category, but the balance was shifting and within ten years, island time could show only traces of natural time within its larger contours.

Island Time and School Time

Between the timescapes of school time and island time sharp contrasts emerge between the location, duration, and sequence of events.

Consciously or not, students register and respond to the differences and contrasts that emerge as follows: Schools start and end at the same time of day without regard to the season. Work organised by island time, on the other hand, varies each day because of people's need to respond, for example, to hours of daylight, demands of running a home, and motivation to earn money.

Time allocated for each school activity varies in the elementary schools by up to twenty minutes from one day to the next, but the length of class periods in grades seven through twelve is constant. The duration of work done within the frames of island time, however, can vary by up to several hours from winter to summer.

The daily sequence of subjects from kindergarten through twelfth grade shows little evidence of logical connections between the sort of thinking required by each subject. The rotational schedule of the high school only emphasises that subjects are taught without regard for the possibility of an integrated curriculum. In the community the sequence of activities within each day and season are related to the project of making a livelihood in a setting that demands close attention to its natural rhythms.

Attendance in school is required for each day of the school-year but then stops abruptly in the summer. This situation leads students to question the long-term importance of an activity that can stop for one whole quarter of the year. Yet ten days of unexcused absence in the other three quarters will result in loss of credit for course work, with probable suspension. In contrast, life-sustaining activities in the community are continuous, even though they follow a seasonal round. Work rhythms seldom recognise the individual's need for a holiday.

In these comparisons, disjunctions emerge between how the timescapes of school time and island time are realised. Students respond to these differences in several ways. Many students accept and passively adapt to the constraints of school time. Others complain periodically and then resign themselves because they see the shape and values of school time as beyond their meaningful control. Students like Mark, Jeff, and Andrea who reacted actively against school time were punished in various ways. Mike and Alton chose to forfeit their schooling before graduation.

From teaching in these schools, I would argue that pathologies are associated closely with temporal disjunctions. Those of my own students who came late, wanted to leave early, or skipped class, who refused to complete writing on time and tried to negotiate deadlines, who refused to write or read when asked, who talked during writing time and remained silent during discussion, all attempted in their own ways to establish some control over their time. To create and find identity in school often causes conflicts around such issues, as students challenge the time limits of school.

In this discussion of temporal values, one key issue is how students perceive the ways in which values are enforced. In school, teachers support their time decisions by appealing to the objective measures of calendar and clock. The teacher has the authority to discipline students by referring to a system of political time values over which students have neither control nor input. In the community, on the other hand, sanctions are applied by natural agencies, which appear more real because they often have economic consequences; when activities are restricted in that realm, the individual does not believe that he or she has been placed within a context of power relations or punished by the dictates of a machine. From the students' perspective, the criteria against which teachers make decisions often appear arbitrary and without practical basis or justification in their lifeworld. Sanctions also appear to be directed at them personally rather than as consequence of the students' own actions against school regulations.

In this discussion, I have emphasised values to underscore the argument that issues of time are intelligible only within a context of values. If local administrators and teachers agreed that the time order of school deserved rethinking, then changes would need to go beyond structurally reorganising the timescapes of school to be more like that of the island, if indeed this was judged to be appropriate or even possible. Solutions to the problems of sociotemporal mismatches between home and school will need to consider the relationships between the values inherent to the timescapes of school and island life. Successful long-term solutions are unlikely to come, for example, by altering the sequence or duration of classes or changing the length of school day and year. This is not to dismiss the need, however, for discussion of these factors, since they are one aspect of the influence of time on students' responses to schooling.

In the above section, I have considered how island time and school time relate and the consequences of that relationship for learning. I will return now to the more difficult question of whether we can find evidence of students' prior experiences of time and language at home in their narrative writing in school.

Narrative Time and Prior Texts

The writing of island students shows evidence of a strong oral base that reflects the modes of discourse particular to their community. Because language and time both serve to orient students and to allow them to make meaning in their lives, we need to recognise the ways in which these referential systems relate to each other and to anticipate how the relationships will be visible in student writing. In the writing of island students, time is apparent often in forms and constructions that often appear as deviant to their teachers. Since writing is an activity in which students attempt to create their identities, teachers need to watch carefully for the play of temporal aspects within students' writing.

The linguistic resources that students bring to school are shaped by both time and language and show traces of different forms of time, of talk, and of "language games" that students have learned. In making stories, students draw on how they have heard other people talk about events and situations and on their understanding of how these are organised in time. Their memory of how the events have been located in time and expressed in talk serve as prior texts for written recountings and reworkings; old language is made new when writers make narrative.

The form of Cortinee's "Storm" narrative in Chapter Four reflects the oral rehearsals through which her story has passed. Although as readers we have access only to her written version, in reading it we can ask what prior texts have contributed to its formation. For Cortinee, her prior texts are shaped in talk and situated in the context of island time. Once we accept that these contexts exert a major influence on student writing, we begin to watch for the ways in which they surface. We have seen that the impress of an oral form on writing is often no more than a turn of phrase, a fugitive trace whose fleeting presence from oral language catches the eye as a grammatical error. These traces are often regarded as deviations from what teachers identify as the acceptable forms of writing. Cortinee's story disrupted and displaced the narrative time sequence anticipated by her teacher. We saw a similar example of this phenomenon in Lindsay's "Kitten" story. The temporal configuration of acceptable writing is defined within individual classrooms and embraces aspects of language, from features of form such as tense markers to the organisational patterns of large units of discourse.

Emphasis on "correctness" is conspicuously more evident in the senior high school than in the elementary school. In the case of story writing, students are expected, for example, to establish and to maintain a consistent temporal viewpoint, to maintain consistency of tense and aspect throughout a narrative, and to proceed in a temporally linear sequence from one event to the next. Recall Anita's piece in which she chose to project herself into a future, as yet unrealised, although the writing prompt asked her to write from the perspective of the present. Although teachers' expectations are not always stated explicitly, they are communicated, for example, in "corrections" that change verb forms, punctuation that breaks run-on sentences into separate ones, and the kind of advice that urges students to structure their writing with a beginning, a middle, and an end.

A reader may well ask why this concern for prior texts whose impress on writing is no more pronounced than a trace, a small irregularity that can easily be "corrected" in passing. I have argued that the deviant form, whether in grammar or in the organisation of stretches of discourse, is tied closely to the identity of the writer. When we edit children's language to meet teacherly expectations, students see themselves losing part of their own distinctive means of expression. As teachers we should want to recognise the logic,[2] the origins, and the significance of these traces as we help students use their ability to manage talk as a basis for their writing. By drawing students' attention to how features of their spoken language and markers of their sense of time appear in their writing, we can explain to students why the presence of "deviant" forms can create difficulties for readers from other communities, for readers who expect to see a different temporal logic and a different projection or expression of a writer's voice.

Island Literacy for the Future

My interpretation of resistance to writing in school in the context of the community's time values might suggest a direct causal connection rather than an influence of association. Students watch how adults at home organise their activities, and expect to find some continuation of that approach in schoolwork. Instead, students discover other ways of learning that often perplex and frustrate them. This discovery is potentially educational, if we talk with them about the differences between home and school learning and about the logic for each. To interpret differences in temporal logic as markers of different cultural values does not implicitly endorse resistance to writing. Students like Fay, Mark, Christie and Jeff will need a different kind of literacy than their parents' and grandparents'.

This generation of high school graduates are looking at a broadening range of career options that include both traditional island work and jobs, for example, in the computer industry, the military, and social services. Some of these non-traditional jobs will take young people away from the island, while others will become available in the area with the influx and growth of new businesses in coastal Maine. Consequently, the young, both women and men, are now in a position to choose whether they will follow a traditional career or pursue non-traditional work at home or in another community. Many students continue to choose the traditional paths. But an increasing number are attracted toward not only careers requiring a high school diploma but also those calling for computer literacy.

For young people who choose to remain on the island, literacy will serve an increasingly important role in conferring political power on those who possess it. The people who hold positions of authority, decide how the towns are managed and the schools governed, are accomplished speakers, readers, and writers. An increasing proportion of these people on the island are now from the mainland and other states. If the next generation of island students is to influence the changes that will occur on this island, then they must be able to participate fully in the political, economic, and social decisions that will influence their lives. Such participation requires a broad education and full literacy.

These arguments for promoting literacy in the island schools are instrumental and survival-oriented. But to suggest that these are the only or most important reasons for why members of this island community or indeed of any community need literacy does justice neither to the power of literacy to form and transform one's self-image nor to the pleasure that reading and writing can bring. Several of the island women with whom I spoke described reading fiction extensively, while men reported reading more often to find answers to technical problems. Recent publications of student writing in the genre of *Foxfire* and *Salt* indicate that students are beginning to value writing as a way to record the distinctiveness of island life, of what deserves remembering and celebrating; in turn, those people who are written about value the chance to share what they know.

From Island to Mainland

I have observed thus far that island students are caught in a tension between values located at different positions on the spectrum of time: values conventionally ordered to serve an institution and values derived from the natural world. Because many teachers do not teach in communities where time values are predicated on the activity patterns of rural life, this example might appear to describe an isolated situation, as remote as the island itself, and unrelated to other classrooms. On the other hand, this example will suggest strongly that students in other communities and classrooms may also experience time in ways unfamiliar to teachers.

In the introduction, I have noted that both the quality of teaching and of students' learning are deeply influenced by how we shape time. Given then, that time defines our relationship with the world, whether teaching in a Maine fishing community or in the inner city, this cultural framework of human experience will always be a factor to consider. How the effects of this dimension play out in particular classrooms, however, cannot be predicted. Because of the context-specific nature of ethnographic enquiry, my own rhetorical move from describing an island community to considering mainstream literacies is made not across a bridge of generalisations but by an appeal, an invitation to English teachers to examine the time values evident in their own communities and classrooms and then to assess how these values influence the teaching of writing and, more broadly, the promotion of literacy.

The project of examining the time values that the educational system has inherited from radically different contexts has been initiated in several critiques of the transmission of sociotemporal values. In *Discipline and Punish*, Michel Foucault (1979, pp. 200–203) traces the original form of the contemporary timetable to Jeremy Bentham's concept of panopticism. The panopticon, a centralised observation tower, allowed prison staff to monitor continually the movements of prison inmates and to ensure that they used all time productively. His philosophy offered a broad method of social control to monitor people's movements in both time and space.

> Its three great methods—establish rhythms, impose particular occupations, regulate the cycles of repetition—were soon to be found in schools, workshops, and hospitals (Foucault, 1979, p. 149).

We ask then, what time values are implicit within the timetables that control life in most public schools?

Although the historic connection is a distant one, several features of Bentham's model are evident in the American school system. The timetable makes it possible to supervise people's activities, to normalise their behaviour, and to assess individual performance against educational standards ordered in units of instruction. A timetable aims to ensure that the maximum amount of work is extracted from the available time. As a principle of control, panopticism intends for the individual to internalise the temporal values of the controlling authority. In school this means that, without prompting, the student will respond to the bell, move swiftly to the next class, and again produce the requisite amount of work. To internalise such values would lead students to conform to the authority of the school to the extent that at home they would block out hours in which to do homework. The values of school time are thus insinuated into every aspect of students' lives.

Panoptic time further controls people by rewarding them with a day of rest or punishing them with "overtime." Time as punishment continues to be a mainstay of many school systems. Students are kept in during recess or placed on detention to "pay back" the lost time. Foucault describes this disciplinary use of time as "linear" or "evolutive" (1979, p. 160). This experience of time contrasts sharply with the community's cyclical timescapes predicated on a high degree of responsibility by the individual to organise his or her time to accommodate activities that often cannot be scheduled in advance.

The strictly regimented time order of monastic life has exerted a long-standing influence on the management of time for secular work. As noted by Lewis Mumford,

The order and regularity that was introduced into the monk's day—with every office performed in due succession at stated intervals, the seven "canonical hours"—was timed and paced by the hourglass, the sundial, and eventually, the clock. From the monastery, this time-keeping habit spread back to the marketplace . . . so that from the fourteenth century on a whole town would time its activities to the ringing of the tower clock's bells. (1952, p. 265)

Zerubavel (1981, pp. 31–69) argues that the principles apparent in the monastic table of hours continue to influence the time values of the school day. The bells of Saint Benedict coordinated the medieval activities of work, study, and prayer to ensure that all time was devoted to the service of God. In the eighteenth century, teachers introduced bells into schools to ring the change of activities and to ensure that students moved in one body, quickly and orderly, between their classes.

In *Time Wars: The Primary Conflict in Human History*, Jeremy Rifkin (1987, p. 59) argues that the ideologies of the business community reinforce the ethic of "time is money." This identification reduces time to quantified units of production, a value that our educational system has substantially incorporated into its own practices and ways of accounting for time spent on school tasks and productive learning. Schools are only beginning to recognise that the quality of learning is shaped not only by the amounts of time that we allocate for learning but also by how we situate activities in time. As we reconceptualise time for writing, we need to think not only about time's external dimensions, such as the duration and frequency of writing sessions, but also about the internal rhythms of composing. We need to recognise the problems that confront the English teacher who needs to provide time of a quality that will help students to hear the muse in their own writing and to listen for it in the writing of others.

If we cannot reasonably expect the time values derived from the business community and from settings that feature uniform and normalised codes of behaviour to adequately serve school programmes, then where might we look for time values appropriate to educational objectives? Although we can assume neither that schools can provide nor that students would necessarily benefit by following the practices of professional writers, these practitioners can offer insights and reference points for writing in schools. In *Shoptalk*, Donald Murray (1990) compiled a collection of authors' statements about how they write. By selecting quotations from Horace to Hemingway and Borges to Blume, Murray's work provides a broad historical perspective on writing practices. From this compilation and other sources,[3] the following examples indicate that the four kinds of regularity referred to by Zerubavel are evident in the time rituals of professional writers: the temporal location, duration, frequency, and sequence of their writing.

Time of Writing

Goethe

Use the day before the day. Early morning hours have gold in their mouth. (Murray, p. 53)

Bernard Malamud

You write by sitting down and writing. There's no particular time or place—you suit yourself, your nature. . . . The trick is to make time—not steal it—and produce the fiction. (Murray, p. 58)

Alberto Moravia

When I began my first novel, I decided to follow a precise schedule. In the morning I would "create"; in the afternoon I would "live." Since then I have always worked this way: At twelve I stop writing until the next morning at seven. . . . Morning is the best time; the mind after sleeping is like a white page: blank and clean. (Murray, p. 59)

Duration of Writing

Robert Grudin

A writer sits down to work. It is nine in the morning, and the next four hours are free . . . by his express decision and unequivocal need. He looks down those four hours as down a clear view of unencumbered space; more broadly the regular work periods of the future open up like a long bright hallway of work in freedom. (Grudin, 1982, p. 91)

Walker Percy

Everybody's different, everybody's habits are different. I have to sit down at 9 o'clock in the morning and write for three hours or at least look at the paper for three hours. Some days I don't do *anything*. But unless you do that—punch the time clock—you won't *ever* do anything. (Murray, p. 60)

Ernest Hemingway

My working habits are simple: long periods of thinking, short periods of writing. (Murray, p. 54)

Garson Kanin

A good plumber or a good doctor works a full eight-hour day, and I don't see why a writer is any different. I work ten four-hour sessions a week: six full mornings, two afternoons and two evenings. (Murray, p. 56)

Catherine Drinker Bowen

What the writer needs is an empty day ahead. A big round space of empty hours to, as it were, tumble about in. (Murray, p. 48)

Frequency of Writing

Horace [Pliny, Trollope, Updike?]

nulla dies sine linea, never a day without a line. (Murray, p. 55)

Raymond Carver

When I'm writing, I write every day. It's lovely when that's happening. One day dovetailing into the next. Sometimes I don't even know what day of the week it is. The "paddlewheel of days," John Ashbery has called it. (Murray, p. 49)

Thomas Hardy

I never let a day go without using a pen. Just holding it sets me off; in fact I can't think without it. (Murray, p. 54)

Order of Writing

Anne Tyler

I have to begin all over every day. I get up at 6 or 6:30 to clean the house, and feed the children, and cook our supper ahead of time, so that I can be perfectly free the instant the children leave for school; but then when they're gone I find I'd rather do almost anything than go into my study. (Murray, p. 64)

W. H. Auden

Get up very early and get going at once, in fact, work first and wash afterwards. (Murray, p. 46)

Donald Murray

I find great joy in writing but, for reasons I cannot understand, I find it hard to get to my writing desk. And once there, to write. My wife recently observed that each morning I go down to my writing desk, turn on the computer, get to the right file, put the cursor at the top left-hand corner of the screen, get up and go back upstairs to the bathroom. (Murray, p. 45)

The quotations above are offered not to reach conclusions about each dimension but rather to observe how professional writers draw on an available vocabulary to discuss their creative times. For at least two centuries, clock time has been a pervasive influence on the habits of writers from different cultures. Even as writers admit that individual habits are different, clock time bounds the activity and penetrates their language. Yet it is within the constraints of time that writers find the freedom to create. The close association between time and number evident above is illustrated further in statements about writers' daily quota of writing:

Anthony Trollope

It has . . . become my custom . . . to write with my watch before me, and to requite from myself 250 words every quarter of an hour. I have found that the 250 words have been forthcoming as regularly as my watch went. (Murray, p. 63–64)

Lavinia Dobler

My goal is to write only one sentence a day. I write this on the bus on my way to work. I usually find that I write more than just one sentence, but the important point is that I have accomplished the goal I set by 9:00 a.m. (Murray, p. 51)

B. F. Skinner

I keep a cumulative record of serious time at my desk. The clock starts when I turn on the desk light, and whenever it passes twelve hours, I plot a point on a curve. I can see what my average rate of writing has been at any period. When other activities take up my time, the slope falls off. That helps me to refuse invitations. (Murray, p. 62)

John Fowles

But all this advice from senior writers to establish a discipline always, to get down a thousand words a day whatever one's mood, I find an absurdly puritanical and impractical approach. Writing is like eating or making love; a natural process, not an artificial one. (Murray, p. 52)

In many quotations we notice that where time is quantified, the time measures of the professional writer are longer, often more frequent, and with fewer apparent distractions than for the student writer in school. If we translate what professional writers have to say about the dimensions of their writing time to the classroom, then we see the wisdom of Nancy Atwell's recommendation in *In the Middle* (1987, p. 55)

Writers need time—regular, frequent chunks of time that they can count on, anticipate, and plan for. When we make time for writing in school, designating it a high-priority activity of the English program, our students will develop the habit of writers—and the compulsions. . . . Graves recommends allotting at least three hours or class periods a week in order for this habit of mind to take hold, for students to begin to rehearse their writing offstage and come up with their own topics with some degree of success. ([Graves] 1983, p. 223)

For writers to establish such habits is clearly important and a necessary step toward becoming conscious of a writer's time. We need to know, however, much more than we do about the temporal contours of the writing process itself. One path to such knowledge leads us to consider the beginning and ending of writing, waiting for writing, and the rhythms of composing. Murray's (1990) quotes are useful for these, too:

Beginning and Ending Writing

Jean Anouilh

I write very little, only for two hours in the morning, and then I stop even if it's going well—in fact especially if it's going well, because that's when you write those beautiful scenes like the ones in old plays, which go on and on. (Murray, p. 47)

Paul Horgan

Many writers confess to observing certain professional superstitions which the non-writer would find absurd. Some break off a day's writing in mid-sentence, sure of how the sentence is to continue, so that the next day they can complete it, and thus find themselves in an already forward-moving phase of work. (Murray, p. 55)

Gustave Flaubert

I have the peculiarity of a camel—I find it difficult to stop once I get started, and hard to start after I've been resting. (Murray, p. 51)

Waiting for Writing

Flannery O'Connor

Many times I just sit for three hours with no ideas coming to me. But I know one thing: If an idea does come between 9 and 12, I am there ready for it. (Murray, p. 60)

E. B. White

Delay is natural to a writer. He is like a surfer—bides his time, waits for the perfect wave on which to ride in. Delay is instinctive with him. He waits for the surge (of emotion? of strength? of courage?) that will carry him along. (Murray, p. 77)

Archibald MacLeish

I formed the habit long ago of putting new poems into a desk drawer and letting them lie there to ripen (or the opposite) like apples. . . . I learned early and by sad experience never to publish a green poem. (Murray, p. 57)

Donald Murray

The first thing to understand is there is such a thing as necessary waiting for writing. A writer drains the well with each draft, and it takes time for the well to fill. . . . Now I return to my schoolroom behavior, stare out the window, watch the squirrels play follow the leader, observe a shadow as it climbs over a rock and up a tree, listen to the interplay of a string quartet, relax, let go and then, in its own time, and with its own voice, the writing comes. (Murray, p. 70)

To consider if aspects of professional writers' practices can be applied to writing time in school, we might begin by asking ourselves how we have responded to students, for example, who stop writing in mid-sentence, delay writing, wait for assignments 'to ripen in their desks,' or who follow Murray's own "schoolroom behavior." What assumptions do teachers make about such practices? In the final quotations, writers describe their personal rhythms and how by writing with intense concentration they can find who they are and can become.

Rhythms of Writing

Richard Ford

I think working on a novel is an exercise in the reassurance of belief in what you are doing. I go out to my study at 8 o'clock and by 10:30 I'm reviving the faith in what I am doing and from 11 to 12 I may get something written. (Murray, p. 73)

John Irving

A novel is such a long involvement; when I'm beginning a book, I can't work more than two or three hours a day. I don't know more than two or three hours a day about a new novel. Then there's the middle of a book. I can work eight, nine, twelve hours then, seven days a week. . . . Then when the time to finish the book comes, it's back to those two- and three-hour days. . . . It takes me nearly as long to rewrite a book as it does to get the first draft. (*Writers at Work*, 1988, p. 416)

Mike Rose

I was spending more time writing: Whole afternoons disappeared as I sat in my apartment's little alcove, the window open to the Pacific breeze, saying the words out loud, trying to catch their rhythms, trying to render some curious thing I had seen. (1990, p. 157)

Annie Dillard

If you want to take a year off to write a book, you have to *take* that year, or the year will take you by the hair and pull you toward the grave. . . . You can keep a tidy house, and when St. Peter asks you what you did with your life, you can say, I kept a tidy house, I made my own cheese balls. (Murray, p. 50)

Charles Dickens

"It is only half-an-hour"—"It is only an afternoon"—"It is only an evening," people say to me over and over again; but they don't know that it is impossible to command one's self sometimes to any stipulated and set disposal of five minutes—or that the mere consciousness of an engagement will sometimes worry a whole day. (Murray, p. 50)

Robert Grudin

Such [writing] periods unify us, concentrating our energy, judgment, and emotion upon a single point. Conversely, they relieve us from all other considerations and so give us profound refreshment. They give us, if temporarily, ourselves. They are true acts of freedom, compared with which our normal miscellaneous diversions and indulgences of impulse are like the flutterings of moths. (Grudin, 1982, p. 91)

The first two quotations reveal a cyclical rhythm in the creative process. Ford describes a slow beginning that does not develop momentum until the third hour. Like the rise and fall of the tide, the temporal movement of Irving's prose flows slowly at the beginning of the work, accelerates through its middle phases, and ebbs toward completion. Yet in schools we have often prompted students to write as though the process, once jump-started, could proceed at a uniform rate until the writer ran out of time or ideas.

Dickens tells us that his concentration on the present moment of writing can be invaded by a future engagement of as little as five minutes. Consider how much more distracting writers in school find a day structured around changes of activity every hour and frequent interruptions within the hour. Whole afternoons disappear while Rose writes, and all domestic work is forsaken temporarily in order for Dillard to create. If writing is to offer the writer what Grudin calls "acts of freedom," then teachers will want to consider how the timescapes of school writing can reflect what professional writers say about the design of their own temporal workshops, about writing coming in its own time as the writer listens to and then follows the changing rhythms of his or her own ideas.

Balzac himself provides a memorable example of a novelist involved in writing to such a degree that time, as most of us live it, no longer existed. In *Balzac*, Stefan Zweig (1946) describes in the chapter entitled "Black Coffee" how the author composes.

> He recognized only the law which his work decreed: "It is impossible for me to work when I have to break off and go out. I never work merely for one or two hours at a stretch." It was only at night, when time was boundless and undivided, that continuity was possible, and in order to obtain this continuity of work he reversed the normal division of time and turned his night into day (p. 136)

Each evening Balzac slept from eight o'clock until midnight. Writing in a heavily-curtained room, he then wrote for five or six hours, leaving his desk only briefly to revive himself with black coffee.

> Outside, the day was beginning to dawn, but Balzac did not see it. His day was the small circle of light cast by the candles, and he was aware of neither space nor time, but only of the world that he himself was fashioning. (pp. 138–139)

After eight hours of continuous writing, Balzac devoted the rest of his day to making meticulous revisions to the galley proofs that arrived each morning. I include this example both to illustrate the extent to which time can be shaped to serve our purposes and to suggest the possibility that students, like professional writers, need to experience time as the medium in which they create, in contrast to time as the enemy, the constraint on creativity.

Reshaping Time

We have seen the powerful appeals that Atwell, Graves, and Murray make for teachers to provide regular and extended chunks of time to encourage students to develop the writing habit. Their primary focus in the sections quoted is on how much and how often students need to write, the quantifiable aspects of time. As central as these issues are, we must ask also about the rhythms and cadences of writing that find expression in and over time. What qualities of time are conducive to writing? How can young writers use their time most creatively within the boundaries set by school and classroom teacher?

Whether one is writing in a profession or in school, it is probable that time for writing will always be bounded by limits set by writers and readers. And if we had unlimited time to write, then some writers might never begin, while others would forever defer presenting their work for their readers' responses. Time limits can stimulate writing and maintain its tempo once in progress. Meeting a deadline can bring satisfaction to writers by providing them with a sense of completion and closure to the exploration of their ideas at that particular moment. Deadlines, a term rich in connotations, become problematic primarily when they are imposed without regard for the nature of an activity and the time needs of those involved.

Much recent discussion of educational reform and how to re-structure school systems has addressed the issue of how to promote more unified and integrated learning experiences. Central to discussions of the atomistic character of classroom life has been the question of how to use the available time, or increase it, by extending or re-vamping the school day and year. Ernest Boyer observes:

> Just as the arrangement of space is standardized in the American class-room, so is the use of time. If ideas are to be thoughtfully examined, time must be wisely used. Time is the student's treasure. However, what occurs in the classroom is often a welter of routine procedures and outside interruptions that come to dominate the life of students and teachers alike and, in the end, restrict learning. Time becomes an end in itself. (1983, p. 141)

With a view to using the available time more effectively, Boyer goes on to recommend "that the class schedule be more flexibly arranged to permit larger blocks of time, especially in courses such as laboratory science, foreign language, and creative writing." (pp. 232–233)

John Goodlad (1984), Joseph Carroll (1990), and Albert Shanker (1990) have all considered making learning more efficient by adjusting the length of the class period to the learning activity. In "The Coperni-can Plan: Restructuring the American High School" (1990), Carroll recommends that we redesign the typical six-period day so that classes meet fewer times for longer periods of time over a thirty- or sixty-day period. According to Carroll, the gains would include closer contact between students and teachers in smaller classes, individualised instruction, and greater focus on fewer subjects at one time. In Sizer's words, "Less is more" (1984). While it is essential for us to reorganise the school day to make better use of the available time, we need also to recognise that if students engage in literacy training as an open-ended process, then all conversation, reading, and writing will mushroom out to fill and then exceed the time frames that we provide. Because the play between language and its users can generate multiple and even infinite meanings, bringing absolute closure to these activities is always deferred. Even though the class ends, the conversation of literacy does not. If literacy is presented as possibilities, there will never be enough time.

Timescapes for Literacy

To argue only for more time, which we do need, perpetuates thinking about time in terms of quantity, the mould into which we pour instruction. Ironically, perhaps, in our time-conscious society, we tend to think of time in very limited mechanistic ways. We fail to recognise that, because time is socially constructed, it is many-layered, and multifaceted, like language itself. Gregory Bateson (1972, p. 449) quoting Korzybski cautions that "the map is not the territory," that there is a perceptual difference between our experience of the world and how we represent it in texts. If we are to make visible those experiences of time that are likely to promote creative activity, then we need to explore spatial representations other than the linear ones that pervade and shape so many aspects of classroom life.

Consider for a moment the experience of reading a road map in contrast to studying the kind of large-scale contour map favoured by those who hike over the rise and fall of land. As the gradients rise into peaks and slope into plain and valley, the ringed contour lines alternately bunch up and open out. Such a finely grained map provides a texture of detail appropriate to a mode of travel that is seldom linear for very long. Moving across open country we expect to stop frequently to check our bearings, to backtrack if we get lost, and to allow time to step off the beaten path to explore and to make detours en route to our destination. As the poet Cavafy shows us in "Ithaca," the journey is certainly as important as the homecoming.

In contrast, the movement of students and teachers through a school day is often a different one. There the boundaries, duration, frequency, and sequence of classes are mapped onto schedules, but the effects of temporal organisation on how learning is experienced are seldom considered enough by the cartographers of the time table. Consequently we have the same kind of difficulty orienting students to the temporal contours of class discussion, of getting into a book, or of writing collaboratively as would walkers attempting to find their way across open country with a road map or of being asked to walk in a straight line up a hill. The destination of education appears to be more important than the journey.

Teachers of English have a responsibility to draw on a human scale what I will call "timescapes for literacy." I use the term "timescape" to suggest that because time has many dimensions we need to attune its configurations to how we perceive literacy activities developing in and over time. The larger contours of a timescape will be boldly marked by the constraints of the schedule, yet its details grained finely enough to represent time of a quality conducive to reflective thought, unhurried discussion, and engaged writing. Teachers need to consider the qualities of reading, writing, and conversation that they seek to promote and then design within the schedule's linear contours appropriate timescapes. Whole language needs whole time.

Teachers frequently ask students to accommodate their rhythms of language use not only to the constraints of the schedule, but also to the time needs that we project for each activity. "You have five minutes to free write, twenty minutes to read, and fifteen minutes for peer editing," a teacher might say. While there are occasions when these constraints will be appropriate and effective, if students' efforts to make meaning through language are routinely cut off because "time is up," one message that this communicates is that teachers are more concerned about observing the time etiquettes of school and classroom than about respecting the time needs of the work itself.

The shape of our students' experience in learning to use language becomes conditioned by the internal time limits that we set for various activities and more broadly by the length of the class period. One major consequence of such limits is that students become accustomed and attuned to the rhetoric of the class hour, as with the packaging, for example, of televised information into sixty-second sound bites.[4] They come to expect and learn how to negotiate, for example, the internal pacing and attention span required by this measure of instruction. Their orientation to learning is governed and defined more by the clock than by the potential scope of the particular language activity, its complexity and potential to engage the student. The experience of learning is then consonant not with the rhythm of the activity itself but with the time frame within which it is situated.

Writing Communities and the Politics of Time

As we continue to define the kinds of literacy that our society will need, an increasing number of teachers report the success of their class when conceived as a community of writers and readers. Students and teacher write together, interpret textual meanings collaboratively, and develop empathic rather than autocratic relations among writers. Teacher and students participate democratically in decisions not only about the forms and topics of writing, but also about each writer's time needs. When writers attempt to develop such communities within a context of time values that model hierarchical and economic power relations, however, their practice runs counter to many of the principles on which writing communities are based. If students are to own the writing by which they define who they are and who they want to become, then both students and teachers need to negotiate the politics of time entailed in this process. We need to conceptualise time in ways that are congruent with our philosophies of teaching students to become literate and that will enhance our students' experiences with language.

We value our schedules, time frames and due dates because they allow us to coordinate our various activities so that we can predict with a fair degree of certainty the location, duration, and rhythm of the key events in our lives. Yet as teachers, we often believe that we cannot change the institutionally determined structures of time that control our classrooms. If we cannot easily reconstruct the time values of our institutions, we can at least negotiate time with our students. To negotiate is not to give up a major principle of social organisation in the classroom in favour of always allowing students to write spontaneously, nor is it to share writing without considering the time needs of the readers. To negotiate time is to observe how the time values of teacher and institution relate to those of the students; it also is to recognise that each group has distinctive values and needs. Both groups then can plan work together with mutual respect for the time needs of each other.

Teachers from grade school to college often claim that their students cannot handle yet the responsibility of managing their own time. If this is true, then in fact we need to involve students more directly in making decisions about the temporal aspects of their education. My students on the island involved me in such decisions as they taught me by the character of their responses how important it was that I recognise and respect the time perspectives from which their own rhythms of writing derived. They asked to write without interruption, to work at their own pace as well as time to be silent.

From the premise that whole language needs whole time, it follows that students need to learn how to attune the available time to the scope, purpose, and audience of an activity. Directives will be less appropriate than questions. We ask, for example, "When can we talk about your work? How much time do you need? How often do you want to have peer editing? Since we have three activities for today, which order makes sense to you?" Questions rather than imperatives allow students and teachers to negotiate the politics of time, thereby to promote values appropriate for a humanistic rather than a factory-model enterprise.

In *Shopping Mall High School* (1985), Arthur Powell observes that time treaties are tacitly negotiated around both teachers' expectations and students' commitment to learning. Powell describes how agreements that only so much work will be required by teachers and handed in by students maintain peace and harmony in the classroom but often undercut the quality and intensity of active engaged education. The kinds of negotiations that Powell describes occur typically in the context of the mechanistic one-time-fits-all model of schooling. Because students' temporal needs for reading and writing vary—for example according to their prior knowledge, perception of task complexity, motivation, and ability—this model cannot accommodate individual and group time needs as adequately as can a timescape that students and teachers design for each activity. We suggest here that teachers and students negotiate time treaties that lead to both classroom harmony and to an interactive, committed education.

Learning in small groups is one powerful way to raise students' awareness of how the uses of time and language are related. By leading students to consider the different time values of group members, collaborative learning situates students experientially both within time and language. Students who work together experience time less as an abstract constraint on their lives and more as part of the process of making meaning. As students work together, for example, on a class publication of oral histories about members of their community, students and teachers will need to make a wide range of decisions.

Rhetorical choices will be made, for example, about how best to shape interviews into written text and the kinds of editing acceptable if the integrity of voice is to be preserved. Students will discover that collaborative writing and reading is necessarily recursive, as students return both to their informants and to their transcripts to understand the complex human realities that they aim to portray. As students research and write together, they learn that, because their rhythms of talking, reading, and writing vary, then accomodation, flexibility, and respect for individual differences are essential if successful collaborations are to occur.

Choices will also be made about how to develop timescapes appropriate for such different tasks as conducting life-review conversations, translating talk into writing, and coordinating individual projects into class publication. Working at the scheduling level, students will plan flexibly the times when each phase of the individual work needs to be completed for the next to begin. Within the interviews themselves, students will discover, if they have not done so already, that the timescape of a conversation between older and younger people needs careful attuning and patience if the elder are not to feel rushed and exploited. It takes time for student interviewers to establish trust and to show that they care about the stories that their respondents have to tell. The open-ended enquiry of collecting and presenting life histories takes different kinds and uses of time and language at each stage of the process, as will any other language activity.

This example of a class project that teaches students about both time and language will suggest others. We do not want to consider time as an issue separate and abstracted from the activity; we want to make time visible as an influence that informs everything that happens in our English classes, from the pauses between questions and answers to those existential moments when reader, writer, and text become one. A major part of our task of making time visible will be to find ways to think and talk about time that will be more adequate than the mechanistic vocabulary that we have inherited, to find a discourse sufficiently complex to address all we do under the rubric of language education. Because all teaching and learning occur within the culture of time and language, we want our students to be engaged also in these conversations and to be exposed to a wide variety of language-learning experiences construed in various modes. My purpose in the discussion above has been to invite teachers to explore with their students the possibilities for drawing on the many different qualities of time that can promote literacy. What literacy comes to mean in classrooms, schools, and society will be influenced by the timescapes that teachers, students, and administrators design.

Given that ethnographic enquiries are designed to be issue-raising and exploratory in contrast to problem-solving, it will be appropriate then, to close with four questions that emerged as I studied the problem of time in the island community. The questions are illustrative of the issues that teacher researchers might want to consider in their own classrooms. Because time assumes a wide spectrum of modes, from diurnal rhythms to the nanoseconds of computer education where, according to Rifkin (1987, p. 182) "time is information," our answers and further questions will evolve within the contexts in which we teach. Our students can help us by reflecting on the qualities of time that will enable them to discover and shape their identities as they talk, read and write.

1. In school, how can teachers establish connections between the community-based time values that students already know and the concepts of time particular to the subjects that they study? Specifically, how can teachers help students attune their own activity rhythms to the temporal logic of writing as a process?

2. How can teachers encourage students' experience of reading, writing, and talking with each other to be one of existential rather than of regimented panoptic time?

3. What opportunities are we currently providing in our schools for students to learn how to become responsible for organising the timescapes of their learning activities? How can this goal be incorporated into the curriculum?

4. How can we engage students in conversations about the meanings of time in the different social contexts they encounter? In what ways other than those described in this study do our students talk about time?

Chapter Seven

FIELD NOTES: TOWARD THE FUTURE

The impulse to return is strong. Ethnographers, no different from the rest of us, return to note the changes occurring in "their" communities. Accounts of such homecomings are presented often as an afterword or epilogue. If only from the narrator's viewpoint, the convention of a visit to the past follows chronology and appears to complete the story. The community's ongoing life is not disturbed, of course, by the observer's departure. And even to suggest the possibility of closure is surely fictive.

What follows here are edited field notes that record both an end and a new beginning to my work. In a community that does not segment time rigidly into past, present, and future, "end" and "beginning" can mark only the temporal perspective of the observer. In this chapter, I present my observations in the form of field note entries, to resituate this study in the continuing history of the community. My uses of the ethnographic present in Chapters one through five might otherwise suggest that the descriptions themselves are ahistorical and that change was not already and always in progress.[1] In the words of George Hicks (1976, p. 2), "Subsequent visits revealed only the working out of changes that had long before been set in motion."[2]

Because of time constraints, I have been able to revisit only a very limited number of the classrooms, workplaces and people that provided my fieldwork in 1984 and 1986. People again have given their time generously and with openness and interest: "Come and see what we are doing now." I chose to work primarily in the junior and senior high school since resistance to literacy was most noticeable after the elementary school years. The following images of life in school and community reflect people's working through and attempting to come to terms with the broad issues of literacy and education for an uncertain future. Based on the preceding chapters, the reader will observe what is changing as well as what appears to remain the same.

September 3, 1990

In previous years, Labor Day has marked the time by which the summer people leave and the island returns to itself. But this year many out-of-state license plates, including my own, line the streets. "They come even earlier and stay longer each year," a local storekeeper comments. More Bed & Breakfast and real estate signs than ever before.

Sept 5

John Holt would be proud to see the imprint of his homeschooling conversations on a new generation of children learning at home. "They will teach themselves," Pattie remembers his telling her when she was anxious that she would not know everything that Jessica, age 8, and Emma, age 6, would need. Nancy continues to homeschool Tia, age 4, and Megan, age 6, and has begun also a pre-school programme. When I listen to nine-year-old Amy play her violin, watch eight-year-old Eben discuss mechanical problems with his father, hear Jessica weave stories around travel photographs and see Megan and Tia's art work, the quality of what these homeschooled children have gained from extended close contact with their parents is very apparent.

Homeschooling has increased on the island since 1986 but continues to be the educational choice for college-educated parents from away. Many of the homeschoolers take this option, arguing that formal education stifles learning. For Nancy, homeschooling allows her to both introduce her children to resources and in turn learn from what they experience. Given the time that fishing families devote to economic survival, it is hard to see that many could keep their children at home and teach them. Much of what island-raised students value in education is already learned at home.

Sept 7

I thought I had heard most of the local expressions likely to shed insight into the lives of island people. Jeff, who came to the island in the

1970s, described the occasion when a professional was inspecting the lines and frames for the lobster boat that Jeff was building. The pro began with, "Praise in the face is an open disgrace," but then went on to self-consciously commend Jeff's work.

Had I heard this expression when I was trying to encourage my junior high students to write, then I would have understood, in part, why they neither sought out nor welcomed the encouragement of their teachers. Jeff explained that if a young person did something well, then nothing was usually said. But if he or she did not do it right, then....

Sept 8

I stop by the local library which continues to open two days a week. The librarian says that book circulations which increased each year until 1985 have not changed since then. She reports that more older than younger people use the library and that the high number of check-outs by summer visitors account for the healthy number of circulations. More of the stores now have racks displaying videos.

Sept 9

Recalling the cold and damp of Maine autumns, I order a cord of hardwood. Joe promises delivery as soon as he has pulled ten cords out of the woods. Remembering me as his English teacher, he tells me that he has planned to get some help with his reading this winter but that his new wife is very good at doing the books for his newly-started construction business.

Sept 10

In 1986, students who wanted to take college courses had to be prepared to leave the island for extended periods. Many returned before graduation. By means of Interactive Television (ITV), students can now try a college course or two without going further than the high school. Through "electronic classrooms," the Community College of Maine now offers a wide range of courses between 7 a.m. and 10 p.m. both to degree-seeking students and to people requiring job training, for example in accounting or workplace safety.

In the first term of the programme, thirty of our students are enrolled in eleven different courses, including economics, art history, workplace safety, and accounting. Most of these students would have been unable previously

Faculty discuss school restructuring.

to attend college, keep a job, and raise a family, often as single parents. Although distance learning is currently serving an increasing number of adult ed. students, Kim in her junior year is taking a psychology course for college credit. The opportunity for students to talk directly with their teachers when the class is in progress appeals to those of our students who have found college learning to be impersonal and text-based.

Sept 11

Mike is making a go of fishing but living off-island with Andrea who is working as a nurse. With hesitation, I ask how the lobstering has been this season. "They've come back again. Never seen so many in a long while. I think they've moved in from the South East. Loads of 'em now. Price ain't any better for the fisherman, though, at $1.78 a pound. Restaurants are still charging $5.95 for a lobster supper. We aren't any better off than when there were fewer of 'em around."

Sept 12

Restructuring was the topic for today's faculty meeting at the high school. We watch Ted Sizer's video on restructuring. Discussion afterwards explores some of the ways in which his nine principles might be applied to *local school reform. Working in small groups, teachers identify the key issues that they think should be addressed here, such as how to make learning more personal and students more responsible for their own education: flexible schedules and focusing goals to achieve greater clarity of purpose. The teachers have read several articles on restructuring over the summer. Conversation is lively, engaging a broad sweep of school and community issues.*

George, the high school principal, is now attending a graduate seminar in social contexts of learning. He writes:

> Restructuring has been an issue of study, discussion, and minor implementation for over a year now in our school district. Recently an islandwide coalition of 36 people was established to rethink our educational programs and to establish a "vision" for our schools. The process is not unlike that which produced the Maine Common Core of Learning. Also similar is the backing and support, both in expertise and dollars, of several major Maine corporations.

Sept 14

When I first came to this island rising on ledges of granite out of the North Atlantic, the stone itself came to represent what I saw in the community as permanent. I saw this intractable medium on which town and spirit were built as a bulwark against the kinds of changes occurring in the lives of those in the small coastal towns along U.S. 1. Today, I read in Time's Arrow/Time's Cycle *(Gould, 1987, p. 6):*

> Two key Huttonian observations fueled the discovery of deep time — first, the recognition that granite is an igneous rock, representing a restorative force of uplift (so that the earth may cycle endlessly, rather than eroding once into ruin).

If in geologic time, earth's most stable forms bear the signature of change, then how much more deeply will change be inscribed on human lives, if we can only recognise the signs.

Sept 15

Linda stops me in the hallway to tell me about her new course in American culture, a new class that combines American history and Ameri-

can literature that she and Clare are team teaching. Linda excitedly describes how this will be a class in which she will not lecture, in which the shape and themes of discussion will emerge as students become responsible for their own learning.

Sept 17

Brenda, who graduated in 1982, has been working as a court recorder after completing a business degree. She likes her work but does not plan to study further. "I am more concerned now about family time, being at home, having children and being with people." In her junior year, she was a very bright student but strongly resisted writing. Might those days have been different if we had been able to glimpse her career now?

Sept 19

Pleased to find Kim back on the island and taking a term off from college before beginning a teacher education programme. She and I discuss the possibility of getting together a small group of adults who would like to work together on their reading and writing. We run an ad in the local paper but know that word of mouth is more likely to encourage people. I call Joe to see when the wood is coming. "Have it to you real soon now."

Sept 20

In this classroom, I used to teach English to 10C and wonder if I could make it to the last bell. When I ask Michael, a fellow teacher, if teaching has changed since he and I started here together in 1978, he smiles and replies, "It's easier, never easy, but many of the kids seem different now. But perhaps it's me who has mellowed. Now we have more to offer them in terms of options and programs." Michael directs the "Island Alternative Program" for students at risk. Working each day with small groups, he closely monitors students' progress in their academic subjects. In addition, the program offers a work component that helps students to maintain a positive self-image. When problems occur at work or in school, Michael can counsel those involved. Fewer students quit school now than in the mid eighties.

Sept 22

Michael asks me to work with Steven on his English. Steven and I last talked in 1984 when he was in grade six. Now in his senior year, English hasn't gotten any easier for him, and he tells me straight off that he can't get the sentences onto the page. "Its a big muddle in my head." We talk through his assignment to write a paper that will "explode a popular belief or myth." Even in one-on-one conversation, Steven's ideas come out so slowly. I can see why Linda struggles to find time to talk with him in class.

Sept 23

George asks me when I am going to take some pictures of Kendal and his math students writing in their response journals. If the changes in philosophy that underly writing as process and the social construction of texts are supported by how other subjects present knowledge and determine meanings, then writing across the curriculum might yet become a reality.

Sept 24

Grade Seven class: 8:05–9:09 a.m.:

English Sucks. A declarative sentence from 1978 greets me from the inside cover of Patterns of Communication. I flashback to Charlie, Joe, or was Judy the author who so thoughtfully inscribed a message for me to find in 1990? The teacher reads from the same book that our class had inherited twelve years ago. The book is still in "fair condition!" Darcy asks her seventh graders to create a noun phrase plus determiner to complete the predicate "swarmed around the singer." For over an hour students quietly predicate subjects and subjugate predicates; I wait for the public protests that I had heard but there are none. John comes over to borrow my pencil and tells me, "I'm good at English, but I hate this grammar. I got the idea of these exercises after ten minutes, but we had to keep on doing 'em."

Having heard that the middle school[5] English teachers have been developing a new programme to incorporate, for example, personal writing, cultural journalism, and small group work, I ask Darcy and Deborah why they continue to teach grammar: They tell me that by satisfying the community pressure to teach the basics, they can then make innovations in other areas.

Sept 25

I overhead Darcy talking with Kendal about how today Gary, the fourth teacher in their middle school team, came to her door and held up

Net making.

ten fingers. "The kids didn't even notice that we had come to the end of the period; they were too busy writing! We kept on working and that gave him extra time to finish up his class on health science. No bells. It's great!"

Sept 27

In today's faculty meeting we discussed a recent newspaper-selling headline, "11th Graders Bomb on Assessment Tests." Criticisms of several programmes resulted. The School Board's discussion of the low scores centred around mainstreaming special-ed. students and the apathy of several students among an already small class. Darcy pointed out that to break the cycles of academic failure and to enhance motivation is difficult when students themselves do not value the skills and accomplishments measured by the assessments. Some of the junior class see few reasons to take seriously tests in literacy and numeracy or to change their "depressed image" in the eyes of the school.

When I first talked with George about the changes occurring in the junior and senior high, one of the items to which he referred me was the 1990 Maine Educational Assessment. The district scores for writing have been lower at grade eleven over the past five years than those of schools with a comparable socioeconomic back ground. For reading, the scores were close to the state average until last year when they fell quite dramatically. At grade eight the scores for both reading and writing have fallen well within the comparison score bands over a five-year period.

If the ongoing efforts of the senior high English teachers to make curricular reforms are not yet reflected in higher test scores, then teachers' changes in approach are evident in the subgroup reports based on a questionnaire. For example, in answer to a question that asks students to indicate how often they have an opportunity to write drafts, island students reported significantly more time than did other students across the state. Similarly, island students shared their writing more often than the state average showed. Island students now engage in prewriting only marginally less than did their mainland counterparts.

Sept 30

Many new businesses cater to the tourist trade with antique shops, water sports, and art work. One new business plies the traditional craft of net hanging for ground fishing. The husband and wife team who net 14—

16 hour days told me, "When we opened, a lot of locals came in to say how pleased they were to see this building being used for something that shows we are still a working waterfront."

Joe calls about the wood. He got behind in cutting in order to close in his barn before the winter. "You'll have it next week." (His first reference to calendric time.)

October 1

Met with Steven after school in the library. He had with him an old iron socket chisel that he had just found while working in the yard. He turned it over in his hands explaining how he had ground out the pitted sections and trued the edge. He planned to turn a handle for it on his father's lathe. When I tried coaxing Steven into writing a piece about his find, he ended our conversation by opening Eric Sloane's Museum of American Tools *and comparing his own tool with Sloane's illustrations. As we talked about Steven's latest English assignment on Robert's* Rabble in Arms, *Steven pared the title off his assignment sheet. He offered to think about writing something on early American hand tools.*

Oct 2

Kim called to tell me about her latest efforts to recruit people for our literacy circle. Friends tell her, "Yes, this is a good idea," but as yet nobody has agreed to come. Other people are offended by an invitation that they see as condescending. She believes that people see no reason to enhance abilities adequate to the task of getting them through the day. "Why should they?" she asks.

Oct 3

Tony relays the familiar story of trying life away from the island. By the time he was eighteen, living on the island felt like "being in a bottle." After two years in the Marines, he returned to Maine and enrolled in a vocational training course. "I needed to know a computer language and calculus, so I quit to go fishing." Two years later, married with a baby on the way, he joined his father's plumbing business where he could make steady money.

Oct 4

Met with the middle school teachers who have a new schedule. In the morning: language arts, sixty-six minutes; math and science, thirty-three minutes each; and forty-five minutes for integrated studies. In the afternoon, the junior high follows the senior high school schedule, hence there is no time flexibility. Period five is for tutorial make-up work, period six for health or phys-ed, and period seven for exploratories (technology, art, home ec., computers).

All five teachers like their morning uninterrupted by bells and office announcements. "It took about a week to get used to the new schedule. I didn't like it at all at first, but we now have more control of learning than in the past." When I ask the team why they have kept the minute-counting class lengths as part of a flexible schedule, they explain that while they are free to structure their own time, the decision to do so has to be made in advance and agreed on by all. They see the school reform movement far more evident in the middle school than in the high school.

"The group argues about when to host a parent's evening:

First teacher: We have a calender of agreed commitments and should not have to do more. It's time we are not paid for.

Second teacher: You are right, of course, but because this is so important to me, I want to do it anyway."

As the teachers balance contract time against personal time, the tension between the positions feels productive. The parent-teacher conferences are planned to occur from 12–7 pm in quarter-hour sessions, with one half-hour dinner break.

Oct 6

A low-drain tide, so I head for the clam flats to watch the action. But this year no tracks lead down to the water's edge. Now only two blue herons dip regally into the mud that a decade ago would have been covered with diggers. I hear more people than ever before saying, "clamming is almost gone, a thing of the past." Pumpkin heads on the porch announce the beginning of the Halloween season. Neatly stacked woodpiles grow daily by everyone's door and barn—except mine! "Friends" tell me that I should have ordered wood in the spring, if I wanted it dry for the fall. Kevin and John begin to rig up their boat for the beginning of the scallop season on November 1. Off the causeway, Old Man Hardy loads his truck with seaweed for his garden before the ground sets up. Each day more V-shaped flights of geese head to the South—in Anderson's words, "pulling in winter."

Oct 7

George describes a recent class visit to a science class. Students role-played a town meeting of concerned citizens gathering to discuss what's to be done about a fish kill caused by excess oxygenation of the river. Each group argued who was responsible for the death of the fish and subsequent loss of revenue from fish tournaments. Rebuttals to accusation were made, for example, by the power company, chemical corporation, and local conservationists. To see if consensus could be reached, open discussion closed the session—a tough process for this class. Students then wrote Letters to the Editor of the school paper to express their opinion as to who was responsible.

To the Editor:

I would like to make a few comments on the recent fish kill that has been attributed to the "Gas Bubble Disease." I believe that the dilemma can be directly related to faulty structure and poor dam design. . . . As a plan to assure the problem will not occur again, I suggest that the Power Company be forced to make structural changes on the dam if they wish to continue business in Riverwood. As for the water that was shipped in during the panic of the matter, I suggest that the cost be picked up by the taxpayers of this great city. In conclusion I would hope that a valuable lesson has been learned by the people of Riverwood. Get the facts and appreciate what you have while you can: It may not always be there. For the time being, enjoy the fishing!

Sincerely, John

The editor,

As a tax payer to the town of Riverwood, I feel that no one group is responsible for the fish kill. I believe that the power company is to blame because of the lack of interest, the engineers because of lack of effort and cooperation, scientists for being incompetent, the sanitation committee for not performing accurate tests, and finally the tax payers for polluting the water in various ways. . . .

Kimberly

Little remarkable in this way of teaching, George observed, but he then pointed out that group work was not being done at all two years ago and particularly not this kind of writing in science classes. Kimberly recognises shared responsibility for the problem. So often in the past, students and parents have taken good-guys-and-villain stands on issues. How will this kind of learning encourage writing across the curriculum?

Oct 8

Talked with Skip down at the Co-op: lobster up to $1.98 a pound. Skip's proud of what's happening in the schools and sees the state recommendations to the school district being instrumental in raising teachers' aspirations for their students. He thinks that teachers are responsible for bringing parents and community round to seeing different futures for the young people. I asked him about why he thought Kim and I aren't getting any takers on the adult literacy programme. "People are so embarrassed about not being able to read that they are not going to come forward. You can be standing right next to a non-reader. He knows that you know, but he'll never admit it."

Oct 10

When I first visited Linda's College English class in 1986, she was lecturing. Students told me then that there were right and wrong answers in her class. Today, students move their chairs into a circle and choose a record keeper and moderator. The group are preparing to explore Hawthorne's concepts of innocence, guilt, and punishment in The Scarlet Letter. *She does not orchestrate discussion, only occasionally asking students to clarify judgment and observation.*

Linda watches and listens as the class works away from defining guilt as an absolute state toward guilt as perception, individual and cultural. Students' pace allows them to reflect and to confront their uncertainties as they try out ideas. "I think we are dealing with two different things here: being guilty and feeling guilty." No timekeeper to limit the direction or depth of discussion, and students wait for each other to answer. After discussing guilt and innocence in the context of a much publicised hunting accident, the class is prepared to assess tomorrow the actions of Hester and Dimsdale in the 19th century.

After class, Linda and I talk about her teaching style. "I was so sick of students' defining themselves and me in particular ways, of not being responsible for their own learning." She and her colleagues kept saying

Seniors discussing literature.

"something has got to change." After she read Horace's Compromise, *took a graduate course in teaching reading, and attended a state conference, she gradually began to change, first modifying one aspect of her teaching, and then another. When I comment that discussion learning can be slow, Linda replies, "I am not concerned about time because I am interested in how students get there. Doing it on their own, using their own resources to the best of their abilities, not dependent on me or anyone else to do their learning for them." One student tells me that he loves this class because he gets to think and to hear the views of his classmates. Another comments, "We never get anywhere at the end of a discussion."*

Oct 12

Recognising my truck from a decade ago, Kevin followed me home and proudly introduced me to Sandra, his new wife. She works down at the factory cutting and packing herring. Sandra tells me that she would like to have her high school diploma. "Why?" I ask. "To have it. I just want it. I would like to be able to go on to college, if I wanted to." When I asked her why she quit school in her senior year, she told the familiar story of being failed out of school because she missed more than ten days without make-up privileges.

Kevin talked as though the high school was a closed pot where he couldn't do anything, couldn't have any fun. "Junior high, my best years. You and Mr. W let us get away with stuff, and we needed to." Perplexing how much former students want to talk about school now, to make sense of who they were? Who were we then in relation to who we are now?

Kevin reiterated the importance of people who come here taking the time to get to know people, to be a part of the community, whether as a teacher or a sheriff.

Oct 14

Check-out line at the market: Two sixth-grade girls buy writing pads and tell me that they will use them to record sales for their conservation club. The girls are selling bracelets and pins to raise money to support a scheme that buys parcels of Amazonian rainforest to protect it against development. Alton and Sylvia still haven't been able to find an affordable lot to park their trailer on. To illustrate the difficulty of finding land, they tell me about an elderly woman who sold her 15 acres of shore-front property to a developer for $15,000 in 1987. He put in a road, subdivided the property into five-acre parcels and sold each for many times the original purchase price. Property taxes have risen to where owning family land becomes a major financial burden. Is education an antidote to subdividing this island rainforest?

Oct 18

Steven gets back an English assignment. "50 — Unfinished" is scribbled across the top. Because I know how long it took him to write even this much, I had hoped to see just one comment that would keep him writing and encourage him to finish his piece. He tells me that he can never catch up and keep up with his English classes. He fails an in-class literature test because he didn't have enough time to finish the questions; his teacher says that he did have. Not to be beaten by his recent defeats, though, he shows me the new maple handles he has turned for his old chisels, and together we look over the draft for his history paper.

Oct 20

When I arrive home, Joe is in the driveway unloading my wood, fat rounds of oak, ash, and birch. The time is finally right. His brother Tom is being tutored in reading so that he can pass the basic skills test to sign up for the Navy. When Kim and I tried to start our literacy group, I talked with Marion about her own work with one-on-one tutors using Laubach's assessment program. She is interested in moving away from a skills-based approach to working with small family groups in a whole-language programme. The methods of instruction that Literacy Volunteers of America use in adult literacy programmes are beginning to get talked about on the island. These kinds of instructional changes occur slowly, however.

Oct 21

The first session for the newly formed community coalition on school restructuring is planned for November. I meet with Becky, Joshua, Duane, and Jim, the student representatives, to understand what they think school reform might address. "I see restructuring as evaluating what your current situation is, interpreting what a school is doing. It's projecting. What can we do to change our school and to improve it?" Jim tells me. Before looking at the changes students would like to see made, we discuss what is working well, for example, small classes in which teachers provide students with one-on-one time both for academic help and to discuss what is happening in their lives.

The major concern in this first meeting is that the college-bound students, a good third of the senior class, "fill all our time in meeting requirements." The perceived demands of the future do not allow students to take courses of immediate relevance, interest, and pleasure and they are unable to schedule elective courses. The group are developing a questionnaire to poll both junior and senior high students on their concerns.

Oct 22

I substitute teach for Marine Studies. We watch a film about the building and loss in 1979 of the *Leavitt* on her maiden voyage. Ned Ackerman built and captained the two-masted schooner and planned to trade her under sail. Talk about dream and reality goes slowly for these fishermen's sons in their junior and senior year. We shift into a session on knots and splicing. With hands and eyes fully occupied, the talk now *begins to flow in preparation for writing an argument for or against a place for sail in the transportation system.*

Oct 23

After chatting with each other, the group settles into the writing almost willingly. Within fifteen minutes, however, most are finished and asking for the rope again. One student writes:

> Today's age I dont think that there is any Room for Sailing Schoners Because they aint as fast as the Big Cargo Ships they cant carry As much and if you cant carry as much you are going to get shut down Because if a company wants to send cargo to some place they want to send the whole shipment not half and there going to want it there in a horray.

> I just dont thing that a 97 ft Boat can carry as much as a 600 ft cargo ship and as safly As the cargo ship, Because Like in the movie when the were out in that storm it is Like that every Winter and in the sumer During hocains and outher Stom's. Let me Ask you were your cargo would be safer on a 97 ft Wooden Boat or a 600 ft Steal Boat.

This is a double period, and by the end of the second period most of the class are very restless. I watch the clock too. Few students are willing to add more information or explain their position in more detail. But they will talk me down the bay and back about lobster boat races and ask again to be shown the quick way to tie a bowline.

Oct 25

Students in grade eight are beginning a unit on immigrants. Deborah asks her class "to walk in the shoes" of those who have crossed cultures, to feel the problems of making a home in a new country. Students' initial judgments of Bette Bao Lord's Year of the Boar and Jackie Robinson *are that it is "stupid" and "weird." They joke playfully about the year of the Lobster and the Crab. Their comments mimic Chinese pronunciations. "I don't like that kind of stuff. I don't like to think about it." Deborah gently pushes Timmy to say why. "I don't know. Because it's retarded." I am reminded that there are very few families on the island from different ethnic groups.*

Calligraphy lesson.

Holli then takes the response session in another direction by commenting, "But it's a different culture, and that's hard for us to understand." Her classmates agree that to live in China would be odd, and imagine some of the differences. Molly asks about the practice of numbering the grandchildren: "Isn't that impersonal?" Slowly students make connections. "So you could say the grandmother is the big cheese," Danny offers. Deborah's reading aloud deepens the interest. When she announces that she doesn't have time to read any more, I hear, "Oh no, now we have to write." But the students appear willing to write in their journals about how they would respond to a new family moving in next door.

Oct 26

Deborah, who trained in Art and now teaches both Special Ed. and English, goes for a hands-on approach to cultural understanding. She brings in a mimeo showing the strokes and stroke-order for Chinese characters. She explains to the class that the Chinese written character is a form of personal expression and that you write what you are. Using India ink and brushes, students copy the signs and clearly enjoy an exercise in calligraphy. Lindsay tells Molly, "I haven't done this since second grade. Fun, ain't it!"

Oct 27

A local columnist observes that, although well past mid-October, "The leaves are still on the trees, flowers still bloom on our garden, and a few veggies are still in the ground." He adds details of the recent but late departure of the warblers. Earlier in the month a newscaster for the area commented that this fall the oak, birch, and maple were changing colour out of sequence—a time marker I had missed.

Oct 28

Not much clamming going on right now, but Alton can still find a couple of bushels a tide and make a hundred dollars a day. We plan to go three hours before low tide. He tells me to meet him at 10:30 a.m. Having forgotten to put back the clock, I arrive at 9:30 a.m. After talking for 45 minutes, he asks me if know what time it is. "I didn't know whether you just wanted to talk some, or didn't know the clocks changed last night." When I ask him how he knows the clocks changed, he laughs and tells me that he watches TV. Alton and Sylvia do not own a clock or a watch and walk over to his mother's house when they need to know the time.

When I ask Jeff about people's responses to changing the clock back, he reminds me that some of the fishermen still do not change their clocks for standard and day-light savings time. Given that the sun and not the clock affect their workday, he wonders why they react strongly to the change with their comments, like, "I wish they would just leave the clock alone and stop messin with it. I am not changing my friggin clock." He explains that some fishermen get mixed up with whether they should turn it forward or backward.

I ask Jeff if he hears the term "island time" used much. "Less so than in the past," an observation that I have now heard from several other people. "The island is getting more competitive now, and people have to learn how business is done in other communities." The expression tends to be used in the context of explaining, perhaps justifying, why events and services do not happen for the convenience of visitors.

Oct 29

For the past two weeks, fishermen have been trucking ashore swaying mounds of lobster traps out of the Co-op. Close to shop or barn, neatly stacked piles of traps and brightly coloured bunches of pot buoys wait for repairs and fresh paint. Almost the end of the season for most inshore *boats. Fishermen report a good season despite soft-market prices. For the past couple of weeks, boats have been on the dock rigging up the long steel booms needed to tow scallop drags. More guns begin to appear across the rear windows of pick-up trucks in readiness for the start of hunting season. Time to wear blaze orange for pets, children, and those who walk the woods to collect brush for Christmas wreath making.*

Oct 31

The faculty meet to discuss proposals for school reform. Working in groups of three, teachers identify what they see as forces for and against effecting change in such areas as making learning more personal, encouraging students to be more responsible for their own learning, achieving greater intellectual focus, and getting the faculty to commit themselves to essential school philosophy and mechanisms. Roadblocks to achieving these include conditioning students to work in particular ways, rigid scheduling, traditional expectations, lack of time for team planning, and standardised testing.

In the open discussion that followed, the recent experiences of the middle-school teachers with their new block scheduling and integrated learning offer one set of reference points for how the high school might proceed next year. While the faculty are critical of some of Sizer's principles, his work is offering one valuable starting point for school reform. Teachers willingly consider options such as increasing the length of the school day and year to use school resources more efficiently.

November 1

First day of scalloping season. Like a plow making furrows, from first light to dusk the boom-rigged boats tow their steel buckets across the bottom of the bay. The cycle of drag, haul, dump, sort, drop the boom, and drag again continues until dark. The excitement comes in sorting the scallops from among sea urchins, sculpin, rocks, and the occasional fish. Down at the market, I ask Skip whether the fishermen believe they will have a good season. "They aren't braggin, but I know they aren't hurtin too awfully bad." Price is fair at $4.50 a pound on the dock. Back in '86, Mike was diving for scallops, sometimes through ice holes.

Nov 3

Second meeting with student coalition members. Joshua and Becky want to listen to the community group and watch what is going on at the coalition group meeting before speaking. In contrast, Jim wants the students to identify their immediate concerns to the group. Much of the subsequent discussion is about the rights that students have to be heard out by their teachers, to be treated in ways that respect students in the final years of school as they fast approach adulthood.

Nov 5

For the first coalition meeting, the School Board have invited a facilitator from one of the large high-tech corporations interested in forming school-business alliances. He devotes the first hour and a quarter of the two hours to explaining group process, elements of a vision statement, and theories of change. Periodically, he apologises for what he describes as necessary preparation for their work that will save time down the road. The group, however, want to get on with the task at hand, discuss issues, stake out individual concerns. Town meetings have given them practice enough in talk!

The meeting ran over by forty-five minutes, and many thought that meetings should be longer and more frequent than once a month to get the work done. The facilitator announced that next session the group will use some right-brain activities to visually represent what a restructured school district might look like. After requested explanation of right- and left-brain functions, wide-spread skepticism was reported that this activity would be time well spent.

Nov 9

When I ask Kim whether it continues to be difficult for fishermen to save money over the season, she replies, "Yes, very," but goes on to explain that her parents both like to go shopping up to the big cities and come back with a lot of gadgets for home and the boat. Her father recently purchased a top-of-the-line voice-activated tape recorder. Bemused by his expensive purchase, she asked him why he needed this item on his boat. He explained that he would use it to record the location of his pots and how well they were fishing as he moved them up and down the bay. Previously he had scribbled down cryptic notes to himself on paper or on a bulkhead. High tech reintroduces the spoken word where writing had a toehold!

Nov 12

Last night's nor'easter dumped record-breaking rain down the New England coast. Throughout the night, trucks pulled down to the dock to *check the moorings. Headlights picked out the blurred shapes of storm-hazed boats still riding safely at their moorings. Hard to imagine only a 1" line between the rocks and an investment of up to $100,000.*

Nov 15

Naomi is home from college for the Veterans Day weekend. When I last spoke with her in 1988, she and her teachers were unsure that she and her six closest friends would graduate, let alone go on to college. She tells me proudly that all six are in college and that she is in a course for law enforcement training. She would like to work with young people on probation or in care, a group whose needs she believes she can understand well.

In 1989, Naomi had invited me to her graduation. Remembering that I was unable to come, she pulls out the speech that she gave, one that had elicited much support from the students but criticism from some parents. She prefaces her reading of it to me with "My English teacher helped me with the grammar."

THE WORLD IS MINE; I'M THE CLASS OF 1989

I would at this time like to say my farewell to my class, the class of 1989.

For years we have sat in class after class together, sharing the same thoughts, but never expressing them. Now as seniors, we have realized if we didn't express them now it would be too late. We all opened up this year and shared them. I feel we have gotten closer to each other than in the past eleven years of school.

Though we feel tired from the struggling to make it to be seniors, we also have in each one of us the ambition and determination to succeed and reach our dreams.

Looking back over the years, I was saddened by the number of students we lost due to pregnancies, drug abuse, and fear, fear they would not make it in school. We are all tired because we had those fears also. Now is the time we need the most energy. We face life, the final test. Can we make it in society?

We've been listening to our elders tell us "they went through the same things." Well, tell me, mom, was AIDS becoming an epidemic, did the country have a trillion plus dollar deficit, were cars $20,000, apartments $600 a month and was there an Oliver North as a national hero? On top of this you want us to be more successful than you?

I hear a lot of my classmates ask "Is it worth it?" The seniors who found the answers are on the stage today.

Those things facing our lives that are going to fight like hell to bring us down, are going to make us fight twice as hard to stay up!

So mom, you tell me you "know what I'm going through." The world has changed and the world is cruel, but for the members of my class, the unspoken it-doesn't-need-to-be-said pact, is that we will all make it or we will die trying. I will let you all know, we are all survivors.

Part of what frustrated Naomi and her friends in school is now being more actively recognised by teachers and administrators as legitimate areas to address. Students are beginning to be regarded as active participants in education who have rights and responsibilities, who need more personal contact time with teachers and with each other. Questioning the rules and time-honoured conventions is regarded less as mindless rebellion and more as part of the critique essential to a critical education.

Nov 18

When I meet writers like Ms. P, the daughter of a local sea captain, I think that I play at writing. I ask her how her own writing is going. (Since she was a young woman she has written articles for publications such as Yankee Magazine, Down East, *and* Audubon.) *She tells me that she has been getting to her desk by about 2:30 a.m. "That just seems to be a good time to write. I lose track of the hours and the days of the week. My friend calls me up when it's Sunday. I once wrote for 36 hours straight until I couldn't read the page anymore."*

After she has left the store, David, the check-out person, tells me that he is finishing a long story that he hopes to get published one day. His former English teacher, Mrs. G, has been helping him with it. Both accounts of this young adult and an elderly person writing remind me to avoid drawing quick conclusions about the amounts and kinds of writing going on in some homes.

Nov 21

Grade Seven class: 9:45–10:15 a.m.

For the next session, Darcy and Deborah change groups. Darcy has been working on vocabulary words particular to the unit on immigrants.

Time to talk.

Her focus is on reading for meaning, using new words like "environment" and "steerage" in context, and on correct spelling. The class is now broken into small groups each to discuss one of four questions on Saroyan's "The Summer of the Beautiful White Horse." In each group of three to four students, one acts as the recorder while the others discuss possible answers. For example:

Aram's family lives in "comical" poverty. Did Aram think that being poor was funny? What makes him describe his family's financial situation in that way?:

He was so poor that it was unbelievably unbelievable, it [was] beyond belief, it was also beyond sadness and had reached the point where you just want to laugh it was so bad They had nothing to lose by laughing and it was how they survived.

No aram did not think being poor was funny it was just that he knew he was poor and their was nothing they could do about it but make the best of it. They made up for their money shortage by being honest, proud, and hard working.

Neighbors all think that Aram and Mourad belong back in the "old country." Why?:

This is because the people are lower class, they can't talk the language very well, they are too honest, and they might take over some jobs. They might be smelly, they might loaf around, they might deal drugs, they might be night people.

As students discuss the questions, Darcy moves from group to group coaching and encouraging students to take their observations further and to see how issues of identity, ownership and honesty change with age and across cultures. Darcy localises the issue of an Armenian boy taking the horse by asking, "What if you found a bike and used it for yourself? How would your parents regard your decision to keep it?" After she has primed a group with further questions and encouragement, the tempo of conversation picks up dramatically and sustains itself. She paces herself deliberately, grimacing at the clock when it reads 10:10 a.m.

I did not observe middle school students collaborating in this way on classroom visits made in 1984–86. Part of the reason lies in teachers' trying different approaches encountered, for example, through attending conferences and in-service workshops, and reading books like Atwell's In the Middle. *Successful conversation and small group work, however, are possible now largely because these students have had several years of group share, peer-editing, and supportive listening practice through the writing process, taught in elementary school. The social interactions of these students are far less agonistic than I recall them being in the past.*

Nov 26

The parking lot in front of the old junior high gym is packed solid but not for a basketball game, town meeting or budget hearing. Tonight is the second annual literature fair to celebrate a generation of children in grades 3–6 reading for pleasure and instruction. Inside the gym, small children proudly tow both fathers and mothers around dioramas that display the books their children are now reading. Parents pause to read the carefully written reports. Amanda writes: "The House in the Snow *is so exciting! Its about a boy who runs away during the winter."*

The Literature Fair is the combined idea of Sue and Pat, special-ed. teacher and fifth-grade teacher. When I ask Sue to compare the reading of elementary students now with five years ago, her answer is in terms of a much higher number of class book orders for the Hog Wild on Reading Program. "In the past we had very few children with books in their homes.

That's changing now. And students are taking a lot longer to choose books now. They don't just grab the first one like they used to do. Now they read the cover blurbs and say 'I read this one. You should read it too. It's all about a girl. . . .'" Many of her students now say that their parents are reading the books at home with them.

In 1981, Paul, then the elementary school principal, introduced the process approach to teaching writing in the district with so much energy, enthusiasm and expertise. He would be proud to see the directions that his ground-breaking work has taken. Pat and Sue were both deeply involved in implementing the approach within K–6 classrooms. On my returns to the island in 1984–86, the influence of a process approach was very evident in the writings of elementary students and beginning to take hold in the junior high English classes. Yet when I ask Sue and Pat now about their current work on writing, they both say that they are emphasising reading more and working less on writing than in the past. They have found "the process" to be a time-intensive approach to teaching writing that has not allowed them, for example, to work with literature as much as they would have liked. Clearly the reasons for their shift in emphasis are complex and warrant a new round of classroom observations and further conversations.

Nov 27

"Winds north to northeast at 20–25 knots; seas 3– 4 feet, tempera-ture 30–35 degrees, small-craft advisory. . . ." Tomorrow will be a good day for a fire, revise Chapter 5, and read The Scribal Society *by Alan Purves. The phone rings. "Do you still want to go to haul?" Sniffing at my reported bad weather report, Mike assures me that this is for the New Hampshire coast. In '84, I had fished with Mike no later than October.*

Nov 28

At 5:30 a.m. we take on bait at the Co-op. In the half light Herbie, an ex-student, recognises me and greets me with "I'd rather be in school than out here today." Eighteen months ago, Mike bought his uncle's boat, and with his younger brother Dana as sternman, realised his ambition to run his own boat. In 1988 Dana quit school in grade nine, having lasted one more year than Mike.

Ice on the decks and a storm watch for the evening, but Mike will haul whenever he can in these late-season days to make boat, house, and truck payments. Over the VHF, this morning's talk is about trying to haul gear with a record tide holding the pot buoys under; several boats return very early. Country and Western music is punctuated by further storm watches and then a toll-free number to call for a guaranteed phonic reading programme. Mike turns down the station and begins to tell me about his reading tutor.

The literacy volunteer, an electronics repairman, has been coming to Mike's house for one evening a week over the past year. Mike likes him a lot because he doesn't look down on him as he felt some of his classmates did. "I find myself reading on my own now, magazines, fishermen's papers, stuff like that." He and his tutor are reading Death of a Salesman, *which Mike finds tough but enjoys. Dana joins the conversation. "I ought to go, too. I'd like to be able to read and write more."*

When I ask why, Dana says, "So I know what I'm signing. Applications for buying a truck." Mike would like to be able to write letters, "once I get the reading down." Finding his lobster pots used to be a matter of remembering their location and siting the marker buoys on the water. Now he has a Loran Navigator that can pinpoint each buoy for him. I gaze dumbly at the changing number references and ask how he figured out the system. "I kept reading the manual and practicing till I got it right." Dana and Mike haul a few more strings and band the lobster. "If me and Andrea have kids, and they ask you to read 'em a story and you can't, then you feel kind of stupid." The last boat on the bay, Mike calls it a day, and we head for home away from the grey cloud banks thickening to the south.

APPROACH: MAPPING THE TIMESCAPES OF LITERACY

Pat Conroy opens his novel *The Water Is Wide* (1972) with a superintendent interviewing a school teacher for a position on Yamacraw Island off the South Carolina coast. Based on his teaching experience, Pat Conroy writes what others have described as a "true story," from which the reader learns much about teaching and learning in a remote sea-island community. My own teaching on another of America's edges also began in conversation with a superintendent and prompted me to write about my students' experiences of coming into the cultures of time and literacy. In *Family Literacy* (1983, p. 102), Denny Taylor refers to her own approach to describing literacy activities in their context as "field research undertaken in the spirit of ethnography."

Recent scholarship on the written construction of social realities (Clifford and Marcus, 1986; Van Maanen, 1988) points to the interdisciplinary character of cultural descriptions and the attendant blurring of genres. If sharp lines can no longer be drawn between the literary and the non-literary, or between what is a fiction and what claims to mirror reality, then the truth values of our representations and interpretations become problematic also. I have framed my own descriptions of life in school and community by describing them as an ethnographic research project, one grounded in a matrix of experience similar to that from which Conroy's "true story" emerged. Although Conroy's style is novelistic, each of our works raises issues of genre, such as how forms of representation shape the meanings that readers attach to the lives of those represented, and how we weigh the truth value of fiction, true stories, and ethnography.

Since the appearance in 1983 of Shirley Brice Heath's *Ways with Words*, ethnography has become an increasingly accepted route for studying the life and work of language communities. Although debate over the value of ethnographic enquiry continues, the legitimacy of this approach to research in its varied forms appears to require less justification now than a decade ago. So that readers can decide what my current study might bring to exploring and understanding our students' engagements with time and literacy, I will now describe the procedures adopted and difficulties encountered. A reader who wants a more detailed discussion of the validity of this approach can refer to rationales found in such works as those by Polakow (1982), Taylor (1983), Fishman (1988), and Neilsen (1989).

‌ ‌

When I returned to the island in 1984 to begin my study, I first sought out several students who had strongly challenged and resisted schooling during my three years of teaching there. I followed the lives of several of my former students who by grade nine had dropped out of school. With pride, skill, and patience, these young adults now taught me about a way of life they knew and cherished. In their homes, on the clam flats, and in lobster boats, we talked of their present employment. When I asked about their work, school often became the topic of our conversation. We all needed to understand and make sense of those last few years in school together.

A second set of students who provided insights into the character and quality of time in school were those currently in kindergarten through second grade, and in sixth and twelfth grade. Many of those whom I had taught in middle school between 1978 and 1981 were now in their junior and senior years in high school. Although I had not taught any students younger than the current juniors, many of their elder brothers and sisters had been in my classes six years ago. In a corner of the library and in empty classrooms, I talked with individuals and with small groups during English class, in study periods, and after school. Teachers supported our conversations by arranging times when their students could leave the regular classes to talk about their experience of learning to write.

A third group of people who explained island life to me were the adults, several of whom were parents of my students. These people in turn led me to other adults patient enough to help me to understand their interpretations of what was going on in this small fishing community. A common refrain in answer to my questions was, "You need to go and talk to my grandmother/grandfather. S/he'll tell you everythin you want to know about that."

A fourth group to support the study were the teachers and principals of the elementary and high school. Although my focus has been on the students' perspectives on their English courses, English teachers have read each of the chapters on schooling and have commented on my accounts of how students regard English instruction. The teachers' readings often led me to look again at quick conclusions I had drawn on the basis of scant evidence. Teachers' insights, and suggestions about students with whom to talk, proved invaluable.

Without the help of each of these four groups, the study would have remained as only an idea. Their perspectives were often different, and as I proceeded they reminded me that I was studying a community whose members themselves held a broad range of views on any given topic. Attitudes, values, and behaviours were far more variable than had initially appeared to be the case. As I wrote the study, I asked people from each category to read the descriptions and respond to what they saw as the accuracy of my accounts—to ask how accurately the texts that I had constructed presented the lives of the people described. As community members provided additional information, I incorporated it. Where differences emerged between my accounts and readers' perceptions of a situation, I noted the divergences.

Yet attempting to validate my descriptions in this way, although essential, was problematic on several counts. First, some students and adults appeared reluctant to critique the writing of someone whom they remembered and still regarded as a teacher. Second, because people had few occasions to read descriptions of their own lives, they had little practice in evaluating written accounts of lived experiences. Third, as willing as people were to assist me in this stage of the work, I placed a greater value on the importance of producing accurate written descriptions than did most readers, who while interested in the writing, tended to regard it as merely an abstract representation of experience.

In contrast, I regarded my descriptions as interpretations of experience that invited critique. This difference in perception reflects both on the quality of my descriptions and on what many community members perceived to be the primary function of writing. Despite these problems, I learned much from sharing the writing in this way. Without such responses, I would feel less certain that this study begins to portray how these students and adults view their lives in school and at home. The practice of checking my perceptions with others shows that authorship of this text was in many respects shared, although the work itself bears only my name.

The stories that I use to depict the life world of these students and adults focus on four major characters with a small network of friends and relatives. I choose the term "character" in contrast to the more clinical terms of "respondent," "interviewee," or "informant" in part to indicate that my representations of the dramatic engagements of students and school are themselves literary constructs based on my interpretations. The characters are Fay in first grade, Mark in sixth grade, Christie in twelfth, and Mike who quit school in ninth grade. Whenever possible, I have preserved the individual voices of the people interviewed and have attempted to be scrupulous in representing details of their language and daily activities. When it would have required several speakers to present the requisite information, I have created composite characters to avoid the problem of presenting a cast that changes with each new topic. In combining information in this way, my aim has been to present particular portraits and not to suggest typical or "common denominator people" (Marcus and Cushman, 1982, as cited in Van Maanen, 1988, p. 49).

I do not claim to be some kind of transparent scribe who has simply written down what others have reported; my act of composing is dialogic and is indebted to many voices. My purpose has been to write a single story about this community, yet the descriptions of these members' lives have been constructed from a pool of information drawn from many hours of taped interviews and still more of informal conversation. My own memories of what people said and did during the three years that I taught on the island provided another source of information. Little of what happens in this community escapes the pages of the local newspaper, and my understanding of life here was enriched by reading its pages and by talking with its editor and staff.

I organised my study around a family to portray the ways in which the family provides one key centre of community life. My own teaching here soon brought me into contact with the families who had provided the children with such fundamental ideas as the roles and identities of men and women, and with models for how language and time are used and valued in the home. While their instruction was conducted informally, it established expectations against which students compared learning in school.

While I am the narrator of this story, I am also a character in it, and in both roles, I observe, participate, and interpret. The precise ways in which my presence influenced activities, however, and the extent of the influence are difficult to determine. As a participant, I assume that my presence in the classroom influenced the ongoing school activities, and it certainly slowed down the fishing, as my questions were answered and procedures explained. I was often struck by the same disarming candour of student's comments at work as I had been in my own classroom teaching. When I came to take photographs, at first students would pose for the camera, most especially when I asked them to continue with their work. After a short time, however, even the loud click of the shutter did not appear to distract them. The photographs are intended not only to provide visual images of school and community life but, more importantly, to show the interplay of time and place and the different kinds of social interactions that people experience in these contexts.

In James Clifford's words, "'Cultures' do not hold still for their portraits" (1986, p. 10), despite the stillness of photographs. I returned to the island on three separate occasions: for the autumn term of 1984, in the winter of 1986, and in the fall of 1990. My purpose was not to make a longitudinal study but to attempt to make the descriptions sufficiently "thick." With each visit, the island appeared to increase in size and the project to become yet more complex. By the fall of 1990, the changes that had been in motion were dramatically visible in the surface texture of school and community life; the need to write "Field Notes: Toward the Future" became apparent.

When I arrived for each new round of fieldwork, people routinely asked where I had been, would I be teaching again, and when I would leave — the latter was sometimes the first question. Since the island is home to an increasing number of temporary residents, my coming and going was regarded with less curiosity than were accounts of my purpose. Briefly I explained that I would be talking with students in school about their experiences of learning to read and write and how they responded to time in school. I would then add that I was interested also in learning more about the different kinds of work engaged in by island men and women and the changes occurring in the community.

Responses to how I accounted for my presence in the community varied from polite nods to questions as to whether I was planning to actually do any work—after I had done watching others. I was often asked would I be teaching again. Since the schools are a central topic of island talk, to declare interest in schooling usually prompted a series of strong opinions about specific educational issues. When I elaborated on my interest in describing different experiences of time, people would often smile or comment on what they saw as the complexity of the task. Others would equate time with memory and recount earlier times; this occurred with both younger and older people. I was asked several times why I was interested in studying a remote island community in contrast to city life, as I was asked also why I didn't settle down here. Those with whom I had the most daily contact would often enquire how my writing was coming along—a gentle reminder of my purpose.

The rituals of leaving and leave-taking after each field visit had much in common. Always I felt surprise, if not outrage, that my time was up. So much remained to be collected, and my understanding was at best still partial. The sense of having been given and trusted with much of what was particular and special in people's lives always eased the transition from fieldwork to ethnographic writing. Because people understood that the purpose of our conversations was to produce a written text, there was also an ethical motivation for me to write up the parts into a whole. Writing about the community was a powerful way to deal with the loss of conversations that once started I wanted to continue. Fieldwork thus served both professional and personal needs. In addition, fieldwork can have educational value for those who participate in the interviews.

At the end of the 1984 visit, the sixth-grade teacher pointed out what he saw as the value of students' reflecting on their writing practices. After my term-long series of interviews, he thought that those in the group with whom I had worked were more willing and able to talk about their writing process than those in the class who had not participated in our discussions. He believed that this awareness was developed further as students read through my observations and descriptions of their language instruction and commented on how these related to their own perceptions. Working with students in this way, I too saw a possible approach to teaching writing through teachers and students collaboratively describing the shared social context of community and school.

As a narrator, what I have observed has been influenced by my own particular agenda of interests and questions, and more broadly by my prior teaching experience in this and other communities. Recognising that the situations of fieldworkers and teachers are both different and comparable, I sought to suspend conclusions about school and community to which my teaching had brought me, for example, that the kinds of alienation that many students experienced in school were related to temporal disjunctions between home and school. Although I could not completely eliminate such conclusions, I made a conscious effort to search anew for the contrasting meanings of school and community life.

Believing that neither the ethnographer nor language itself can make an unmediated representation of a culture, I see myself as one who has participated in the construction of the many stories from which this story is written. Most often I believe the descriptions require no further interpretation than what a thoughtful reader will make. For me to interpret each of them is to run the risk of stating the obvious and to distract the reader's attention from character and situation. The evaluations interlarded between descriptions may themselves already appear intrusive enough to those readers who would prefer to read all analyses at the end of each chapter and in the conclusion. But readers have commented that because ethnographic texts do not speak for themselves, such commentary is not only desirable but needed.

Readers are likely to ask how the different categories of time presented in Chapter Six evolved. The specific categories which pre-exist the community in the sense that each can be found in other settings, emerged as I looked for ways to account for the complexity of temporal experience in this particular context. During my three years of teaching on the island, I observed that time in school and time in the community were conceived of in contrasting ways. The differences led me to look more closely at how time was experienced in each setting, with a view to distinguishing among time's different dimensions. This observation was one that Alton L. Becker in particular encouraged me to explore further, for example, by viewing the community from a "wave perspective" (Young, Becker, and Pike, 1970). My interest in the categories is less in providing a comprehensive description of the various kinds of time found in the community than in showing that different and sometimes conflicting imperatives for action are associated with each form. Other observers in other contexts will describe time in different ways and expand or modify the categories offered here. Any value in this task is to reveal the multiple facets of a stratum of human experience often regarded as linear and one-dimensional or equated only with its technical measures.

As a narrator, I have had to decide what material to include and what to exclude. Because my own experience in this community began with attempting to teach English, my first concern has been to emphasise the material that reveals what was problematic in the school lives of these students. I have done this not to provide one more account of education failing but to make visible the impact of time on students' experience of learning by examples that illustrate the frictions and fault lines that occur when we neglect the role of differential temporal experience. What I have not featured are the stories of those students who would describe as successful their experience of schooling and becoming literate. The roles that different kinds of time played in these stories must be the focus of another study.

Notes

Introduction

1. While process approaches to the teaching of writing vary, the method in evidence in this school district after 1981 owes much to a series of in-service workshops broadly following the pedagogy of Donald Graves (1983).

2. It would be easy to regard these differences as deficits that schools need to reduce to prepare students for the "real" world. While differences can be detrimental in certain contexts, my concern here is to recognise the home and community as significant educators. Several of the ways in which the temporal organisation of home and community influence education are discussed by Hope Jensen Leichter (1974), pp. 33–35 and (1975), pp. 51–54.

3. The limits of ethnographic enquiry as an approach to research in composition is discussed by Stephen North (1987), pp. 272–313. For a broad discussion of the limits to enquiry, see also Max van Manen (1990), pp. 21–24.

4. Such statements surely echo the influence on education of Frederick W. Taylor's scientific management and his efforts in the early years of this century to organise labour by a rational model relating output to the efficient use of time on each task. See Jeremy Rifkin (1987), pp. 106–109, for a summary of the principle features of scientific management.

5. See Rifkin, pp. 59–61, for discussion of how schools attempt "to establish a pace and rhythm in the classroom that mimics the tempo in the larger world for which children are being prepared."

6. Central here is the idea that we perceive time as reified, and seldom recognise the extent to which it is a human product grounded on social convention. See Eviatar Zerubavel (1981), pp. 42–43.

7. For discussion of the consequences of the separation of human rhythms from the cyclical rhythms of nature and our entente with the sun, see Michael Young (1988).

8. Miriam Ben-Peretz and Rainer Bromme (1990) ask,

   Why is it so natural—some argue so trivial—to use the concept of time as a yardstick, and apparently so difficult to analyze time as experienced, perceived, and managed by teachers and students? The reason may be that the metric of time, counted in minutes and hours, has so strongly formed our concepts about time that it is quite difficult to understand and to analyze other frames and experiences of time. (p. vi).

9. In the word of Shirley Brice Heath from her epilogue to *Ways With Words* (1983), "Patterns of language use in any community are in accord with and mutually reinforce other cultural patterns, such as time and space ordering, and problem-solving techniques. . . . " (p. 344).

10. For one approach to such a study, see Kaoru Yamamoto, *Children in Time and Space* (1979).

11. Lauren B. Resnick observes that if we define literacy in terms of cultural practices, in contrast to competency or ability, then we pose key questions for ourselves.

    Examining literacy as a set of cultural practices rather than as skills or abilities leads to questions that are not often posed in discussions of the literacy crisis. These are questions about the kinds of situations in which literacy is practiced, that is, in which people engage with written texts. (1990), p. 170.

12. For an extended discussion of this concept of literacy see Thomas Newkirk (1986).

13. Ben-Peretz argues that, "This aspect of time should become part of educational deliberations. Insights into the personal meanings of time, which are significant to all participants in an educational situation, may then become part of the knowledge base of teaching." (1990), p. 73.

14. In the words of Peter Berger and Thomas Luckman,

     Temporality is an intrinsic property of consciousness. The stream of consciousness is always ordered temporally. . . . The temporal structure of everyday life confronts me as a facticity with which I must reckon, that is, with which I must try to synchronize my own projects. I encounter time in everyday reality as continuous and finite. All my existence in this world is continually ordered by its time, is indeed enveloped by it (1964), pp. 26–27.

15. For those interested in the relationship between time and identity, see especially the work of Martin Heidegger, the philosopher who framed out the major dimensions for how we now think about this subject from a phenomenological perspective. (1962).

16. Bernard Comrie is careful to distinguish between the nature of time as we experience it and the grammar of a language. To maintain the distinction, he defines tense as "grammaticalised location in time." (1985), p. 9. Although tense is a problematic index of lived time, time relations are marked by parts of speech, by aspect, and by discursive time, what Oswald Ducrot and Tzvetan Todorov call "the instance of enunciation." (1972), p. 318.

Chapter One: Ways with Lobsters

1. The accuracy of this information is verified and supplemented by sources from the local historical society. For an account of fishing on the Maine coast from the time of sail to that of power, see Harold B. Clifford, *Charlie York: Maine Coast Fisherman.* (1974).

2. T. M. Prudden (1962), pp. 6–10.

3. I use the term "lobsterman" or "men" to describe the gender of the population currently fishing. To my knowledge, there is only one woman in this area who currently holds a lobster licence. More common are sternwomen, referred to in this community, like their male counterparts, as "sternmen." While the term "fishermen" refers primarily to individuals engaged in the seasonal work of lobster fishing, the term includes also those dragging for scallops in winter and long-line fishing in early spring.

4. Readers interested in the ability of seafaring people to find their way using not only knowledge of the movement of astronomical bodies but

also of sea life and one's relationships to it should see the discussion in
Thomas Gladwin (1970) and in Steven Thomas (1987) of the navigational
practice known as Etak.

5. The above account of lobster fishing is written with a particular focus on
   how time is conceived of and realised in the work. Those interested in
   broader descriptions of the industry by one who has fished for over half a
   century should read *The Great Lobster Chase* (1985) by Mike Brown. For
   those interested in the work from a sociological perspective, in particular
   the kinship networks, see *The Lobster Gangs of Maine* (1988) by James
   Acheson. *A Part of the Main: Short Stories of the Maine Coast* (1973) by
   Edward Holmes offers memorable narrative accounts of life and work in
   coastal and island communities.

Chapter Two: Work on the Island

1. The contrast between cyclical and linear time is a pervasive one in the
   literature about the philosophy of time and the history of its conception.
   For example, the contrastive time orders of different religious groups is
   discussed by J. T. Fraser (1987), pp. 17–22. Michael Young (1988) explores these two representations of time to show the relationships between natural rhythms and human timetables. In the context of portray-
   ing the "counter-school" culture, Paul Willis (1981), p. 135 argues that by
   asserting individual rhythms and movement patterns, working class youth
   challenge the linear timetables of British schools, institutions driven by
   capitalist time values. Stephen Jay Gould (1987) uses the controlling
   metaphor of time's arrow and time's cycle to present the alternatives in
   conceptualising geological time. See also Comrie (1985), pp. 2–7, for discussion of the issue of cyclical and linear time in language.

2. I use the term "natural" in contrast to the mechanical measure of the
   clock. I am not suggesting here, however, that our access to forms of
   temporal reference, natural or mechanical, is unmediated by language.
   The changing movements of the sun, tide, and seasons are independent of
   language, but our perceptions, descriptions, and evaluations of these movements are shaped by language and culture.

3. See discussion by Geoffrey Leech (1980), pp. 14–30 of time and its progressive aspect.

Chapter Three: Fay

1. For a full discussion of this approach, see Graves (1983).

2. The exceptions to this observation would be the day, the lunar month and the year, which originate in astronomic cycles, in contrast, for example, to the number of days in a week and hours in a day, which are determined by social convention. Time has become progressively a social and mechanised phenomenon separated from natural periodicities and rhythms.

Chapter Four: Mark

1. Many thanks to Alton L. Becker, Professor Emeritus at the University of Michigan, for his insights into how writers take the prior texts of their language and make them new. Ludwig Wittgenstein describes this phenomenon in terms of a "language game" (1953), no. 7, pp. 53.

2. For a discussion of the interplay between time and narrative, see Paul Ricoeur (1980), pp. 169–190.

Chapter Five: Christie

1. Through extended conversation with me in 1984 and 1986, these students taught me about their experiences in being seniors in high school. As a check on the accuracy of my descriptions, students who are currently enrolled in the high school, or now working, or in college critiqued the chapter. Where appropriate, I have included the qualifying comments, in particular those of Naomi, Kim, Steven, and Ashley.

Chapter Six: Timescapes for Literacy

1. Readers familiar with the work of Heidegger (1962) will recognise in this next section that I begin to apply to the lifeworld of students Heidegger's concepts of *dasein* — being in the world; of *geworfenheit* — the situation of being "thrown" into a world without referential orientation; and *appropriation* — the acts of making that world one's own.

2. The importance for teachers to determine the logic that underlies errors in writing is argued convincingly by Mina P. Shaughnessy (1977).

3. The series *Writers at Work: The Paris Review Interviews*, edited by Jean Plimpton, offers many accounts of how authors produce, for example, a

work of fiction, an essay, or a biography. Sometimes time is referred to explicitly in the interviews, but more often time is the activity of writing.

4. I am indebted to Professor Ralph Williams at the University of Michigan, Ann Arbor, for drawing my attention, by precept and example, to the need for teachers to regard the class hour as no more than a flexible, if not an arbitrary, reference point for shaping the scope of dialogue between students and teachers.

Chapter Seven: Field Notes

1. John Van Maanen, *Tales of the Field: On Writing Ethnography* (1988), p. 72.

2. For a full discussion of the contradiction between the "temporal conditions experienced in fieldwork and those expressed in [ethnographic] writing," the phenomenon of "temporal distancing," see Johannes Fabian, (1983), pp. 71–104.

3. Since 1986, grades seven and eight have been increasingly referred to as the middle school. In this chapter, I use both the newer term "middle school" and the older term "junior high," as used in the previous chapters, reflecting the teachers' current interchangeable usage.

Bibliography

The bibliography includes the works that are referred to in the text and also identifies several other readings that have been helpful.

Acheson, J. (1988). *The Lobster Gangs of Maine.* Hanover, N.H.: University Press of New England.

Agar, M. (1980). *The Professional Stranger: An Informal Introduction to Ethnography.* New York: Academic Press.

Armstrong, M. (1980). *Closely Observed Children: The Diary of an Observed Classroom.* London: Writers and Readers Publishing Cooperative Society.

Arnove, R., and H. Graff. (1987). "National Literacy Campaigns: Historical and Comparative Lessons." *Phi Delta Kappan* Vol. 69, No. 3, pp. 202–206.

Atwell, N. (1987). *In the Middle: Writing, Reading, and Learning with Adolescents.* Upper Montclair, N.J.: Boynton/Cook.

Barritt, L. S., and A. J. Beekman. (1982). *Educational Research in the Social Sciences.* Ann Arbor: University of Michigan Press.

Barnes, D., J. Britton and M. Torbe, eds. (1986). *Language, the Learner and the School.* London: Penguin.

Bateson, G. (1972). *Steps to an Ecology of Mind.* New York: Ballantine.

Becker, A.L., and A.A. Yengoyan, eds. (1979). "Communication Across Diversity." *The Imagination of Reality: Essays in Southeast Asian Coherence Systems.* Norwood, N.J.: Ablex. pp. 1–5.

Ben-Peretz, M., and R. Bromme, eds. (1990). *The Nature of Time in Schools: Theoretical Concepts, Practitioner Perceptions.* New York: Teachers College, Columbia University.

Berger, P. L., and T. Luckmann. (1967). *The Social Construction of Reality: A Treatise in the Sociology of Knowledge.* Garden City, N.Y.: Anchor.

Britton, J., T. Burgess, N. Martin, A. McLeod, and H. Rosen. (1975) The Development of Writing Abilities (11–18). Houndsmills: Macmillan.

Boyer, E. L. (1983). *High School: A Report on Secondary Education in America.* New York: Harper and Row.

Brody, H. (1981). *Maps and Dreams.* New York: Pantheon.

Brown, M. (1985). *The Great Lobster Chase.* Camden, Me.: International Marine Publishing Company.

Carroll, J. M. (1990). "The Copernican Plan: Restructuring the American High School." *Phi Delta Kappan* Vol. 71, No. 4, pp. 358–65.

Clifford, H. B. (1974). *Charlie York: Maine Coast Fisherman.* Camden, Me.: International Marine Publishing Company.

Clifford, J., and G. E. Marcus, eds. (1986). *Writing Culture: The Poetics and Politics of Ethnography.* Berkeley and Los Angeles: University of California Press.

Comrie, B. (1976). *Aspect: An Introduction to the Study of Verbal Aspect and Related Problems.* Cambridge: Cambridge University Press.

———. (1985). *Tense.* Cambridge: Cambridge University Press.

Conroy, P. (1972). *The Water Is Wide.* Boston, Mass.: Houghton Mifflin.

Cottle, T. J., and S. Klineberg. (1973). *The Present of Things Future: Explorations of Time in Human Experience.* New York: Free Press/ Macmillan.

De Grazia, S. (1962). *Of Time, Work, and Leisure.* New York: The Twentieth Century Fund.

Ducrot, O., and T. Todorov. (1979). *Encyclopedic Dictionary of the Sciences of Language.* Baltimore, MD.: The Johns Hopkins University Press.

Dyson, A. (1988). "Negotiating Among Multiple Worlds: The Space/Time Dimensions of Young Children's Composing" Berkeley and Pittsburgh: Center for the Study of Writing.

Elkind, D. (1981). *The Hurried Child: Growing Up Too Fast Too Soon.* Reading, MA.: Addison-Wesley Publishing Co.

Ellison, H. (1965). *Paingod and Other Delusions.* New York: Pyramid Books.

Erickson, F. (1977). "Some approaches to inquiry in school-community ethnography." *Anthropology and Education* 8: pp. 58–69.

Fabian, J. (1983). *Time and the Other: How Anthropology Makes Its Object.* New York: Columbia University Press.

Fishman, A. (1988). *Amish Literacy: What and How It Means.* Portsmouth, N.H.: Heinemann.

Foucault, M. (1979). *Discipline and Punish: The Birth of the Prison.* Trans. by Alan Sheridan. New York: Vintage.

Fraser, J. T. (1987). *Time, the Familiar Stranger.* Amherst: University of Massachusetts Press.

Friere, P. (1970). *Pedagogy of the Oppressed.* New York: Continuum.

Freire, P., and D. Macedo. (1987). *Literacy: Reading the World and the Word.* South Hadley, Mass.: Bergin and Garvey.

Geertz, C. (1973). *The Interpretation of Cultures.* New York: Basic Books.

Gladwin, T. (1970). *East is a Big Bird: Navigation and Logic on Puluwat Atoll.* Cambridge, Mass.: Harvard University Press.

Glassie, H. (1982). *Passing the Time in Ballymenone: Culture and History of an Ulster Community.* Philadelphia: University of Pennsylvania Press.

Goodlad, J. I. (1984). *A Place Called School: Prospects for the Future.* New York: McGraw-Hill.

Goody, J., and I. Watt. (1968). *Literacy in Traditional Societies.* Cambridge: Cambridge University Press.

Gould, S. J. (1987). *Time's Arrow/Time's Cycle: Myth and Metaphor in the Discovery of Geological Time*. Cambridge, Mass.: Harvard University Press.

Graves, D. H. (1983). *Writing: Teachers and Children at Work*. Portsmouth, N.H.: Heinemann–Boynton/Cook.

Grudin, R. (1988). *Time and the Art of Living*. New York: Ticknor and Fields.

Gurvich, G. (1964). *The Spectrum of Social Time*. Dordrecht, Holland: Reidel.

Hall, E. T. (1959). *The Silent Language*. New York: Doubleday.

———. (1966). *The Hidden Dimension*. New York: Doubleday.

———. (1983). *The Dance of Life: The Other Dimension of Time*. Garden City, N.Y.: Anchor.

Heath, S. B. (1980). "The Functions and Uses of Literacy." *Journal of Communications* Vol. 29, No. 2, pp. 123–135.

———. (1983). *Ways with Words: Language, Life, and Work in Communities and Classrooms*. Cambridge: Cambridge University Press.

Heidegger, M. (1962). *Being and Time*. Trans. by John Macquarrie and Edward Robinson. New York: Harper and Row.

Hicks, G. L. (1976). *Appalachian Valley*. New York: Holt, Rinehart and Winston.

Holmes, E. M. (1973). *A Part of the Main: Short Stories of the Maine Coast*. Orono, Me.: University of Maine Press.

Jewett, S. O. (1981). *The Country of the Pointed Firs and Other Stories*. New York: W. W. Norton.

Kintgen, E. R., B. M. Kroll, and M. Rose, eds. (1988). *Perspectives on Literacy*. Carbondale, Ill.: Southern Illinois University Press.

Labov, W. (1972). *Language in the Inner City.* Philadelphia: University of Pennsylvania Press.

Leech, G. N. (1971). *Meaning and the English Verb.* London: Longman.

Leichter, H. J. (1980). "A Note on Time and Education." *Teachers College Record* Vol. 81, No. 3, pp. 360–363.

Leichter, H. J., ed. (1974). *The Family as Educator.* New York: Teachers College, Columbia University.

———. (1979). *Families and Communities as Educators.* New York: Teachers College, Columbia University.

Lippitz, W. (1983). "The Child's Understanding of Time." *Phenomenology + Pedagogy* Vol. 1, No. 2, pp. 172–180.

Lunsford, A., H. Moglen, and J. Slevin, eds. (1990). *The Right to Literacy.* New York: Modern Language Association.

MacLeod, A. (1988). *The Lost Salt Gift of Blood.* Princeton: Ontario Review Press.

Merleau-Ponty, M. (1962). *Phenomenology of Perception.* London: Routledge and Kegan Paul.

Mumford, L. (1952). *Art and Technics.* New York: Columbia University Press.

———. (1967). *The Myth of the Machine: Technics and Human Development.* New York: Harcourt Brace Jovanovich.

Murray, D. M. (1990). *Shoptalk: Learning to Write with Writers.* Portsmouth, N.H.: Heinemann–Boynton/Cook.

Nachtigal, P.M., ed. (1982). *Rural Education: In Search of a Better Way.* Boulder: Westview Special Studies in Education.

Nash, R. (1980). *Schooling in Rural Societies: Contemporary Sociology of School.* London: Methuen.

Neilsen, L. (1989). *Literacy and Living.* Portsmouth, N.H.: Heinemann.

Newkirk, T., ed. (1986). *Only Connect: Uniting Reading and Writing.* Upper Montclair, N.J.: Boynton/Cook.

————, ed. (1990). *Understanding Writing: Ways of Observing, Learning, and Teaching.* 2d ed. Portsmouth, N.H.: Heinemann.

North, S. M. (1987). *The Making of Knowledge in Composition: Portrait of an Emerging Field.* Portsmouth, N.H.: Heinemann.

Ong, W. T. (1982). *Orality and Literacy: The Technologizing of the Word.* New York: Methuen.

Piaget, J. (1969). *The Child's Conception of Time.* New York: Basic Books.

Plimpton, G., ed. (1988). *Writers at Work: The Paris Review Interviews*, 8th ser. New York: Viking Penguin.

Polokow V. P. [Suransky, V. P.], (1980). "Phenomenology: An Alternative Research Paradigm and a Force for Social Change." *Journal of the British Society for Phenomenology* Vol. 11, No. 2, pp. 163–179.

————. (1982). *The Erosion of Childhood.* Chicago: University of Chicago Press.

Powell, A., G. E. Farrar, and D. K. Cohen. (1985). *The Shopping Mall High School: Winners and Losers in the Educational Marketplace.* Boston: Houghton Mifflin.

Prudden, T. M. (1962). *About Lobsters.* Freeport, Me.: The Cumberland Press.

Purves, A. C. (1990). *The Scribal Society: An Essay on Literacy and Schooling in the Information Age.* London: Longman.

Rabinow, P. (1977). *Reflections on Fieldwork in Morocco.* Berkeley and Los Angeles: University of California Press.

Resnick, L. (1990). "Literacy In School and Out." *Daedalus* Vol. 119, No. 2, pp. 169–187.

Ricoeur, P. (1980). "Narrative Time." *Critical Inquiry* Vol. 7, No. 1, pp. 169–180.

Rifkin, J. (1987). *Time Wars: The Primary Conflict in Human History.* New York: Henry Holt and Company.

Robinson, J. L. (1990). *Conversations on the Written Word: Essays on Language and Literacy.* Portsmouth, N.H.: Heinemann–Boynton/Cook.

Rose, M. (1989). *Lives on the Boundary.* New York: Free Press.

Scribner, S., and M. Cole. (1981). *The Psychology of Literacy.* Cambridge, Mass.: Harvard University Press.

Shanker, A. (1990). "The End of the Traditional Model of Schooling and A Proposal for Using Incentives to Restructure Our Public Schools." *Phi Delta Kappan* Vol. 71, No. 5, pp. 345–357.

Sher, J., ed. (1977). *Education in Rural America: A Reassessment of Conventional Wisdom.* Boulder: Westview Special Studies in Education.

Shaughnessy, M. P. (1977). *Errors and Expectations: A Guide for the Teaching of Basic Writing.* New York: Oxford University Press.

Sizer, T. R. (1984). *Horace's Compromise: The Dilemma of the American High School.* Boston: Houghton Mifflin.

Spring, J. (1972). *Education and the Rise of the Corporate State.* Boston: Beacon.

Taylor, D. (1983). *Family Literacy: Young Children Learning to Read and Write.* Portsmouth, N.H.: Heinemann–Boynton/Cook.

Thomas, S. D. (1987). *The Last Navigator.* New York: Ballantine.

Thomson, P. (1983). *Living the Fishing.* London: Routledge.

Turnbull, C. (1962). *The Forest People.* New York: Simon and Schuster.

Tway, E. (1984). *Time for Writing in the Elementary School.* Urbana, Ill.: ERIC/NCTE.

Van Maanen, J. (1988). *Tales of the Field: On Writing Ethnography.* Chicago: University of Chicago Press.

Van Manen, M. (1990). *Researching Lived Experience: Human Science for an Action Sensitive Pedagogy.* Albany: State University of New York Press.

Vygotsky, L.S. (1962). *Thought and Language.* Cambridge, MA: MIT Press.

Wigginton, E., ed. (1972). *The Foxfire Book.* Garden City, N.Y.: Doubleday. (subsequent volumes by the same title)

Willis, P. (1981). *Learning to Labor: How Working Class Kids Get Working Class Jobs.* New York: Columbia University Press.

Wittgenstein, L. (1953). *Philosophical Investigations.* Trans. by G. E. M. Anscombe. Oxford: Blackwell.

Wood, P., ed. (1977). *The Salt Book.* New York: Anchor.

Yamamoto, K., ed. (1979). *Children in Time and Space.* New York: Columbia University Teachers College.

Young, M. (1988). *The Metronomic Society: Natural Rhythms and Human Timetables.* Cambridge, Mass.: Harvard University Press.

Young, R., A. L. Becker, and K. Pike. (1970). *Rhetoric: Discovery and Change.* New York: Harcourt, Brace and World.

Zerubavel, E. (1981). *Hidden Rhythms: Schedules and Calendars in Social Life.* Berkeley and Los Angeles: University of California Press.

Zweig, Stefan. (1946). *Balzac.* Trans. by W. and D. Rose. New York: Viking Press.

Index